ERRORS AND MISTA
PROTECT

C000052517

International Discour
and Strategies

Edited by Kay Biesel, Judith Masson,
Nigel Parton and Tarja Pösö

P

First published in Great Britain in 2021 by

Policy Press, an imprint of
Bristol University Press
University of Bristol
1-9 Old Park Hill
Bristol
BS2 8BB
UK
t: +44 (0)117 954 5940
e: bup-info@bristol.ac.uk

Details of international sales and distribution partners are available at
policy.bristoluniversitypress.co.uk

British Library Cataloguing in Publication Data
A catalogue record for this book is available from the British Library

ISBN 978-1-4473-5070-5 hardcover
ISBN 978-1-4473-5093-4 paperback
ISBN 978-1-4473-5094-1 ePub
ISBN 978-1-4473-5092-7 ePdf

Cover design: Robin Hawes

Bristol University Press and Policy Press use environmentally responsible
print partners.

Printed in Great Britain by CPI Group (UK) Ltd, Croydon CR0 4YY

FSC
www.fsc.org
MIX
Paper from
responsible sources
FSC® C013604

Contents

List of figures and tables

Figures

Tables

List of abbreviations

BHS	Board of Health Supervision
Bufetat	Office of Children, Youth and Family Affairs
CAPA	Child and Adult Authority
CISMAI	Coordinamento Italiano Servizi contro Maltrattamento e Abuso all'Infanzia [National Network of Services Against Child Maltreatment]
CRC	United Nations Committee on the Rights of the Child
CRIP	Centre de recueil de l'information préoccupante [Centre for Collecting Information of Concern]
CWA	Child Welfare Act
CYPA	Care of Young Persons Act
DP	direct provision
ECtHR	European Court of Human Rights
FHNW	University of Applied Sciences and Arts Northwestern Switzerland
HSE	Health Service Executive
IGQK	Association for Quality in Child Protection in Switzerland
IP	information préoccupante [information about concern]
KESCHA	Contact Point for Child and Adult Protection
KOKES	Konferenz für Kindes- und Erwachsenenschutz [Conference for Child and Adult Protection]
LIRIK	Licht Instrument Risicotaxatie Kindveiligheid [Light Instrument Risk Assessment Child Safety]
LJ	Lord/Lady Justice
LSCB	Local Safeguarding Children Board
NBIC	Swedish National Board of Institutional Care
NBHW	National Board of Health and Welfare
NCCIS	National Child Care Information System
NSPCC	National Society for the Prevention of Cruelty to Children
OAG	Office of the Auditor General of Norway
Ofsted	Office for Standards in Education, Children's Services and Skills
ONED	Observatoire national de l'enfance en danger [National Observatory for Children in Danger] from 2004 until 2016
ONPE	Observatoire national de la protection de l'enfance [National Observatory for Child Protection] (from 2016, formerly ONED)

ORBA	Onderzoek Risicotaxatie Besluitvorming AM(H)Ks [Investigation Risk Assessment Decision Making AM(H)Ks]. AM(H)K = Advies- en Meldpunt Huiselijk geweld en Kindermishandeling [Advice and Report Center Domestic Violence and Child Abuse]
PRM	predictive risk modelling
SCC	Swiss Civil Code
SCR	serious case review
SNATED	Service national d'accueil téléphonique de l'enfance en danger [National Agency for Phone Calls Regarding Children in Danger]
SSA	Social Services Act
UNCRC	United Nations Convention on the Rights of the Child

Notes on contributors

Jill Duerr Berrick serves as the Zellerbach Family Foundation Professor in the School of Social Welfare at the University of California, Berkeley, USA. Berrick's research focuses on the relationship of the state to vulnerable families, particularly those touched by the child welfare system. She has written or co-written 11 books on topics relating to family poverty, child maltreatment, and child welfare services. The most recent, *The Impossible Imperative* (New York: Oxford University Press), examines child welfare professionals and the morally contentious and intellectually demanding choices they regularly face in their work with children and families.

Teresa Bertotti is an associate professor of Social Work at the University of Trento, Italy. She has a professional background in the field of child protection. Her research interests include decision making in child protection, professional identity and social service organisation, and social work education. She is currently President of the European Association of Schools of Social Work (EASSW). She published several books and articles, for example in the *European Journal of Social Work* on 'Ethical consideration in social work research' (2018) and on analysing the impact of austerity in child and family social work.

Kay Biesel is Professor of Child and Youth Welfare focusing on child protection at the University of Applied Sciences and Arts Northwestern Switzerland. He has published widely on topics such as quality development, error and mistake management, and case understanding in child protection. He conducted the first empirical study on errors and mistakes in child protection in Germany (Transcript, 2011) and has developed with Reinhart Wolff an approach to reviewing serious or fatal cases: *The Dialogical-Systemic Case Laboratory* (Transcript, 2014). With Stefan Schnurr, he promoted the development and implementation of a process manual for the assessment of the child's well-being in German-speaking Switzerland (Haupt, 2017).

Jaclyn Chambers is a PhD candidate in the School of Social Welfare at the University of California, Berkeley, USA. Her scholarly interests center on the intersection of social work and law, with a focus on improving decision making and equity in the child welfare system. She has direct social work experience working with parents and youth, and she has published peer-reviewed articles examining child welfare decision making. She holds a B.A. from Colgate University and M.S.W. from New York University.

Michelle Cottier is Professor of Private Law at the Law School of the University of Geneva, Switzerland and Director of the Center for Legislative and Evaluation Studies (CETEL). Michelle Cottier conducted one of the first empirical studies in Switzerland on the participation of children in child protection proceedings (Stämpfli, 2006). Since then she has continued to publish on the topic of child-friendly justice in the area of child protection as well as in family law in general. Michelle Cottier is also a specialist in sociology of law and on the theoretical and methodological implications of interdisciplinary collaboration between law and social science.

Christine Gerber works at the German Youth Institute. She is part of a research project that has developed and field-tested a method for analysing problematic child protection cases in Germany located at the National Centre on Early Prevention in Childhood (NZFH, 2018). Subsequent to her training as social worker, she has gained extensive experience in child protection practice. After changing into science she was part of several inquiries into child maltreatment related incidents.

Staffan Höjer works at the Department of Social Work, University of Gothenburg, Sweden as a professor in social work. His research interests are knowledge, professionalisation and organisation in social work. He has among other things studied privatisation, decision making in child protection, children influence in child protection processes and work overload in welfare organisations. Recently he co-authored several articles in international journals on decision making (2018, *Nordic Social Work Research*), on motives of Ugandan social work students and resilient child protection workers in Europe (2017/18, *European Journal of Social Work*).

Hélène Join-Lambert is assistant professor and head of the Department of Education at University Paris Nanterre, France. Her research examines support for at-risk youth and children in state care and their parents, including cross-national analysis of practices across Europe. A main area of interest is the participation of young people and their parents in decision making. Recently she has co-edited a special issue on ethical matters in research with vulnerable young people in an open access journal (*Sociétés et jeunesses en difficulté*, 2017) and has also published a paper on parental involvement in *Social Policy and Society* in 2016.

Essi Julin is Doctoral researcher at Tampere University, Finland. In her forthcoming (2020) doctoral dissertation she examines multi-professional and inter-organisational child abuse investigation process from a parent perspective. She is experienced social worker in different fields of Finnish child protection. Currently she works as social worker in forensic child psychiatry unit at University Hospital and she has done a report for Finnish Ministry of Social Affairs and Health in 2018 on activities of these units. This report is a first general view on these units during their operation period. She also contributes to development of other Finnish child welfare practices.

Heinz Kindler works as a senior researcher at the German Youth Institute. He has directed research on risk assessment tools and case trajectories in child protection. In addition, he has authored and edited several books on child protection including the *Handbuch Kindeswohlgefährdung* [*Handbook on Child Protection*] (German Youth Institute, 2006) which is an important handbook for practitioners. He serves as expert in child protection court cases and was member of several commissions on the future of child protection in Germany.

Inger Kjellberg works in the Department of Social Work at the University of Gothenburg, Sweden, as a senior lecturer. Her thesis (University of Gothenburg, 2012) focused on complaints procedures and mandatory reports of mistreatments in elder care. Her key topics of research include integrated care and collaboration in social and health care, abuse of older people and quality management in social work.

Susanna Lillig works at the German Youth Institute. She is part of a research project that has developed and field-tested a method for analysing problematic child protection cases in Germany located at the National Centre on Early Prevention in Childhood (NFZH 2018). Trained as a psychologist she has extensive work experiences in child protection services. She has served as one of the editors of the *Handbuch Kindeswohlgefährdung* [*Handbook on Child Protection*] (German Youth Institute, 2006) which is an important handbook for practitioners and was part of several inquiries into child maltreatment related incidents.

Mónica López López is an associate professor at the University of Groningen, the Netherlands. She teaches decision making in child welfare in the master's programme Youth, Society and Policy. Her research interests include disparities in child protection decisions and the participation of children and families in decision-making processes in the child protection system. She is a board member of the European Scientific Association on Residential and Family Care of Children and Adolescents. She is an editor of the forthcoming handbook *Decision Making and Judgement in Child Welfare and Protection: Theory, Research, and Practice* (Oxford University Press, 2020).

Judith Masson works at the University of Bristol, UK, where she is Professor of Socio-Legal Studies in the School of Law and teaches family and child law. Her empirical research focuses on the operation of child care and child protection systems, particularly the interactions between social work organisations, police, health services, lawyers and the courts, the participation of children and parents, and children's outcomes, using mixed methods research: *Protecting Powers* (Wiley, 2008) examined emergency child protection interventions. She is co-author of *Principles of Family Law* (Thomson, 8th edn, 2008).

Brigitte Müller, PhD, psychologist FSP, is a Senior Research Associate at the School of Social Work, University of Applied Sciences and Arts Northwestern Switzerland. Her work in the past years covers a broad range of activities at the intersection of science and practice, which includes counselling, concept development and evaluations in child and youth welfare as well as child protection services. She also specialises in the topic of families where a parent has a mental illness. Recently she co-authored an article on laypersons help for parents with mental help problems (in *Child & Youth Services*, 2019).

Nigel Parton worked for more than 40 years at University of Huddersfield, UK, now on a part-time basis, as Professor of Applied Childhood Studies. His main research interests are concerned with child protection, social welfare and social work. He has written or edited 25 books, recently including *The Politics of Child Protection* (Palgrave Macmillan, 2014), and more than 100 journal articles and book chapters. He is currently the Editor in Chief of the open access online journal *Social Sciences*, and from 1996 to 2006 was co-editor of the journal *Children & Society*.

Tarja Pösö is Professor in Social Work at Tampere University, Finland. She also works as a part-time professor II in the Centre for Research on Discretion and Paternalism at the University of Bergen, Norway. She has studied child protection for a number of years with a keen interest in social work practice, ethics and methodologies as well as comparative child protection research. She is one of the co-editors of

Child Welfare Removals by the State (Oxford University Press, 2017) and *Lasten haastattelu lastensuojelussa* [*Interviews with Children in Child Protection*] (PS-kustannus, 2018).

Fred Powell is a Professor of Social Policy at University College Cork – National University of Ireland, where he served as Dean of Social Science between 2008 and 2014. His recent books include: *The Politics of Civil Society* (Policy Press, 2013), *Dark Secrets of Childhood: Media Power, Child Abuse and Public Scandals* (Policy Press, 2015) and *The Political Economy of the Irish Welfare State: Church, State and Capital* (Policy Press, 2017), which won the Richard Titmuss Book Prize 2018 in the UK. He previously wrote *The Politics of Social Work* (Sage, 2001).

Clarissa Schär works in the Department of Social Pedagogy within the Institute of Education at the University of Zurich, Switzerland. She is a teaching and research assistant. Her research interests are child protection, childhood and youth, body and gender and cultural studies. Among numerous publishing activities she is author and co-author of articles on how children, adolescents and parents experience the assessment of the well-being of the child (including 'Wenn es um das eigene Kind geht' [' When It Comes to Your Own Child'], in *SozialAktuell*, 2018). She has contributed to the initial research findings on this topic becoming visible both nationally and internationally.

Gilles Séraphin is full Professor of Educational Sciences at the University of Paris-Nanterre, France – UPL (CREF-EA1589) and editor-in-chief of the scientific journal *Recherches Familiales*. Between 2012 and 2017, he was Director of the National Observatory for Child Protection (ONPE). Today, his research are on public policies in favour of families and public policies of protection. His latest publication in English is 'Child Protection in France', in Lisa Merkel-Holguin, John D. Fluke and Richard D. Krugman (eds), *National Systems of Child Protection: Understanding the International Variability and Context for Developing Policy and Practice* (Springer, 2018).

Caroline Shore is a college lecturer at University College Cork, Ireland. She has worked as a senior social work practitioner in child protection. She continues to practise in the Irish child care courts as a freelance guardian *ad litem*. Her research and teaching interests are in the areas of child protection, values and ethics in social work practice, the scholarship of teaching, and professional development. She co-authored several articles, among which 'What Social Workers Talk

About When They Talk About Child Care Proceedings in the District Court in Ireland' in *Child & Family Social Work* (2018).

Marit Skivenes is a professor at the Department of Administration and Organisation Theory (University of Bergen, Norway), and director of the Centre for Research on Discretion and Paternalism. She completed her PhD in Political Science at the University of Bergen in 2002, and is a leading international scholar on discretionary decision making, children's rights and child protection systems. Skivenes has an extensive record of scientific publications, as well as being Principal Investigator for numerous research projects, and she recently received the prestigious Consolidator Grant from the European Research Council.

Øyvind Tefre works at the Western Norway University of Applied Sciences, Department of Welfare and Inclusion as a lecturer. He is a PhD candidate in Political Science at the Department of Administration and Organisation Theory at the University of Bergen, where he is also affiliated with the Centre for Research on Discretion and Paternalism. His research is comparative and focused on policymaking and professional decision-making in different welfare states and child welfare systems.

Tom van Yperen works at the Netherlands Youth Institute. He is also a special professor of Monitoring and Innovating Youth Care at the University of Groningen. Much of his research is on the outcome services. He helps many municipalities and institutions to further develop these services by using outcome monitoring as a tool to gradually improve the effectiveness of methods and interventions. He is chief editor of *Zicht op effectiviteit* [*A View on Effectiveness*] (Lemniscaat, 2017), which has become an important handbook for many researchers and practitioners in the field.

Kirti Zeijlmans works as researcher at the WODC, the research and documentation centre of the Ministry of Justice and Security in the Netherlands. Her current project focuses on the distinct approach to young adults in the criminal justice system. Her research interests focus on social work, decision making, youth care (in particular foster care), child abuse and youth delinquency. Prior to her current position, she conducted her PhD research titled 'Matching Children with Foster Carers' at the University of Groningen (2019), which focused on the decision-making process of matching in foster care.

Acknowledgements

This book would not be possible without the support of the University of Applied Sciences and Arts Northwestern Switzerland, School of Social Work, Institute for Studies in Children and Youth Services (FHNW) and the Swiss National Science Foundation (SNSF). The SNSF funded an international exploratory workshop to bring together several contributors of this book and to discuss policies, discourses and research on errors and mistakes in child protection. The FHNW enabled editing the book with a several month long sabbatical, from which Kay Biesel, a co-editor of the book, benefited.

The book is also the result of well-functioning international partnerships that were mainly developed in the context of the Interdisciplinary Network for Research on Child Welfare Proceedings and Decision-Making.

The editors would like to thank all contributors of the book for their work. In particular, they would like to acknowledge Paul Maetschke (FHNW) for his checking and formatting activities.

1

Errors and mistakes in child protection: an introduction

Kay Biesel, Judith Masson, Nigel Parton and Tarja Pösö

The central aim of this book is to describe and critically analyse the nature and impact of child protection errors and mistakes in different countries across Europe and the USA. It focuses on the development of policy and practice in relation to errors and mistakes in the different child protection systems, locating such developments in their relevant historical and political contexts. In the process, it will demonstrate how the perceptions, definitions and explanations of errors and mistakes vary both historically and culturally.

The idea for the book arose in the context of an international workshop on errors and mistakes in child protection organised by Stefan Schnurr and one of the editors, Kay Biesel (both FHNW School of Social Work), and took place in Basel in May 2017. The Swiss National Science Foundation funded the international workshop. Most of the contributors to the book were present and provided separate country reports about how errors and mistakes in child protection were understood and responded to in their respective jurisdictions and with what impacts. The book contains a total of 14 chapters: this introductory chapter, a conceptual framework chapter, 11 country-specific chapters (England, Finland, France, Germany, Ireland, Italy, Norway, the Netherlands, Sweden, Switzerland and the United States) and a concluding chapter. It shows how 'Western societies' with different child protection orientations deal with the issue of errors and mistakes. It presents an overview of the various historical and contemporary developments identified in the different countries and attempts to identify where there are similarities and differences, including what might be identified as current and future best practice. It highlights which strategies are seen as helpful in reducing errors and mistakes and in promoting quality in child protection. It is the first book that aims to provide knowledge of how countries in Europe and the United States deal with the issue of errors and mistakes in child protection and it adds to the small number of texts that aim to analyse child protection systems in their international and comparative contexts (Gilbert, 1997; Gilbert et al, 2011a; Burns et al, 2017).

The discovery of errors and mistakes in child protection

In many respects concerns about errors and mistakes have been a key influence on the development of child protection systems ever since the modern (re)discovery of child abuse in the 1960s. In fact, a common explanation of why there is so much child abuse is that it results from the errors and mistakes of welfare professionals – if only we could overcome the errors and mistakes in the identification and management of child abuse, the incidence and prevalence of the problem would be much less than it is. Attempting to address the challenges posed by errors and mistakes therefore becomes a major focus in order to prevent child abuse.

The growing concerns about errors and mistakes in child protection can be seen to be very much related to wider and growing social concerns about risk in society and the way this is understood and responded to in terms of debates about 'the risk society'. Biesel and Wolff (2013) have drawn on this perspective to analyse how the nature of errors and risks in child protection has developed in England and Germany and which is schematically summarised in Table 1.1.

The modern discovery of child abuse in the 1960s followed the publication in the *Journal of the American Medical Association* of an article titled 'The Battered-Child Syndrome' (Kempe et al, 1962). The article claimed that the syndrome could be characterised as a clinical condition in very young children who had received serious physical abuse, usually from a parent, and that it was a significant cause of childhood disability and death. It argued that the syndrome was often 'misdiagnosed' and that it should be considered in any child showing evidence of possible trauma or neglect or where there was a marked discrepancy between the clinical findings and the story presented by the parents. The use of X-rays to aid diagnosis was stressed and the authors recommended that doctors report all incidents to law enforcement or child protection agencies. Science, particularly medical science, was seen as vital for establishing our knowledge of child abuse and intervening where previously we may not have done. Not only did the problem of the 'battered child' quickly become identified as a significant social problem in the US and other Western countries it also helped to usher in major changes in child welfare law, policy and practice (Parton, 1985). While by the late 1970s the term 'child abuse' referred to a wide variety of situations that varied in form and degree, the 'battered-child syndrome'

Table 1.1: Stages in construction and control of errors and mistakes between 1960 and today

Child protection phase	Construction of errors and mistakes	Strategies to control errors and mistakes
Rediscovery of child abuse the 1960s	Denial of errors and mistakes; gradual problematisation of professional misdiagnosis; under-reporting of child abuse and neglect	Information campaigns; development of differential diagnostic tools; passing of special child protection laws; new reporting obligations; more research
Socio-critical debate about reasons for child maltreatment in the 1970s	Parents as error-causers; unreflected system-related errors and mistakes (abusive practices in institutions)	Training for professionals; development of new methods and helps; further law reforms
Expansion of child protection in the 1980s	Over-reporting of child abuse and neglect; resources problems; personnel turnover; increasing costs; heaping child protection scandals	Differential responses; development of new procedures and (actuarial) risk assessment instruments; use of new public management strategies
Child protection in the risk society in the 1990s and the beginning of the 21st century	Professionals as error-causers (standard and procedure deviations); discovery of system-related errors and mistakes (abusive practices in institutions); problematisation of organisational mismanagement; lack of contact and trust with families; quality problems	More training for professionals; development of quality standards; use of risk, quality management and early prevention strategies and so on

remained the root metaphor. It is also important to point out that the original work by Henry Kempe and his colleagues was significant in bringing the problem of child abuse to a wide audience in many countries. For example, the book by Ruth and Henry Kempe called *Child Abuse* (1978) was translated into eight languages. The focus was not only on the importance of professionals recognising the problem but also emphasising the importance of providing services to families to help them.

However, by the mid-1980s it was being increasingly recognised that much of the clinical and scientific research was not nearly as rigorous as was assumed and that there were a number of unforeseen and unintended consequences in the dominant approach to policy and practice. In particular, it seemed that some children were continuing to suffer while others were being wrongly identified as being at risk – what we might call the problems of both false negative and false positive error.

The problem of false positives was explicitly demonstrated in a high-profile scandal in Middlesbrough, an industrial town in the north-east of England. Some 121 young children were kept in the local general hospital against the wishes of their parents on emergency protection orders (then called Place of Safety Orders) in the summer of 1987 on suspicion of sexual abuse but based on highly contentious methods of investigation. This led to a major public inquiry published the following year (Secretary of State for Social Services, 1988).

It seemed that the systems established to identify, regulate and prevent child abuse and avoid professional errors and mistakes were themselves culpable. Reviewing the system in the USA, Waldfogel (1998) concluded there were problems of: *over-inclusion* – where some children and families were inappropriately subject to intervention; *under-inclusion* – where some children who should have been included were missed; *capacity* – where the number of reports to the system had increased so dramatically over the previous 30 years that the system could no longer cope with the demands being made of it; *service delivery* – where even those cases that crossed the threshold for appropriate inclusion did not receive the right sort of service or any service at all; and *service orientation* – where the obsessive focus on forensic investigation meant that the needs of the children and families concerned were not being addressed.

In many respects, by the 1990s concerns about child protection systems, certainly in the USA, England and Germany seemed to characterise many of the elements associated with the 'risk society' where society has become increasingly sceptical about providential reason – the idea that increased secular understanding of the world leads to a safer existence. There was a growing view that science and modern technologies were double-edged, creating new harms and negative consequences as well as offering beneficial possibilities. In relation to child protection, it seemed that the systems established to prevent child abuse had a series of unintended negative consequences and that the identification and prevention of the problem was much more contentious and complex than had been previously assumed.

The growing concerns about errors and mistakes in child protection can be seen to be very much related to wider and growing concerns about risk in society and the way this is understood and responded to in terms of debates about the 'risk society' (Beck, 1992). This does not simply refer to the fact that contemporary social life introduces new forms of danger but that living in the 'risk society' means living with a calculative attitude to the open possibilities of different actions with which we are continually confronted. The 'risk society' is thus a self-critical, reflexive society. According to Giddens 'the reflexive monitoring of risk is intrinsic to institutionalised risk systems' (1991: 119). It is in this context that concerns about errors and mistakes in child protection can be seen as almost emblematic of the times in which we live. However, this is likely to vary considerably in different cultural contexts and it will be interesting to see how these ideas – including the summary Table 1.1 developed from Biesel and Wolff (2013: 21) – applies in the different countries included in this book. The table was developed originally in relation to developments in England and Germany and we do not know if a similar historical developments and processes has taken place in other countries.

What is child protection in a cross-national perspective?

While the focus of this book is errors and mistakes in child protection, we have to recognise that what we mean by the term 'child protection' it is not straightforward. UNICEF uses the term broadly to refer to the prevention and responses to exploitation and abuse of children in all contexts (Bissell, 2015) and a child protection system is defined as 'certain formal and informal structures, functions and capacities that have been assembled to prevent and respond to violence, abuse, neglect and exploitation of children' (UNICEF et al, 2013: 3). However, trying to determine what 'child protection' is for the purposes of cross-national comparison is difficult. A consequence of the social, historical and cultural contexts of different countries is that what is meant by a child protection system differs considerably: basic words and concepts may have different meanings; statistics may differ and refer to different things; there may be major differences in the division of tasks and responsibilities between different organisations; and systems, policies and practices change rapidly (see for example Hearn et al, 2004). Translation itself brings an extra layer of complexity, potential misunderstanding and oversimplification when trying to compare different countries (Pösö, 2014).

However, a number of studies have attempted to compare child protection systems (see Parton, 2017 for a summary overview). *Combatting Child Abuse: International Perspectives and Trends* (Gilbert, 1997) was an early and influential attempt to compare child protection systems. Academic researchers were recruited to analyse the child protection systems in Belgium, Canada, Denmark, England, Finland, Germany, the Netherlands, Sweden and the USA. The key finding was that there were important variations between the countries concerning the extent to which systems emphasised a *child protection* or *family service* orientation, and the two orientations were distinguished along four dimensions.

The first dimension, and perhaps the most significant, was the way the problem of child abuse was framed. In some systems abuse was conceived as an act that demanded the protection of children from harm by 'degenerative relatives', whereas in other systems abuse was conceived as a problem of family conflict or dysfunction that arose from social and psychological difficulties but which responded to help and support.

Second, the response operated either as a mechanism for investigating deviance in a highly legalistic way, or as a service response responding to a family's needs. As a result, third, the child welfare professionals functioned either in the child protection orientation, in a highly adversarial way, or in the family service orientation, in a spirit of partnership – particularly with parents. Finally, while there seemed to be a high rate of voluntary arrangements with parents in making out-of-home placements with the family service orientation, in the child protection orientation the majority of out-of-home placements was compelled through the coercive powers of the state, usually in the form of court orders.

What the research suggested was that there were important differences in the way Anglo–American child welfare services were organised and the way they responded to concerns about child abuse, when compared to northern European and Nordic countries. The researchers argued that while the details of different programmes and policies were important, the way different systems operated was also influenced by wider cultural and societal conditions.

The book was published when a number of policy makers and politicians were looking at other countries to see if they could learn any lessons about how to organise their own child protection systems and the two orientations seemed to provide something of a benchmark for discussions and analyses in a number of research studies and government reports. Parton (2017) summarised the key elements and differences between the two orientations (see Table 1.2).

A child-focused orientation

More recently, there has been an attempt to update the comparative research originally reported in *Combatting Child Abuse* (Gilbert, 1997), this time comparing ten countries – the same countries as

Table 1.2: Difference between child protection (Anglo-American) and family service (northern European) systems

Broad type of system	Child protection (Anglo-American)	Family service (northern European)
Type of welfare state	Tendency to residual and selective provision	Tendency to comprehension and universal provision
Place of child protection services	Separated from family support services	Embedded within and normalised by broad child welfare or public health services
Type of child protection system	Legal, bureaucratic, investigative, adversarial	Voluntary, flexible, solution-focused, collaborative
Orientation to children and families	Emphasis on individual children's rights. Professionals' primary responsibility for child's welfare	Emphasis on family unit. Professionals usually work with the family as a whole
Basis of the service	Investigating risk in order to formulate child safety plan	Supportive or therapeutic responses to meeting needs or resolving problems
Coverage	Resources are concentrated on families where risks of (re)abuse are immediate and high	Resources are available to more families at an earlier stage

Source: Developed from Parton (2017).

before (Belgium, Canada, Denmark, England, Finland, Germany, the Netherlands, Sweden and the United States) plus Norway. The overall conclusion (Gilbert et al, 2011a) was that while the two original orientations – child protection and family service – were still relevant they needed to be revised in the light of the developments in the various countries during the intervening 15 years up to 2008/09.

The findings suggested that approaches to protecting children from abuse had become much more complex. Countries previously identified with the child protection orientation, for example England and the USA, had taken on some of the elements of the family service orientation. At the same time, there was also evidence that those countries that had previously operated according to a family service orientation had made efforts to respond to increasing concerns about harm to children. This seemed to be the case in all the Nordic countries (with the possible exception of Sweden) and all the north European countries studied.

It was also possible to discern the emergence of a new approach – a *child-focused orientation* (Gilbert et al, 2011b: 255). This orientation concentrated its focus on the child as an individual with an independent relation to the state. It was not restricted to narrow concerns about harm and abuse; rather the object of concern was the child's overall development and well-being. The programmes aimed to go beyond protecting children from risk to promoting children's welfare. In this context, concerns about harm and abuse were relevant as just one set of factors that might affect a child's development and well-being. If for any reason there was concern about a child's development, the state sought to intervene to offer support or more authoritative intervention if this was required. With a *child-focused orientation* the state takes on a growing role in terms of providing a wide range of early intervention and preventive services. The *child-focused* orientation also aimed to take into account the views and wishes of the child and took seriously the United Nations Convention on the Rights of the Child. Overall, the *child-focused orientation* puts children's rights above parents' rights and emphasises parental obligations and responsibilities as carers.

The United Nations Convention on the Rights of the Child can be seen as a unifying factor, given its ratification by all countries except the USA. However, its influence varies markedly both between countries and in relation to the different rights it promotes. It provides a lens through which policies and practices can be viewed and criteria – rights – against which they can be measured. Article 12, the child's right to participation in decision making, further explained in General Comment 12, has begun to change attitudes and practices among professionals and agencies enabling children to have a voice in decisions about their lives by listening to their views and experiences. As such practices become more widespread, former approaches can come to be viewed as mistaken.

The three orientations identified by Gilbert et al (2011b: 255) were derived from an analysis of a country's principal policies and aims and may not necessarily have been evident in practice; they are summarised in Table 1.3.

Recent developments

Gilbert et al (2011b) also identified several common trends that characterised the development of child protection systems in all the countries studied since the mid-1990s. First, the systems had expanded. More children, and hence more families, received services and interventions, although the degree of expansion was uneven and varied among countries and the orientation of the system. Second,

Table 1.3: Three orientations on the role of the state vis-à-vis child maltreatment

	Child focus	Family service	Child protection
Driver for intervention	The individual child's needs in a present and future perspective / societies need healthy and contributing citizens	The family unit needs assistance	Parents being neglectful towards children (maltreatment)
Role of the state	Paternalistic/defamilialisation – state assumes parent role; but seeks to refamilialise child by foster home/kinship/adoption	Parental support – state seeks to strengthen family relations	Sanctioning – state functions as 'nightwatchman' to ensure child's safety
Problem frame	Child's development and unequal outcomes for children	Social/psychological (family systems, poverty, inequality)	Individual/moralistic
Mode of intervention	Early intervention and regulatory/need assessment	Therapeutic/needs assessment	Legalistic/investigative
Aim of intervention	Promote well-being via social investment and/or equal opportunity	Prevention/social bonding	Protection/harm reduction
State–parent relationship	Substitutive/partnership	Partnership	Adversarial
Balance of rights	Children's rights / parental responsibility	Parents' rights to family life mediated by professional social workers	Children's/parents' rights enforced with legal means

Source: Developed from Gilbert et al (2011b: 255).

child protection operated in an increasingly volatile atmosphere where practices could come under critical media and political scrutiny and which was more intense in some jurisdictions than others – something we consider further later. Third, due in part to professional vulnerabilities, as well as the highly sensitive and complex nature of the work, there was an increased emphasis on legalistic and procedural thinking and decision making. Finally, there was a growing recognition of the issues posed by racial and ethnic disparities and the challenges posed by the growth in migration and asylum seeking.

Perhaps most significantly there were changes in the social, political and economic contexts during the previous 15 years. While these did not affect all countries equally and countries responded in different ways, there was no doubt they had an impact on child protection policy and practice. The growing significance of neoliberal ideas, the influence of globalisation, and the increased awareness of uncertainty and insecurity were all significant. The period had seen an intensification of global competition, wide-ranging mobility of capital and labour, the speeding up of economic and communication processes, and the increasing interdependence of national economies, which have contributed to the erosion of individual nation states' abilities to control their economies. The massive global downturn following the 'credit crunch' of 2007/08 and the crisis in the global banking and financial sectors demonstrated this very starkly.

In many respects these trends have become even more significant since Gilbert et al's comments in 2011. We have witnessed the continuing intensification of neoliberal policies and global competition and growing evidence of income and wealth disparities between the rich and the poor. The richest 0.1 per cent of the world's population increased their combined wealth by as much as the poorest 50 per cent between 1980 and 2016 (Alvaredo et al, 2017). Inequality is high in North America and Europe and has grown considerably in recent years. In the USA the richest 1 per cent accounted for 39 per cent of the nation's wealth in 2014, up from 22 per cent in 1980, while in Britain the richest 1 per cent control 22 per cent of the wealth, up from 15 per cent in 1984 (Alvaredo et al, 2017). It seems that inequalities are growing not just in income and wealth but also in family and community environments, life chances and political influence. We have witnessed the decline of long-established centre-ground political parties and the growth of nationalist and populist parties in a context of growing economic and social insecurity There is a growth in racism, particularly in relation to immigrants and refugees, which has had a significant impact on child welfare and protection systems (Skivenes et al, 2015).

For example, in the UK there is growing evidence that the decade since the financial crisis, with the squeeze on living standards, has brought these inequalities into sharp focus. Concerns abound that the poor are being left behind by the rich and that social mobility has completely stalled (Social Mobility Commission, 2019). Technological change and globalisation are threatening settled ways of living. Children have been particularly hard hit by recent austerity policy measures resulting in an estimated growth in child poverty between 2010 and 2021/22 of 1.5 million children, an increase from 31 per cent to 41 per cent of children and young people below the age of 18 (Portes and Reed, 2018).

Triggers for changes and reforms

One of the issues we are interested in is whether there are any notable differences in the way errors and mistakes are understood and responded to according to the overall orientation of the country concerned. Do the family service, child protection and child focused orientations develop different ways of handling errors and mistakes?

We are also aware of the differences between policy *action*, *reaction* and *inaction* in relation to errors and mistakes, where an *active* approach attempts to anticipate possible problems in advance so that policies and practices are put in place so that these can be avoided; a *reactive* approach responds to problems after the event and tries to correct whatever has gone wrong after the error or mistake has taken place; and finally an *inactive* approach simply does very little or nothing either in anticipation of or in reaction to any errors or mistakes. Do different orientations tend to favour a particular approach to errors and mistakes in terms of *action*, *reaction* and *inaction* and are there any notable differences in the triggers for change?

 For example, we were aware that in the UK and the US high-profile scandals had acted as major triggers for change and that the media had played a major role in this so that the overall policy approach tended to be more *reactive* (Gainsborough, 2010; Butler and Drakeford, 2011). In some countries, politicians have responded to errors and mistakes in child protection in increasingly moralistic and emotional terms (Warner, 2015), responses that reflect wider cultural anxieties which may not apply in all jurisdictions. We were interested to see how far such reactions were evident in the countries studied in this book and how far these differences might relate to these three different orientations.

What is clear is that scandals and catastrophes in a number of countries have shaken the image of child protection as an institution for promoting children's well-being and have helped shape the image of errors and mistakes to a wide audience. Testimonies from former residents about abusive practices in foster care and residential care as well as in educational and religious facilities have been heard in many countries in recent decades. Sköld (2016) estimates that investigations into historical institutional abuse have become the focus of political attention in at least 19 countries. These countries are mainly European but also include Australia, New Zealand and Canada. Former residents of child welfare institutions have made demands for recognition, reparation and justice due to devastating physical, sexual and emotional abuse and neglect experienced during their placements, some of them exceptionally cruel and constant. Their demands have brought media attention, which according to Sköld (2016), eventually forced governments to take action, and pursue prosecutions. Some governments have expressed an official apology and provided redress schemes to acknowledge past errors in the care provided. These responses are by their very nature public: as distinct from single incident reviews, these responses on historical institutional abuse reflect community expectations of transparent investigative processes and publicly available reports (Wright, 2017). Furthermore, the role of practitioners as carers for children in most vulnerable situations of out-of-home care and as wrongdoers in those situations highlighted in the scandals has challenged child protection professionals to revise their practice and ethical commitment to care critically (Kendrick and Hawthorn, 2015).

Public inquiries into historic, institutional abuse have underlined the importance of the institutionalisation of children's rights within national child protection systems as they have recognised the needs and rights of victims and survivors and given voice to them (Wright, 2017). It could therefore be argued that the scandals related to historic abuse have increased awareness of errors and mistakes in child protection.

These inquiries have also underlined the changing and contested nature of knowledge. The nature of 'truth' is especially contested when studying sensitive, normative and emotional issues as lived experiences, particularly in the past. Johanna Sköld (2016) has pointed out that investigating historical abuse is a complex act of balancing positivist empiricist and postmodern constructivist approaches to what can be truthfully said about the past. For, on the one hand, there are inquiries, which rest primarily on the voices of victims/survivors over other types of data, and on the other, those who claim that victim/survivor stories should be treated as constructed narratives. What should be treated as reliable, valid and credible knowledge is far from straightforward.

These discussions of historical abuse are a reminder that what we subjectively might think of as a social problem such as abuse in child protection facilities may not be – or may be – the same as the objective characteristics of the phenomenon (Loseke and Best, 2003). Likewise, scandals and catastrophes are not simple and straightforward reflections of errors and mistakes; rather they are accounts presented through lenses and filters, which magnify some aspects and shade others. Parton's historical analysis of the emergence of child abuse as a significant social problem in the UK provided an early example of drawing on social constructionist perspectives (Parton, 1985).

Child deaths, especially of children known to child protection services, are often at the core of scandals and investigations related to errors and mistakes. Child deaths are 'sentinel events' (Chen and Isaac, 2006: 265) but statistics relating to child homicides due to maltreatment do not provide an accurate indication of the prevalence because of difficulties in diagnosis and limited investigations. While recorded figures for such child (aged 0–15) homicides are low for the European counties represented here, ranging over 5 years from 0.20 per 100,000 children in Italy to 0.72 in Switzerland, including deaths with 'undetermined' intent (WHO, 2013: Tables 2.2–3) actual rates are likely to be far higher. The World Health Organization estimates that, globally, only a third of deaths due to maltreatment are recognised as homicides, a figure that varies widely, even within Europe.

Book summary

The next chapter explores some of the more conceptual and theoretical approaches to errors and mistakes and how these might inform our thinking about errors and mistakes in child protection more specifically. This is followed by the 11 different country chapters looking at England, Ireland, the Netherlands, Finland, Norway, Sweden, Switzerland, Germany, France, Italy and the USA. Each country chapter provides an outline of their respective child protection system, the key elements of its structure and the main orientation adopted. Each then attempts to address a series of interrelated questions as they apply to their particular country:

• How are errors and mistakes in child protection defined and constructed?
• What is understood by errors and mistakes in child protection and who defines these?
• Historically, when have errors and mistakes in child protection been identified and why?
• Which errors and mistakes in child protection are the main focus of concern both now and in the past?
• What has been the impact of changing demographics (such as changes in birth rate, ageing population, changes in immigration and the impact of refugees) in this context?
• Are there any specific groups of children who have been particularly the subject of errors and mistakes?
• What strategies have been developed to respond to and manage errors and mistakes in child protection?

- Have these strategies changed over time and, if so, how?
- Has the way errors and risks in child protection been managed encouraged risk averse approaches on the part of professionals and child protection agencies?
- What role have politics and the media played in the way that errors and mistakes have been both identified and responded to?
- In what ways has the child protection system taken account of the rights of both children and families when responding to errors and mistakes?
- What research is available on errors and mistakes in child protection? What are the research gaps and methodological challenges in this area of work?

The final chapter tries to identify the key similarities and differences identified across the 11 countries in the ways that errors and mistakes are identified, defined and responded to. It explores whether there are any significant differences in approach between the different child protection orientations, which we have outlined in this introduction, and looks at how far the responses could be characterised as *action, reaction* or *inaction*. We also discuss what the implications might be for policy and practice and whether some approaches to the way errors and mistakes are responded to are more productive than others in attempting to improve both learning and the child protection systems themselves and, most crucially, for helping to prevent child abuse.

References

Alvaredo, F., Chancel, L., Piketty, T., Saez, E. and Zucman, G. (2017) *World Inequality Report 2018*, Paris: World Inequality Lab.

Beck, U. (1992) *Risk Society: Towards a New Modernity*, London: Sage.

Biesel, K. and Wolff, R. (2013) *Expertise: Das dialogisch-systemische Fall-Labor – Ein Methodenbericht zur Untersuchung problematischer Kinderschutzverläufe* [*Expertise: The Dialogic-Systemic Case Laboratory – A Methodological Report for the Investigation of Problematic Child Protection Processes*], Cologne: Nationales Zentrum Frühe Hilfen.

Bissell, S. (2015) 'Protecting Children from All Forms of Violence', *Child Abuse & Neglect*, 50: 9–14.

Burns, K., Pösö, T. and Skivenes, M. (eds) (2017) *Child Welfare Removals by the State: A Cross-Country Analysis of Decision-Making Systems*, New York: Oxford University Press.

Butler, I. and Drakeford, M. (2011) *Social Work on Trial: The Colwell Inquiry and the State of Welfare*, Bristol: Policy Press.

Chen, J. and Isaac, R. (2006) 'The Relation Between Child Death and Child Maltreatment', *Archives of Disease in Childhood*, 91(3): 265–9.

Gainsborough, J.F. (2010) *Scandalous Politics: Child Welfare Politics in the States*, Washington, DC: Georgetown University Press.

Giddens, A. (1991) *Modernity and Self-Identity: Self and Society in the Late Modern Age*. Cambridge: Polity Press.

Gilbert, N. (ed.) (1997) *Combatting Child Abuse: International Perspectives and Trends*, New York: Oxford University Press.

Gilbert, N., Parton, N. and Skivenes, M. (2011b) 'Changing Patterns of Response and Emerging Orientations', in N. Gilbert, N. Parton and M. Skivenes (eds) *Child Protection Systems: International Trend and Orientations*, New York: Oxford University Press, pp 243–57.

Gilbert, N., Parton, N. and Skivenes, M. (eds) (2011a) *Child Protection Systems: International Trends and Orientations*, New York: Oxford University Press.

Hearn, J., Pösö, T., Smith, C., White, S. and Korpinen, J. (2004) 'What Is Child Protection? Historical and Methodological Issues in Comparative Research on *Lastensuojelu*/Child Protection', *International Journal of Social Welfare*, 13(1): 28–41.

Howitt, D. (1993) *Child Abuse Errors: When Good Intentions Go Wrong*, New Brunswick, NJ: Rutgers University Press.

Kempe, C.H., Silverman, F.N., Steele, B.F., Droegemueller, W. and Silver, H.K. (1962) 'The Battered-Child Syndrome', *Journal of the American Medical Association*, 181(1): 17–24.

Kempe, R.S. and Kempe, C.H. (1978) *Child Abuse*, Cambridge, MA: Harvard University Press.

Kendrick, A. and Hawthorn, M. (2015) 'Dilemmas of Care: Social Work and Historic Abuse', in J. Sköld and S. Swain (eds) *Apologies and the Legacy of Abuse of Children in 'Care'*, London: Palgrave Macmillan, pp 172–80.

Loseke, D.R. and Best, J. (eds) (2003) *Social Problems: Constructionist Readings*, New York: Aldine de Gruyter.

Parton, N. (1985) *The Politics of Child Abuse*, Basingstoke: Macmillan.

Parton, N. (2017) 'Comparing Child Protection Systems: Towards a Global Perspective', in P. Dolan and N. Frost (eds) *The Routledge Handbook of International Child Welfare*, Abingdon: Routledge, pp 225–42.

Portes, J. and Reed, H. (2018) *The Cumulative Impact of Tax and Welfare Reforms*, London: Equality and Human Rights Commission.

Pösö, T. (2014) 'Translation as a Knowledge Transformation Practice: The Ambiguous Case of Presenting Finnish Child Welfare in English', *European Journal of Social Work*, 17(5): 616–26.

Pösö, T. (2018) 'Experts by Experience Infusing Professional Practices in Child Protection', in A. Falch-Eriksen and E. Backe-Hansen (eds) *Human Rights in Child Protection: Implications for Professional Practice and Policy*, London: Palgrave Macmillan, pp 111–28.

Secretary of State for Social Services (1988) *Report of the Inquiry into Child Abuse in Cleveland*, Cmnd 412, London: HMSO.

Skivenes, M., Barn, R., Kriz, K. and Pösö, T. (eds) (2015) *Child Welfare Systems and Migrant Children: A Cross Country Study of Policies and Practices*, New York: Oxford University Press.

Sköld, J. (2016) 'The Truth About Abuse? A Comparative Approach to Inquiry Narratives on Historical Institutional Abuse', *History of Education*, 45(4): 492–509.

Social Mobility Commission (2019) *State of the Nation: Social Mobility in Great Britain 2018–19*, London: Social Mobility Commission.

UNICEF, UNHCR, Save the Children and World Vision (2013) *A Better Way to Protect ALL Children: The Theory and Practice of Child Protection Systems*, Conference Report of Conference 13–16 November, in New Delhi, India, New York: UNICEF.

Waldfogel, J. (1998) *The Future of Child Protection: How to Break the Cycle of Abuse and Neglect*, Cambridge, MA: Harvard University Press.

Warner, J. (2015) *The Emotional Politics of Social Work and Child Protection*, Bristol: Policy Press.

WHO (World Health Organization) (2013) *European Report on Preventing Child Maltreatment*, Copenhagen: WHO Regional Office for Europe.

Wright, K. (2017) 'Remaking Collective Knowledge: An Analysis of the Complex and Multiple Effects of Inquiries into Historical Child Abuse', *Child Abuse & Neglect*, 74: 10–22.

2

Errors and mistakes in child protection: understandings and responsibilities

Kay Biesel and Michelle Cottier

Introduction

Child protection is a practice that is often assumed to be prone to errors and mistakes. Decisions that must be made, based on the assessment of current and future family situations and of risks to children's well-being, are well intended but may nevertheless go wrong. This is tragic for children and parents as well as for professionals and their organisations. In particular, if children are harmed or even die due to wrong decisions or inappropriate interventions, the disaster potential of child protection becomes clear. Also, assaults (including sexual assaults) on children by professionals shed light on how vulnerable children can be in institutions that are intended for their protection.

Howitt (1993) was one of the first authors to point out that child protection is affected by errors and mistakes. In his book, *Child Abuse Errors: When Good Interventions Go Wrong*, he suggested a typology that is still pertinent today. He differentiated between *true positive, false positive, true negative* and *false negative* diagnoses in child protection (compare Howitt, 1993: 31), whereby *false positive judgements* describe situations in which professionals diagnose child maltreatment wrongly, and *false negative judgements* are situations where professionals do not identify child maltreatment as such. These wrong decisions by professionals can have life-changing effects for children and their families, especially when parents are incorrectly suspected of abusing or neglecting their children and in consequence children are removed from them (*over-involvement*) or when children remain in families where they suffer maltreatment and nothing is done to protect them (*under-involvement*). Even worse, however, is when children, who are placed for their safety, are sheltered in institutions of poor quality where they are not loved, and where they grow up suffering abuse or neglect. Such cases demonstrate that decisions in child protection are rarely harmless. According to Howitt, errors and mistakes can emerge in the stages of reporting, diagnosis, identification of the perpetrator and in the actions which are taken to protect children (compare Howitt, 1993: 188).

An important contribution of Howitt's book is the insight that errors and mistakes in child protection are *socially constructed*. Whether they are recognised and criticised as such depends on the status and rights of children and parents in society, and the powers of professionals to protect children from abuse and neglect. Similarly, as discussed in the introduction to this book (Chapter 1), what is meant by 'errors' and 'mistakes' varies according to time and place, and these concepts are themselves socially constructed; the definition of errors and mistakes in child protection cannot be universal and constant over time, but is necessarily based on societal expectations, legal regulations, professional values, norms and attitudes as well as quality standards. Also, errors and mistakes in child protection cannot all be defined in a normative way. They are multicausal in origin, and in practice difficult to anticipate and to avoid in real time (compare Biesel, 2011: 70). Often, they are identified only after an event with bad consequences, when it is too late; there is no opportunity to correct them, and it appears that the only possibility remaining is to ask questions of responsibility.

In view of these difficulties, the challenge for a book on errors and mistakes in child protection, aimed at reflecting how countries across Europe and the USA deal with them, is to frame what is being discussed. The purpose of this conceptual chapter is therefore to give an overview of the literature on the understandings of what errors and mistakes in child protection might be, and who or what is responsible for them. In support of this goal, we present a vocabulary of different understandings of errors and mistakes in child protection, making visible their social construction. We further explain how in different societies the question of who or what is responsible for them is a function of different definitions of the causes and consequences of errors and mistakes. Finally, we discuss different legal responses to errors and mistakes and the way they frame responsibility for errors and mistakes in child protection. In doing so, we hope to give readers of the book an analytical entry point into the country chapters (Chapters 3–13) and to show ways to link and compare different understandings of and responses to errors and mistakes across Europe and the USA.

Understanding errors and mistakes in child protection as socially constructed

As will become clear, it is impossible to formulate a universal definition of errors and mistakes for the field of child protection. The understandings of what an error or mistake could be depend on the views of the members of a particular society at a given time. Often it is unclear what is meant with the statement, 'you committed an error' or 'you made a mistake'. This is not particularly surprising, as there are different terms for errors and mistakes such as bug, fault, failure, lapse, slip, deviation, misconception, misunderstanding, misbelief, misjudgement, wrongdoing, offence, violation, crime or mismanagement. All these terms are used for actions in child protection that went wrong, thereby framing them in particular ways. What can, therefore, be understood by an error, mistake, failure, wrongdoing and violation and how do these terms frame who or what is responsible for them?

The term *error* can be interpreted as a deviation from a standard, regulation, goal, condition or result. It indicates that an obligation has not been fulfilled or a target has not been met. In contrast, the term *mistake* has a different meaning. It emphasises not a deviation but a misunderstanding, a misinterpretation of a situation or a misbelief, which in consequence causes the wrong decision or choice in practice. The word *failure* in turn underlines that a person, project or object has been unsuccessful. The term *wrongdoing* accentuates an action which is unjust from a moral point of view. The word *violation* is used to designate actions that violate legal norms (see Figure 2.1).

Reason (1990: 9, 53), for example, suggests an error classification that is based on research on organisational accidents in the technology sector, derived from Rasmussen's skill–rule–knowledge classification of human performance (compare Reason, 1990: 53, 42–4). He uses the generic term *error* to distinguish between skill-based *slips and lapses, rule-based or knowledge-based mistakes* and *violations*. He understands slips and lapses as actions, which do not proceed close to plan because of inattention or over-attention by individuals. Distinct from that, he classifies rule-based and knowledge-based mistakes as actions, 'where the plan itself is inadequate to achieve its objectives' (Reason, 1990: 17). Rule-based mistakes arise because of the misapplication of good rules or application of bad rules in organisations. Conversely, knowledge-based mistakes occur because individuals are limited in their rationality or in their knowledge. In contrast, violations are situations in which individuals routinely, for reasons of optimisation or necessity,

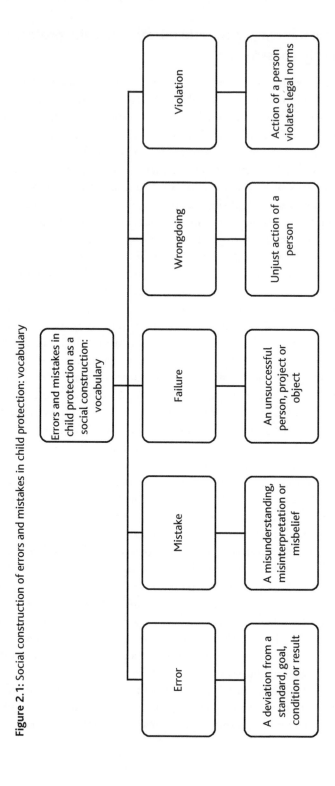

Figure 2.1: Social construction of errors and mistakes in child protection: vocabulary

break rules, disrespect standards or regulations, or offend against laws (compare Reason, 1990: 53, 1997: 72–83, 2008: 29).

An alternative vocabulary can be found in a book by Biesel (2011), which is based on research in youth welfare offices in Germany. He distinguishes between errors and mistakes by their consequences and not by their causes. He categorises the following types of errors and mistakes: *fatal errors and mistakes* that result in the death of a child; those that have harmful effects for a child (*damaging errors and mistakes*); and those that can be reversed in practice with no significant harm or costs (*harmless errors and mistakes*). In addition, he also discusses violations by professionals as legally relevant errors and mistakes.

The existence of such a variation of vocabulary and understandings used to criticise, scandalise or blame erroneous child protection practice confirms our argument that errors and mistakes in child protection are always socially constructed. They are based on ever-changing ethics for what a society sees as right or wrong practices in child protection. These ethics in turn are influenced by concepts about how children in families should grow up, what is expected from parents in bringing up their children, and how children should be protected from abuse and maltreatment (compare Biesel, 2011: 84); these concepts can be child-focused, family service oriented or based on a child protection approach (compare Gilbert et al, 2011: 255). Ethics are not the only aspect, the status of the rights of service-user also play a role. For example, the United Nations Convention on the Rights of the Child (UNCRC) had a big impact in many countries on the status of children and led to changed views on their need for protection and their participation rights. In countries where children are seen as subjects with their own rights and as current citizens, and where a child-focused orientation is present, it is important to make sure that professionals also take the child's best interests into consideration (compare Gilbert et al, 2011: 252-256). Accordingly, it may occur in these countries that if professionals ignore children's rights and put parents' rights above children's rights, they will be criticised for such errors, or create a scandal. By contrast, in countries where children have fewer rights or limited access to justice, because they are refugees for example, the fact that the best interests of the child are not taken into account and protection against harm in refugee camps is limited may not be considered to be an error.

In this respect, understandings of errors and mistakes in child protection are always a mirror for social developments in societies. There is not one single, universally agreed definition of errors and mistakes in child protection, or if there is one at all, there is only an agreement on the supposition that it includes some kind of deviation (see Reason, 2008: 28). Therefore, it makes sense to differentiate linguistically between errors and mistakes in child protection, because the term *error* refers to a deviation from a standard, goal, condition or result, whereas the term *mistake* denotes a misunderstanding, misinterpretation or misbelief within a situation. There are also terms that indicate more specifically who or what is responsible, such as failure, wrongdoing or violation. Often words are used that are linked to the consequences of errors and mistakes, such as fatal, damaging or harmless errors and mistakes. For this reason, it is essential to think carefully about which word to use and why, in order to make clear when good intentions in child protection went wrong. In child protection it is challenging to judge whether errors have been caused by deviations from standards and regulations or not, and whether professionals should be legally liable for them. Indeed, sometimes it is essential for the protection of a child that professionals do *not* follow standards or rules, if the standards or rules are themselves flawed. An error or mistake in child protection is an undesirable event. It can be avoided if a more favourable and feasible alternative exists (compare Weingardt, 2004: 234), but this is often not known or not recognised by the people making the decision. For that reason, it is essential to accept that it is a meta-failure to think that errors and mistakes do not exist; there is no zero-failure paradise in child protection (compare Sicora, 2017: 45).

Causes of errors and mistakes

It is well known that professionals in child protection are not free to take decisions and to support families as they choose because bounded rationalities and lack of information play a major role in the occurrence of errors and mistakes (Munro, 1996). Professionals are dependent on the cooperation of their clients, the working conditions in their teams and organisations and the resources and possibilities of their collaborating partners (compare Wolff et al, 2013: 15–16). Often, they do not know service-users very well. Despite contradictory or inadequate information they have to take decisions, the effects of which they cannot fully assess. Many errors and mistakes in child protection do not result from professionals not following standards or rules, but from circumstances such as heavy caseloads, which have meant that they have been unable to identify their mistakes and change their decisions in a timely way.

It is known from research, for example, that professionals do not systematically evaluate their hypotheses, due to a lack of information. They tend to use information that is easily obtainable and vivid, and to reconsider their decisions too slowly (Munro, 1996, 1999;

Broadhurst et al, 2010). Other insights from research are that not enough attention is paid to what children say, to how they look and to how they behave (Broadhurst et al, 2010; Wolff et al, 2016). Other causes of errors and mistakes known from research on child deaths or from serious case reviews are insufficient exchange of information and cooperation between organisations; incomplete and superficial recording of information; inadequate assessments and diagnoses; ineffective decision making; poor understanding of the family system; confirmation heuristics and biases; parent-focused thinking and acting; failing to focus on the child as the subject with their own rights and needs; ignoring and not including men, especially aggressive or violent members of the family; insufficient procedures and support; inadequate case-consultation and supervision (compare Biesel and Wolff, 2013a: 122; Axford and Bullock, 2005: 7–15).

In child protection, professionals are influenced by different factors such as:

- *Skills related factors*: lack of competence and skills, trouble with the dual mandate (to support families and to protect children at the same time).
- *Family or user factors*: unstable relationships, social and health problems (unemployment, poverty, housing exclusion or threatened with homelessness, mental health problem), resistant or unmotivated parents.
- *Staff and team factors*: unqualified staff, staff turnover, problems and conflicts in the teams.
- *Organisational factors*: difficult working conditions, high case- and workloads, lack of time, methods and instruments, conflict of objectives, poor or no leadership.
- *Cooperation factors*: problems establishing trust and help relationships with families, lack of coordination in collaborations between agencies, services, departments and authorities, insufficient information exchange.
- *Legal factors*: lack of clear decision criteria or processes, lack of clear attribution of responsibilities to different actors, contradictory regulatory goals, fear of individual legal liability as an impediment for a learning culture.
- *Public opinion factors*: General public criticism of child protection work (too much or not enough intervention), scandals arising from individual cases.

(Compare Wolff et al, 2013: 15–16.)

Because of these different factors that can trigger errors and mistakes in child protection, resulting in harmless but also serious outcomes, a new approach to investigating child abuse deaths has been introduced in more recent years, the systems approach (compare Munro, 2005; Biesel and Wolff, 2013b). The approach is taken from the civil aviation industry. Its original aim was to avoid errors and mistakes in the interaction between humans and machines. It is not directly transferable to child protection. However, it tells us how to respond to errors and mistakes and establish a safety culture through constantly learning from them. It also points out that professionals are at the sharp end of the child protection system where they are responsible for decisions and interacting with children and parents. How they are able to take and monitor decisions and the way they can collaborate with and support families is influenced by various factors (as described earlier), especially by individual factors (knowledge and skills, case dynamics, conflicts of interests), and by organisational factors such as resources, constraints and the organisational culture.

Organisational cultures particularly affect professionals handling child protection matters (compare Reason, 1997: 38; Biesel, 2011: 77; Munro, 2019). They determine whether, and which, errors and mistakes are detected, and how organisations can learn from them. There are, according to Westrum (1993) for example, organisations where nobody is interested in identifying and learning from errors and mistakes (*pathological culture*). More common, however, are organisations that deal with errors and mistakes in a bureaucratic way where it is not required to identify and to report them, but if they are discovered, local solutions will be chosen (*bureaucratic culture*). In contrast, an organisational culture in which mistakes are managed proactively is characterised by strategies that help to locate and eliminate errors and mistakes at an early stage, before they cause significant harm (*generative culture*). Organisations with a generative culture are desirable in child protection, but hard to develop in practice, because professionals are often blamed for errors and mistakes, not least because these can have serious consequences (compare Leigh, 2017). However, the literature highlights that to balance safety for children at risk and avoiding errors and mistakes it is fundamental to have just, flexible and learning cultures within child protection authorities and organisations where errors and mistakes can be dealt with openly (Reason, 1997: 191–220; Dekker, 2012; Weick and Sutcliffe, 2015). To achieve this, child protection authorities and organisations should be more supported to manage the unexpected, and to be able to create generative cultures where professionals will be respected for their knowledge and skill and where the quality of relationships among employees is at the heart of the organisation's activities (compare Weick and Sutcliffe, 2015).

Dekker (2014) considers that it would be helpful if errors and mistakes were no longer seen as the result of the behaviour of individuals but rather as symptoms of trouble deeper inside authorities and organisations; the same, of course, applies to the whole child protection system, in which there are often problems with interagency collaboration. This would widen the view to *why* something went wrong and would better highlight that inside safe authorities and organisations no one works improperly, there are simply well-intentioned people in imperfect institutions. This new view makes it more possible to understand why professionals in child protection who made errors or mistakes, did what they did, and to find out why it made sense for them to do what they did (see Table 2.1). The extent to which this new view in child protection is established is an open question and may be clarified in the country chapters of the book. Whether this new view operates or not depends on how errors and mistakes in a given society are socially constructed and whether only individual professionals are seen as the originators of errors. It depends also on the extent to which the fact that child protection is a risky and error-prone practice, not fully able to protect children against harm, is accepted (compare Berrick, 2018).

It is not particularly surprising that in reaction to fatal cases this new view often does not (yet) play a major role. The difficulty is that cases causing public scandal often influence discourses and debates on errors and mistakes. On the basis of such individual cases, the media generate the impression that professionals alone are responsible for the fatal development of errors and mistakes, without taking into account the factors that influence them. In view of this, it is not surprising that when children are harmed or even die professionals are often scapegoated and, consequently, have little interest in reporting their errors and mistakes openly and assisting learning from them.

Reason (2008: 69–103) differentiates the following reactions to errors and mistakes: *the plague response, the person response, the legal response* and *the systems response*. In the context of the plague response, professionals are seen as primarily responsible for errors and mistakes. In order to keep them away from making errors and mistakes again, it is necessary to formalise and build procedures for their practice with the help of technological measures. Where the person response plays a role, professionals are also seen as responsible for errors and mistakes. However, they are not regarded as a plague. Nevertheless, it is essential to reduce unwanted professional behaviour by using disciplinary, instructive, managerial and inspection measures to control and observe their actions. A variation of the person response is the legal response, but with a strong moral imperative.

Table 2.1: The difference between the old and the new view on the origin of errors and mistakes in accordance to Dekker

Old view on the origin of errors and mistakes	New view on the origin of errors and mistakes
Errors and mistakes are causes of trouble	Errors and mistakes are symptoms of deeper trouble inside of authorities or organisations
Errors and mistakes are separate categories of behaviour, to be feared and fought	Errors and mistakes are attributions, judgements that are established after the fact
Errors and mistakes are the targets; professionals' behaviour is the problem and has to be controlled	Behaviour is systematically connected to features of professionals' tools, tasks and working environment
Errors and mistakes are something to declare war on. Professionals need to practise perfection	Error and mistakes are information about how professionals have learned to cope (successfully or not) with complexities and contradictions of real work
Errors and mistakes are simple problems. Once all things are in place, just get professionals to pay attention and comply	Errors and mistakes are at least as complex as the authority or organisation that helps create them
With tighter procedures, compliance, technology and supervision, it is possible to reduce the problem of errors and mistakes in child protection	With better understanding of the messy details of professionals' daily work, it is possible to find ways to make it better for them to improve their practice
It is necessary to achieve zero errors and mistakes, zero serious cases, zero child death cases	It is necessary to enhance the resilience of professionals and their authorities and organisations

Source: Dekker (2014, p xvi).

Professionals are also seen as responsible for errors and mistakes; they are considered to be highly trained, so they should not make errors and mistakes: they have a duty of care. For that reason, it is required to sanction and punish professionals for their errors and mistakes through civil and criminal law measures, aimed at protecting child protection practice from fallible professionals, or providing financial compensation for victims. In contrast, the systems response (the new view on the origin of errors and mistakes) focuses on the fact that professionals are imperfect. They commit errors and mistakes because of adverse circumstances and factors. For this reason, measures will be used to change poor practice conditions and promote learning from errors and mistakes.

Legal responses to errors and mistakes in child protection

Mirroring different understandings of errors and mistakes and their causes, legal responses can also be framed in different ways. Legal discourse thereby contributes to the social construction of child protection errors and mistakes in an important way (as already described, and see Howitt, 1993). For while we are always constructing and changing the world, we do so in the context of the institutions, laws and frameworks of meaning handed to us by previous generations and, hence, extant in the world. However, law is not monolithic and differences in logic and approach compete in the legal arena. A tension exists between an approach that attributes responsibility for child protection errors and mistakes to the individual on the one hand, and an approach that focuses on the responsibility of local authorities and agencies, or the state, on the other hand.

If we look more closely at the legal response as identified by Reason (discussed in the preceding section), it becomes apparent that he takes into account only one of three possible levels of legal responsibility (see Table 2.2), *individual legal responsibility*. Professionals active in the child protection system are indeed held personally accountable for actions and failure to act. Errors and mistakes in child protection may constitute offences against *criminal law*. For example, the removal of a child without a decision by the competent authority, be it a court or an administrative body, will in many countries constitute the criminal offence of child abduction, kidnapping or child theft (for the position in Switzerland, see Bernard et al, 2016). *Tort law*, the law of civil wrongs, is the basis for claims for financial compensation against individual child

Table 2.2: Levels of legal responsibility

Level of legal responsibility	Instruments
Individual responsibility	*Criminal law*: punishment; *tort law*: financial compensation of victims of errors and mistakes by individual professionals; *labour law and civil service law*: warning, reprimand, termination of the employment relationship
Responsibility of local authorities and agencies	*Control by courts* of decisions of local authorities; *appeals* to higher courts; *supervisory authorities*: quality development and control; *systematic review* of individual cases of child death or serious child abuse; *financial compensation* of victims of errors and mistakes by local authorities and agencies; obligation of creating *risk-averse working conditions* for child protection professionals
State responsibility	*International human rights law*: responsibility of states monitored through international courts and human rights treaty bodies; *national law*: national programmes of reparation for victims of systematic violations of children's and parents' rights by the child protection system

protection practitioners or civil servants who have harmed parents or children through their actions or inactions (Fairgrieve and Green, 2004). *Labour law* and *civil service law* may provide sanctions ranging from warnings, to reprimands, to termination of employment following a serious breach of a duty. However, the new view on the origin of errors and mistakes already discussed (the systems response) is more in line with the two other levels of legal responsibility, the responsibility of local authorities and agencies, and state responsibility.

Local child protection authorities and agencies can, in most legal systems, be held legally accountable for their actions or inactions. Decisions to remove children from the home or restrict parents' rights cannot generally be made solely by child protection authorities and organisations but are under the control of courts or boards, if they are not themselves organised as courts. This is intended to prevent errors and mistakes, such as over-intervention, to ensure decisions are based on evidence, that children and parents are heard, and that intervention is proportionate and respectful of the rights of parents and children. Errors and mistakes by courts and boards can be appealed, a process which may involve redressing violations of the right to be heard, analysing the facts again or just reconsidering the reasons stated for reasons stated for the decision. Control by courts is a classic instrument for dealing with errors and mistakes in that it may be able to correct erroneous decisions, such as the violation of the principle of proportionality, by taking measures that are too strong or too weak. If the complaint is successful, an error or mistake can be corrected: for example, removal of a child in breach of the proportionality principle can be replaced by a less invasive measure. Although appeals to courts have been used to challenge unfair decisions by front-line social workers, in many legal systems decisions, for example, to consider a child is 'at risk', are not reviewed by the judiciary (Berrick et al, 2015).

Second, and in addition to these means for securing legal redress, the law can be used to regulate institutions by establishing *supervisory authorities* or *inspectorates* charged with monitoring and assessing the functioning of child protection authorities and agencies in general, through standard setting and quality assessment. Supervision uses tools such as directives, training and supervisory reviews of the functioning of authorities or of the handling of individual cases.

A third mechanism is the *systematic review* of individual cases of death or serious child abuse and neglect not prevented by child protection authorities or agencies, such as in England and Wales child safeguarding practice reviews put in place by the Child Safeguarding Practice Review and Relevant Agency (England) Regulations 2018.

Fourth, some legal systems provide for a legal obligation of local authorities and agencies to *compensate financially* for damage caused by their actions or failure to act (compare Fairgrieve and Green, 2004).

Fifth, there may be legal obligations on local agencies to create the work conditions necessary to exercise different professional roles in the child protection system in a way that respects the fundamental rights of clients, especially through providing adequate staff resources and training (compare McFadden et al, 2014).

On the level of state responsibility, states, by signing international human rights conventions, assume responsibility for protecting the human rights of everyone living in them; this can include protecting parents and children from child protection errors and mistakes. For example, the European Convention on Human Rights and Fundamental Freedoms sets out positive obligations on states to protect individuals (Articles 2 and 3) and to support family life, and negative obligations not to interfere with family or personal life (Article 8). Errors and mistakes in child protection and the absence of effective remedies may amount to a 'failure to protect'. Individuals whose rights have been breached can (albeit through an arduous and lengthy process) make a claim against the state. The European Court of Human Rights hears these cases, and has developed a body of case law interpreting the state's duties including to protect children against abuse and neglect in care homes (Nencheva and Others v. Bulgaria, Application no. 48609/06, 18 June 2013), and from extreme neglect and emotional abuse by their parents (Z. and Others v. the United Kingdom, Application no. 29392/95, 10 May 2001). Errors and mistakes resulting in over-intervention have also been held to breach parents' and children's human rights (T.P. and K.M. v. United Kingdom, Application no. 28945/95, 10 May 2001; Venema v. The Netherlands, Application no. 35731/97, 17 December 2002; Haase v. Germany, Application no. 11057/02, 8 April 2004). The decisions of the European Court of Human Rights are of importance beyond the individual case, because there is general acceptance in Europe that the decisions of the Court, even if they concern only one Contracting State, will be implemented in *all* Contracting States through law reform, and that the Court's standards will be applied in practice (*de facto erga omnes* effect of the Court's case law, compare Büchler and Keller, 2016).

The United Nations Committee on the Rights of the Child (CRC) has also developed a practice on quality management in child protection and recommends state parties establish mechanisms that allow them to effectively manage, monitor and hold accountable the implementing bodies of child protection at national and subnational levels (Committee on the Rights of the Child, 2011, para 42). The effectiveness of these international standards depends on political will at the national level, as the Committee itself has very limited powers to ensure that its recommendations are followed (Simmons, 2009).

It is also the case that at the *national level*, some states take responsibility for systematic violations of individual rights in child protection through national programmes of reparation (Sköld and Swain, 2015). Examples are the reparations following the National Inquiry into the Separation of Aboriginal and Torres Strait Islander Children From Their Families in Australia (Wilkie, 1997), and more recently the financial 'contribution of solidarity' following the Swiss Federal Act on Compulsory Social Measures and Placements prior to 1981 (CSMPA) from 30 September 2016, and the compensation of victims of institutional abuse following the Report of the Historical Institutional Abuse Inquiry in Northern Ireland (Hart, 2017).

When comparing the advantages and disadvantages of different types of legal response, it becomes clear that there are strong limitations to legal instruments focusing on individual responsibility. While the law clarifies what the desirable and permitted individual actions are and which actions have to be avoided, it cannot provide guidance on how to develop a child protection system in which only desirable and permitted actions take place. The processes in which the law clarifies individual responsibilities and obligations are also cumbersome and costly, and operate retrospectively; that is, identifying liability for errors and mistakes instead of focusing on their avoidance. Also, and most importantly, the clarification of individual legal responsibility does not support the creation of generative cultures of errors and mistakes in child protection authorities or agencies. For example, when only professionals are held accountable for serious cases, they feel blamed and even criminalised. In this situation, judicial proceedings do not support the understanding of errors and mistakes in child protection. On the contrary, they produce fear among professionals and, in the worst case, turn them into secondary victims, who feel guilty and personally responsible because they failed to avoid harm to a child in a case that ended tragically (compare Dekker, 2012: 76, 2014: 24). In addition, there are substantial hurdles in accessing the law, especially for the most vulnerable, the children themselves, but also for disadvantaged groups of parents who do not have the material and personal resources to seek legal redress for violations of their rights (compare Sandefur, 2008), all the more so as many countries have reduced legal aid, thereby making legal advice and access to the courts unaffordable for many (compare Flynn and Hodgson, 2017).

For all of these reasons, it seems most promising to use legal instruments that are situated on the level of the *responsibility of local authorities and agencies* as well as of *nation states* (compare Table 2.2). Quality development and control implemented by supervisory authorities or by authorities and agencies themselves, the systematic review of individual cases of child death or serious child abuse, and instruments aimed at creating risk-aware working conditions and generative cultures on errors and mistakes in child protection could be the best strategies. But errors and mistakes in child protection are not easy to identify and to stop. There is no technological or legal solution to eliminate them once and for all. It is hard to live with them and to accept that they will never go away. This is the big challenge and also the major problem of child protection.

Conclusion

Good intentions in child protection can go wrong. They do not necessarily have to. This is a tragic and a hopeful story. We are of the opinion that professionals should not be held solely responsible for the origin of errors and mistakes in child protection. For this reason, it is important to know that in child protection different levels of legal responsibility exist that are often forgotten in discourses, debates and policies on errors and mistakes, in particular the responsibilities of local authorities, agencies and states.

It is possible to change the practice of child protection and to learn from errors and mistakes. Research is available, especially about mistakes in decision-making, and knowledge exists about strategies to identify and to avoid errors and mistakes (some of it set out in this book). Nevertheless, dealing with errors and mistakes is a difficult and sensitive issue. Committing errors and mistakes is often perceived and portrayed as a private, not a public matter. There are good reasons for this as reactions to errors and mistakes are typically condemnatory and harsh. In order to identify and avoid errors and mistakes in child protection it is necessary to develop new working environments in which professionals are supported in their endeavours to improve their skills and do a better job. The majority of child protection professionals do not come to work to commit errors or mistakes, but with the intention to support families and protect children from harm, effectively. They wish to work in authorities and agencies where the presence of errors and mistakes is not a catastrophe, but an occasion for learning and improving practice. They do not want to become secondary victims due to mismanagement and structural deficiencies or dysfunctions in child protection. They hope for respect and appreciation and wish not to be left to bear the responsibility for errors and mistakes alone.

References

Axford, N. and Bullock, R. (2005) *Child Death and Significant Case Reviews: International Approaches – Report to the Scottish Executive*, Edinburgh: Information and Analytical Services Division, Scottish Executive Education Department.

Bernard, S., Indermaur,, I., Meyer Löhrer, B. and Zihlmann. M. (2016) 'Strafrechtliche Aspekte' ['Criminal Aspect'], in C. Fountoulakis, K. Affolter-Fringeli, Y. Biderbost and D. Steck (eds), *Fachhandbuch Kindes- und Erwachsenenschutzrecht* [*Handbook of Child and Adult Protection*], Zurich: Schulthess, pp 849–912.

Berrick, J.D. (2018) *The Impossible Imperative: Navigating the Competing Principles of Child Protection*, New York: Oxford University Press.

Berrick, J.D., Peckover , S., Pösö , T. and Skivenes, M. (2015) 'The Formalised Framework for Decision-Making in Child Protection Care Orders: A Cross-Country Analysis', *Journal of European Social Policy*, 25(4): 366–78.

Biesel, K. (2011) *Wenn Jugendämter scheitern. Zum Umgang mit Fehlern im Kinderschutz, Reihe: Gesellschaft der Unterschiede Bd. 4* [*When Child and Youth Welfare Aagencies Fail: Dealing with Errors and Mistakes in Child Protection. Series: Society of Differences Volume 4*]. Bielefeld: Transcript.

Biesel, K. and Wolff, R. (2013a) 'Das dialogisch-systemische Fall-Labor. Eine Methode zur Untersuchung problematischer Kinderschutzfälle' ['The Dialogical-Systemic Case-Laboratory: An Approach to Investigate Fatal Cases'], in Bundesarbeitsgemeinschaft der Kinderschutz-Zentren e.V. (ed.) *Aufbruch: Hilfeprozesse gemeinsam neu gestalten* [*Awakening: Redesigning Help Processes Together*], Cologne: Bundesarbeitsgemeinschaft der Kinderschutz-Zentren.

Biesel, K. and Wolff, R. (2013b) *Expertise. Das dialogisch-systemische Fall-Labor. Ein Methodenbericht zur Untersuchung problematischer Kinderschutzverläufe. Beiträge zur Qualitätsentwicklung im Kinderschutz 4* [*Expertise: The Dialogical-Systemic Case-Laboratory – A report About an Approach to Investigate Fatal Cases. Series: Contributions for Quality Development in Child Protection 4*]. Cologne: Nationales Zentrum Frühe Hilfen.

Broadhurst, K., White, S., Fish, S., Munro, E., Fletcher, K. and Lincoln, H. (2010) *Ten Pitfalls and How to Avoid Them: What Research Tells Us*, London: NSPCC.

Büchler, A. and Keller, H. (2016) 'Synthesis', in A. Büchler and H. Keller (eds) *Family Forms and Parenthood: Theory and Practice of Article 8 ECHR in Europe*, Cambridge: Intersentia, pp 501–44.

CRC (United Nations Committee on the Rights of the Child) (2011) *General Comment No. 13: The Right of the Child to Freedom from All Forms of Violence*, CRC/C/GC/13, United Nations.

Dekker, S. (2012) *Just Culture: Balancing Safety and Accountability*, 2nd edn, Boca Raton: CRC Press.

Dekker, S. (2014) *The Field Guide to Understanding 'Human Error'*, Burlington, CT: Ashgate.

Fairgrieve, D. and Green, S. (2004) *Child Abuse Tort Claims Against Public Bodies*, Aldershot: Ashgate.

Flynn, A. and Hodgson, J. (eds) (2017) *Access to Justice and Legal Aid: Comparative Perspectives on Unmet Legal Need*, Oxford: Hart.

Gilbert, N., Parton, N. and Skivenes, M. (2011) 'Changing Patterns of Response and Emerging Orientations', in N. Gilbert, N. Parton and M. Skivenes (eds) *Child Protection Systems: International Trend and Orientations*, New York: Oxford University Press, pp 243–57.

Hart, A. (2017) *Report of the Historical Institutional Abuse Inquiry*, Northern Ireland. Available from: www.hiainquiry.org/.

Howitt, D. (1993) *Child Abuse Errors: When Good Intentions Go Wrong*, New Brunswick, NJ: Rutgers University Press.

Leigh, J. (2017) *Blame, Culture and Child Protection*, London: Palgrave Macmillan.

McFadden, P., Campbell, A. and Taylor, B. (2014) 'Resilience and Burnout in Child Protection Social Work: Individual and Organisational Themes from a Systematic Literature Review', *The British Journal of Social Work*, 45(5): 1546–63.

Munro, E. (1996) 'Avoidable and Unavoidable Mistakes in Child Protection Work', *British Journal of Social Work*, 26(6): 793–808.

Munro, E. (1999) 'Common Errors of Reasoning in Child Protection Work', *Child Abuse & Neglect*, 23(8): 745–58.

Munro, E. (2005) 'A Systems Approach to Investigating Child Abuse Deaths', *British Journal of Social Work*, 35(4): 531–46.

Munro, E. (2019) 'Decision-Making Under Uncertainty in Child Protection: Creating a Just and Learning Culture', *Child & Family Social Work*, 24(1): 123–30.

Reason, J. (1990) *Human Error*, New York: Cambridge University Press.

Reason, J. (1997) *Managing the Risks of Organizational Accidents*, Aldershot: Ashgate.

Reason, J. (2008) *The Human Contribution: Unsafe Acts, Accidents and Heroic Recoveries*, Boca Raton, FL: CRC Press.

Sandefur, R.L. (2008) 'Access to Civil Justice and Race, Class, and Gender Inequality', *Annual Review of Sociology*, 34: 339–58.

Sicora, A. (2017) *Reflective Practice and Learnings from Mistakes in Social Work*, Bristol: Policy Press.

Simmons, B.A. (2009) *Mobilizing for Human Rights: International Law in Domestic Politics*, New York: Cambridge University Press.

Sköld, J. and Swain, S. (eds) (2015) *Apologies and the Legacy of Abuse of Children in 'Care': International Perspectives*, Basingstoke: Palgrave Macmillan.

Weick, K.E. and Sutcliffe, K.M. (2015) *Managing the Unexpected: Sustained Performance in a Complex World*, 3rd edn, Hoboken, NJ: John Wiley & Sons.

Weingardt, M. (2004) *Fehler zeichnen uns aus: Transdisziplinäre Grundlagen zur Theorie und Produktivität des Fehlers in Schule und Arbeitswelt* [*Errors and Mistakes Characterise Us: Transdisciplinary Foundations on the Theory and Productivity of Errors and Mistakes in Schools and the Workplace*], Bad Heilbrunn: OBB/Verlag Julius Klinkhardt.

Westrum, R. (1993) 'Cultures with Requisite Imagination', in J.A. Wise, D.V. Hopkin and P. Stager (eds) *Verification and Validation of Complex Systems: Human Factors Issues*, Berlin: Springer, pp 401–16.

Wilkie, M. (1997) *Bringing Them Home: Report of the National Inquiry into the Separation of Aboriginal and Torres Strait Islander Children from Their Families*, Sydney: Human Rights and Equal Opportunity Commission.

Wolff, R., Flick, U., Ackermann, T., Biesel, K., Brandhorst, F., Heinitz, S., Patschke, M. and Röhnsch, G. (2013) *Aus Fehlern lernen – Qualitätsmanagement im Kinderschutz. Konzepte, Bedingungen und Ergebnisse* [*Learning From Errors and Mistakes – Quality Management in Child Protection*], Opladen: Nationales Zentrum Frühe Hilfen.

Wolff, R., Flick, U., Ackermann, T., Biesel, K., Brandhorst, F., Heinitz, S., Patschke, M., Robin, P. (2016) *Children in Child Protection On the Participation of Children and Adolescents in the Helping Process: An Exploratory Study*, Köln: Nationales Zentrum Frühe Hilfen (NZFH).

3

England: attempting to learn from mistakes in an increasingly 'risk averse' professional context

Judith Masson and Nigel Parton

Introduction

The child population in England in 2019 is 12 million, and it is increasing; children make up approximately 21 per cent of the population. The child welfare system was established in 1948 as one of the pillars of the welfare state (Packman, 1975). Local authorities (in 2019 numbering 152, ranging in size from large cities or counties to medium-sized towns or areas) have responsibility for social services for children and families, including child protection, which they deliver through an array of arrangements including with commercial and third sector organisations. The legislative framework, the Children Act 1989, aimed to establish a family service-oriented system (compare Gilbert et al, 2011) but following the scandal of the death of 'Baby P' (which we discuss later) and the shift to a government policy of austerity after the 2010 general election, there have been substantial cuts to funding for many preventive and family support services (ADCS, 2018). The system is now largely oriented to child protection with children's services' resources focused on investigating and responding to risks and providing care for children in need of protection away from home (Children's Commissioner for England, 2018).

Child protection in England is a multi-agency endeavour involving, among others, local authority children's services departments that have statutory responsibility for protecting children; the police and Crown Prosecution Service who investigate and prosecute crime; the health service, which diagnoses and treats children who are ill, injured or disabled; numerous non-governmental organisations providing support for families or care for children, including the National Society for the Prevention of Cruelty to Children (NSPCC), which historically has investigated child protection cases; and the justice system. Local authority children's services rely on referrals from these other agencies, from families and the public to identify children at risk. Within local authorities, qualified social workers are the lead professionals in investigating and responding to child protection. There are only limited legal obligations to report child maltreatment; rather, this is regarded as a professional responsibility of all who work with children and a moral responsibility in the community, a position supported by media campaigns by the NSPCC. Increasingly children's services teams involve other professionals, including psychologists and support workers, and some are co-located with police child protection services and/or other services for families. Health professionals are central to the identification of both ill-treatment and neglect. The National Health Service provides access to health services, including specialist services for preschool children, including developmental checks and some home visits. Doctors and health visitors routinely refer their concerns to the local children's services department.

Except for police powers of emergency intervention, protecting children, removing them from home or keeping them in care requires a court order (and has done so since such powers were first created). The way the court system operates is central to child protection and has sometimes contributed to, rather than prevented, errors and mistakes, as we will show. Reforms to this system have been made in response to major scandals, where the law and the courts were a factor in the failure of protection, and in recognition that both parents and children have rights under the European Convention of Human Rights. However, the judiciary have not engaged in inquiries except when conducting them, claiming that their position in the state requires their decisions and actions to be immune from such review.

Concerns about professional and system errors and mistakes have dominated policy and practice debates and changes in England ever since the problem of child abuse was (re)discovered more than 40 years ago. The period has been punctuated by a series of high-profile scandals usually where a child has died or been subject to severe abuse and where professionals have been seen to fail to intervene effectively. Such tragedies have had an enormous impact on the nature and development of the child protection system in England. New laws and procedures have been introduced and central government has repeatedly issued official guidance directed to child protection workers; social work training has been continually revised and the profession regulated, all social workers being required to register and a few whose conduct is found inadequate or unacceptable deregistered. The regime for inspecting children's services has been strengthened; the Office for Standards in Education, Children's Services and Skills (Ofsted) grades services, those rated 'inadequate' are reinspected and can be taken over by commissioners appointed by the minister. Throughout, a major policy response has been the use of public inquiries and, more recently, 'serious case reviews' (SCRs) to investigate what has gone wrong, with the aim of learning from the experiences to ensure that such tragedies could be avoided in the future.

No distinction is made in discussions in England between 'errors' and 'mistakes'. Rather, there is a focus on failure by those with responsibility to do what is required. Individuals may be 'named and shamed', disciplined or even deregistered if they are social workers or doctors.

This chapter uses specific inquiries and reviews as examples of failures in child protection and responses to them. It demonstrates that the whole field has become increasingly subject to media and political 'outrage' largely directed at the social work profession. It starts by examining the early development of the contemporary child protection system in the 1970s following the Maria Colwell Inquiry, the first such inquiry since the 1940s, and then considers the importance of inquiries and how their use has grown. Throughout these developments the judiciary, who have a leading role in child protection, have insulated themselves from all review processes. We will also demonstrate that the focus of child protection has broadened considerably and is now concerned with a whole range of extrafamilial as well as intrafamilial abuses; and that the changes introduced have become increasingly complex and involve a wide range of different professionals and the wider public. We will suggest that while the changes introduced may have made for a safer set of systems protecting children, the systems themselves have become more 'risk averse' and reactive rather than being able to develop policies and practices which are able to generate longer-term, preventive strategies.

The establishment of the contemporary child protection system

It was the public inquiry into the death of Maria Colwell in 1973/74 that had the effect of catapulting the issue of child abuse and the errors and mistakes of professionals, particularly social workers, into the centre of public and media attention and helped establish the beginnings of the contemporary child protection system in England.

Maria, one of nine children born to her mother, died, aged seven years, on 7 January 1973. She spent more than five years in court-mandated local authority care fostered by her aunt but was returned to her mother and stepfather after the local authority did not oppose her mother's application for discharge of the order and it was replaced by a supervision order to the local authority. The family was visited by a number of social workers from both the local authority and the NSPCC and concerns were repeatedly expressed about Maria to both organisations by her schoolteacher and neighbours. However, she died of 'extreme violence' at the hands of her stepfather and was found to be severely neglected and underweight. William Kepple, the stepfather, was convicted for Maria's manslaughter and imprisoned.

The decision to establish a public inquiry was taken by Sir Keith Joseph, the government minister responsible, in May 1973 and took place between 10 October and 7 December 1973, with the report published in September 1974 (Secretary of State for Health and Social Security, 1974). During the whole of the inquiry and the subsequent publication of the report, there was high-profile coverage in the national press and television. Maria's death and the failure of the 'helping' agencies to prevent it was seen as a national scandal (Parton, 1985; Butler and Drakeford, 2011). While the report was critical of the work of individual professionals, particularly the local authority and NSPCC social workers, its main conclusion, reflected also in media coverage was that 'it was the "system", using the word in its widest sense, which failed her' (Secretary of State for Health and Social Security, 1974: 86). It was recognised that the lack of a formalised inter-agency system for dealing with child abuse left protecting children to the initiative of individual workers.

The government responded with the publication of a circular to all local authorities entitled *Non-Accidental Injury to Children* (DHSS, 1974) and introduced a system whereby: each local authority would establish an inter-agency committee (area review committee) to oversee and coordinate the work of different agencies; the establishment of multidisciplinary case conferences to be held whenever a suspected case of non-accidental injury came to light; together with a register of such known cases which professionals could consult. The system was refined in a series of further circulars throughout the decade (DHSS, 1976a, 1976b, 1978), and by 1980 the problem to be addressed had been officially framed as 'child abuse' (DHSS, 1980), which was made up of physical injury, physical neglect, failure to thrive and emotional abuse but did not include sexual abuse.

Examining the magistrates' decisions was not within its terms of reference but the Inquiry recognised that the local authority's decision not to oppose the discharge of the care order left the court with an incomplete picture of Maria's care. One member of the panel, Olive Stevenson, emphasised that the social workers were working 'within a legal and social system where there was a strong presumption' (Secretary of State for Health and Social Security, 1974: 109) that the court would return Maria to her mother despite the years she had spent with her foster family. The implication was that changes to the system were needed so that courts were better informed about children's welfare. In response, the Children Act 1975 made provision for a guardian *ad litem* for children in cases of possible conflict of interest between children and parents. Initially, these court guardians were provided for uncontested discharge proceedings but they became a key feature in all child protection proceedings.

The importance of public inquiries

Between the publication of the Colwell Inquiry Report in 1974 and 1985 there were 29 further public inquiries into the deaths of children while under the care or supervision of local authorities. An analysis of 18 of these inquiries (DHSS, 1982) identified a great deal of similarity in the findings:

- a lack of interdisciplinary communication;
- a lack of properly trained and experienced front-line staff;
- too little focus on the needs of the child as distinct from those of the parents.

Crucially, errors and mistakes in sharing information and using the full authority of the law led to the professionals doing 'too little too late' and hence failing to intervene to protect the child. This was reinforced further in the mid-1980s with a series of other tragic deaths and public inquiries that reached similar findings: Jasmine Beckford (London Borough of Brent, 1985); Tyra Henry (London Borough of Lambeth, 1987); and Kimberley Carlile (London Borough of Greenwich, 1987).

In the light of these high-profile and, apparently, fatal errors, the government was in the process of tightening the procedures for professionals and had produced draft guidance for consultation (DHSS, 1986) when a rather different scandal hit the headlines in the summer of 1987. This time 121 children were kept in the General Hospital in Middlesbrough (a declining industrial town in the north-east of England, in the county of Cleveland) against the wishes of their parents on emergency 'place of safety orders' on suspicion of being sexually abused and based on what came to be seen as very dubious diagnostic methods. The government established a high-profile public inquiry which reported the following year (Secretary of State for Social Services, 1988). Not only was this the first scandal and public inquiry into possible professional overreaction – intervening too early and too authoritatively – but also the first where the actions of paediatricians and other doctors, as well as social workers, were put under the microscope and subject to criticism. This was a very different discourse about the nature and impact of child protection errors and mistakes. Again, there were issues of court practice; individual magistrates had granted orders allowing children's removal and preventing family contact without, apparently, assessing applications, keeping records or informing the court clerk. Although a judge, Elizabeth Butler-Sloss LJ, was appointed to chair the inquiry and the terms of reference allowed the review of court decision-making, the magistrates were not questioned, and the inquiry avoided examining their decisions.

By 1988 it seemed that the state, in the guise of a number of health, welfare and criminal justice agencies, was both under-intervening *and* over-intervening. This was a major challenge and helped prompt the passage of the Children Act 1989, which put in place a fully reformed legislative framework and, among other things, tried to ensure that professional practice was much more accountable and transparent. However, the inquiry's suggestion for an Office of Child Protection to scrutinise applications was abandoned: this task remained for the courts alone. There was also considerable redrafting of the government guidance (DHSS, 1988). While the guidance broadened the definition of child abuse to include sexual abuse, it was primarily concerned to ensure that professionals maintained a balance in their work between protecting children from abuse while also protecting the privacy of the family from unnecessary and unwarranted intrusion (Parton, 1991). In addition, the guidance established a new element to the child protection system, which, as we will see, would grow in significance 20 years later. Part 9 of the new government guidance established a new system of 'case review':

> A Case Review by management in each involved agency should be instigated in all cases that involve the death of, or serious harm to, a child where child abuse is confirmed or suspected. Agencies need to respond ... to ensure that their services are maintained and not undermined by the incident, that public concern is allayed and media comments answered in a positive manner. The timely production of a ... report with clear conclusions, and where necessary positive recommendations for action should ... enable

agencies *to ensure necessary lessons are learnt and public concern satisfied.*

(DHSS, 1988: para 9.1, emphasis added)

The introduction of the new case review system was an attempt to learn from errors and mistakes but in a much less public and politically febrile context. What had become evident was that public inquiries had become very expensive. Most inquiries were established and therefore paid for by the local authority concerned and this was proving a major financial burden. But also, inquiries nearly always received huge media attention so that it became difficult to control, politically, the impact and outcome of such a process. As the figures in Table 3.1, produced by Corby et al (1998), demonstrate, the number of public inquiries grew considerably between 1972 and 1992 but began to decline after 1992, suggesting that the introduction of the new case review system had some effect.

There was no clear guidance as to when a case review should be made public and decisions on this were left to the local Area Child Protection Committees and after 2006 by their replacement Local Safeguarding Children Boards (LSCBs). Although it was stated that an overall summary report should be made available, in practice very few such reviews were ever published, and it was never easy to know how many were ever being produced. While of considerable interest (and anxiety) to staff involved in such cases, the public, including the media, were rarely aware of these reviews. This virtual invisibility of SCRs was confirmed by Rose and Barnes (2008) who sought to analyse reports produced between 2001 and 2003. The researchers expected 180 reviews but only received 45 and had to base their study on 40 reports because of the limited information presented in five. However, the invisibility of SCRs was to change quickly and dramatically with the very high-profile scandal arising from the death of 17-month-old Peter Connelly (often referred to as 'Baby P') in the London Borough Haringey in 2007.

Table 3.1: Number of public inquiries and types of abuse investigated 1945–97

Year	Physical	Sexual	Neglect	Institutional	Total
1945–72	1	0	0	1	2
1973–82	29	1	1	0	31
1983–92	18	2	1	7	28
1992–97	3	0	1	9	13
Total	51	3	3	17	74

The growing 'politics of outrage'

Haringey had been at the centre of a previous high-profile child abuse scandal in 2000/01 which had led to major changes in the organisation and delivery of children's services which were designed to prevent any further tragedies. Victoria Climbié had died on 25 February 2000 at the hands of her aunt and her aunt's boyfriend and the case seemed to have many of the similarities of most of the tragic child death scandals of the previous 30 years (see Parton, 2004; Masson, 2006 for critical analyses). The government established a public inquiry which reported in early 2003 (Laming Report, 2003) and then published plans for the fundamental reform of children's services (HM Treasury, 2003) backed by new legislation, the Children Act 2004.

The fact that Peter Connelly also died in Haringey made his death even more scandalous. Not only did it appear to reflect very badly on the ability of the London borough to learn from its mistakes but it seemed that the wide-ranging changes introduced by the government seemed to have failed in their most basic aim.

On 11 November 2008, two men were convicted of causing or allowing the death of a 17-month-old child, Baby P on 3 August 2007. The baby's mother had already pleaded guilty to the charge. During the trial, the court heard that Baby P was used as a 'punch bag', that his mother had deceived and manipulated professionals with lies including smearing him with chocolate to hide bruises. He was subject to a child protection plan with Haringey; there had been more than 60 contacts with the family from health, police and social care professionals and had been pronounced dead just 48 hours after a paediatrician failed to identify his broken spine. The media and political response was immediate and highly critical of the services and professionals involved, particularly the director of the children's services department, social work managers and social workers (Jones, 2014; Parton, 2014: Ch 5; Shoesmith, 2016).

At the centre of the political furore was the independence of the SCR into the case. At a press conference after the end of the trial the Director of Haringey Children's Services, Sharon Shoesmith made positive reference to the findings of the SCR and said that 'while lessons had been learned' and two social workers and a lawyer had been given written warnings, there had been no sackings or resignations, and overall the review of the department's involvement had been positive. However, she was Chair of the Haringey LSCB which had commissioned the SCR report (Haringey LSCB, 2008). The following day, 12 November 2008, David Cameron, then leader of the Conservative opposition party, in Prime Minister's Questio. in Parliament, became embroiled in a very angry and highly charged argument with Gordon Brown, the Prime Minister and leader of the Labour Party, about the handling of the case in which he questioned the independence of the SCR. From this point the issue of SCRs – their efficacy and independence – became contentious and high profile, receiving much political and media attention.

The same evening in an attempt to gain control of the crisis, the government minister responsible, Ed Balls, ordered Ofsted, the Healthcare Commission and the Police Inspectorate to carry out an urgent Joint Area Review (JAR) of safeguarding and child protection in Haringey. He also established a Social Work Task Force to identify barriers that social workers faced in working effectively and to make recommendations for improvements and the long-term reform of social work. This reported the following year (Social Work Task Force, 2009).

On receipt of the JAR on 1 December, which he described as 'devastating', Ed Balls announced he was directing Sharon Shoesmith's removal from her post. Later that month she was sacked with immediate effect and without compensation. Four other members of staff involved with Baby P were sacked the following April. The sackings sent shock waves through children's services throughout the country; such summary dismissals had never taken place on such a scale. It seemed that the discourse associated with errors and mistakes in child protection had reached a new level of outrage and that the consequences for professional staff and senior managers could be considerable. A culture of blame and failure seemed pervasive, encouraging a professional and organisational response which was increasingly risk averse.

This development was reinforced in 2009 with the publication of the new SCR demanded by Ed Balls (Haringey LSCB, 2009). The report argued that the agencies' response was 'inadequate' and that Baby P should have been taken into care. It said that there had been a lack of 'authoritative child protection practice' in the social work with the family and that this approach should be central. From this point a much more *authoritative* approach to child protection is evident in England where intervention in both families *and* local authorities is much more coercive (Parton, 2018). In the ten years since, the number of child protection cases brought before the courts has doubled, resulting in a 'crisis' for the courts (Care Crisis Review, 2018) and huge pressures on all children's social care services (ADCS, 2018).

The focus on SCRs increased. In December 2008, Ofsted produced its first evaluation of SCRs' quality, where it said that 20 of 50 SCRs assessed were 'inadequate' (Ofsted, 2008). Over the next few years the status and quality of SCRs was repeatedly raised as a serious issue; the SCR into the death of Hamzah Khan in Bradford being a very clear example (Bradford Safeguarding Children Board, 2013; and see Warner, 2015: Ch 6 for a helpful discussion). Child protection failures had become significantly politicised and were major vehicles for criticising the Labour government's reforms of children's services and its welfare changes more generally (Parton, 2014).

The coalition government of 2010–15 very quickly introduced two changes for which the Conservative Party had been campaigning since the Baby P scandal, namely: that all SCRs should be published in full (suitably redacted so as not compromise the welfare of the child and siblings), so that 'all agencies can learn from mistakes made'; and that all LSCBs should be independently chaired to increase transparency and accountability. However, the government continued to be concerned about the quality and variability of SCRs and in the 2013 *Working Together* (HM Government, 2013) announced the establishment of a national panel of independent experts to LSCBs to ensure that lessons were learned from serious incidents.

It became clear that the new Conservative government wanted to introduce more changes following its election win in 2015. David Cameron, the prime minister, announced a review of the role and functions of LSCBs including the work of SCRs, chaired by Alan Wood. The review argued there was clear evidence: of bureaucratic processes; too much timid inquiry at practitioner and system level; an unwillingness to challenge partners when they opted out of cooperating; and too much acceptance of less than good performance by agencies and in individual practice (Wood, 2016). These recommendations were accepted and included in the Children and Social Work Act 2017 and in the much-revised *Working Together* (HM Government, 2018).

LSCBs were to be replaced by *Safeguarding Partnerships* covering all local authority areas and to be made up of the local authority, the local health clinical commissioning group and the local chief officer of police. The safeguarding partnership would have similar responsibilities to LSCBs but would only be responsible for carrying out 'local child safeguarding practice reviews'. The guidance states that:

> The purpose of reviews of serious child safeguarding cases, at both local and national level, is to identify improvements that should be made locally to safeguard and promote the welfare of children. Learning is relevant locally, but it has wider

importance for all practitioners and for government and policy makers. Understanding whether there are systemic issues, and whether and how policy and practice need to change, is critical to the system being dynamic and self-improving.

Reviews should seek to prevent or reduce the risk of recurrence of similar incidents. They are not conducted to hold individuals, organisations or agencies to account.... (HM Government, 2018: 82)

The Children and Social Work Act 2017, section 12 also established a *Child Safeguarding Practice Review Panel* to identify *serious* child safeguarding cases, which raise complex issues of *national* importance and which might require changes to law or statutory guidance, and to supervise these reviews.

Over the years a number of reports have been produced providing overall summary findings from public inquiries (DHSS, 1982; DH, 1991) and SCRs (Brandon et al, 2008; Rose and Barnes, 2008; Brandon et al, 2010, 2012). The most recent report (Sidebotham et al, 2016) was based on an analysis of 293 SCRs between 2011 and 2014 but drew on over 1,100 cases that the team had been analysing since 2003. It concluded that once a child is known to need protection, for example when a child protection plan is in place, the system was working well. However, only 12 per cent of children who were the focus of an SCR had a current child protection plan at the time of their death or serious harm despite an increase in the number of these plans from 34,000 in 2007/08 to 63,310 in 2015/ 16. The system seems to work well for those who are identified and subject to close attention. The challenge is to predict accurately which children may be harmed, when and in what manner. In trying to reduce the number of false negatives (where children die or experience serious harm but are not identified for intervention) there is always the strong likelihood of increasing the number of false positives (identifying children for child protection intervention but where there is no likelihood of the child dying or experiencing serious harm). These are very different forms of errors and mistakes which are very difficult to reconcile.

Reviews and the role of the judiciary

The decisions and actions of the judiciary were not included in inquiries or reviews. Respect for the principle of judicial independence, judges' natural desire to avoid criticism, and controls on access to court records protected judicial actions from this external scrutiny. Judicial errors and mistakes are defined by the appeal system; litigants can have *legally* wrong decisions overturned and the Court of Appeal sets guidelines to prevent recurrence. Miscarriages of justice, the conviction of innocent people, including parents for harming their children, have tarnished the criminal justice system. The view that it is better for ten guilty men to go free, than for one innocent person to be convicted (Blackstone, 1769), remains fundamental.

Women's Aid had long been concerned about the failure of the family justice system as a whole, and judges particularly, to recognise the seriousness of domestic violence. As part of their campaign, Women's Aid published *Twenty-Nine Child Homicides* (Saunders, 2004) an account of 13 cases where children had been killed during contact with their father, including five cases where the courts had ordered contact. Partly drawn from SCRs, this material could not be dismissed as anecdotal. The report posed a series of questions about decision making in the cases and highlighted lessons from these deaths.

Elizabeth Butler-Sloss, then President of the Family Division, discussed the Women's Aid report with officials from the Department for Constitutional Affairs and agreed that a senior judge would examine court files for the five cases mentioned (Wall, 2006). Lord Justice Wall's report was quite defensive, stressing the judges' experience and diligence and rejecting any suggestion that judicial accountability required a mechanism beyond appeals. However, any sense that this was sufficient was undermined by the fact that the judiciary were unaware of these tragedies and any 'lessons to be learned' until Women's Aid's report had provoked the review. The report recommended that the Family Justice Council be asked to advise how courts should approach uncontested cases where domestic violence could be a factor. The Family Justice Council's Report, *Everybody's Business* (2007), highlighted how the family court system promoted agreement without knowledge of potential risks, and recommended substantial changes in the handling of cases. Acknowledging that both the SCRs and Homicide Reviews (Domestic Violence, Crime and Victims Act 2004, section 9) could provide feedback for the courts, it advised the involvement of the family justice system. More specifically, it recommended that the relevant government departments should explore how the family court process should be included within these reviews (Family Justice Council, 2007, para 50). The response of the new president of the family courts was equivocal. While expressing concern about judicial independence and the disclosure of court documents he stated: 'while there can be no duty upon the Court to assist if ... a judicial decision may have played a material part in ... it is plainly desirable ... that the review should be acquainted with the course of the proceedings and the material upon which the Court came to its conclusion' (Potter quoted in Munby, 2017: 2).

However, attitudes had changed by the time Alan Wood reviewed LSCBs, and the Chief Coroner was the only judge who took part in the discussions.

Ellie Butler suffered injuries and a collapse in the care of her father when she was only a few weeks old; care proceedings resulted in her placement with her maternal grandparents where she lived for five years having little contact with either parent. Her father was imprisoned for injuring her, but his conviction was quashed when further medical evidence suggested the collapse could have been natural. Subsequently, care proceedings brought for the couple's second child focused on the medical evidence for Ellie's collapse, largely ignoring other evidence of neglect of this child – concealing her existence, paternity and her father's violence. The court appeared to accept that the parents were victims of a miscarriage of justice and their behaviour was all explained by their feelings and loss of Ellie due to this. The judge not only refused any order, she exonerated the father of any wrongdoing, required the local authority to write informing all agencies of this and appointed a small, independent social work agency to plan and undertake both children's reunification with their parents. Less than a year after returning, during which abuse was concealed by absence from school and missed medical appointments, Ellie was brutally murdered by her father.

There are numerous parallels between the lives and deaths of Maria Colwell and Ellie Butler despite the 40 years and major legal reforms that separate them. Family relationships were fractured and the parents' capacity to care was never assessed. Despite the order giving Ellie's grandparents permanent care, the judge and agency social workers appeared to see her return to her parents as inevitable. Numerous professionals expressed concerns, but in Ellie's case there was no uncertainty about responsibilities, rather workers felt 'powerless to act' (Sutton LSCB, 2016, para 7.3.2) in the face of the judge's statement. The judge declined to participate in the SCR, and the Courts Service was not represented on the SCR panel. The SCR was clearly hampered by the lack of explanations for the judge exceeding her role, exonerating the father and excluding the local authority. The Overview Report criticised this lack of engagement which 'raised serious questions for consideration at a national level' and called for the responsibility of the courts to LSCBs to be clarified (Sutton LSCB, 2016, para 9.2.5).

Sir James Munby, President of the Family Division, who had previously promoted his 'transparency agenda', seeking ways to open the family court to public scrutiny (Munby, 2014), responded in trenchant fashion. 'Judges do not respond to questions from SCRs ... do not attend evidence sessions and are under no obligation to provide information to SCRs ... not ... to evade scrutiny or accountability, but in order to protect ... independence and the independence of individual judges' (Munby, 2017: 1–2). Despite Wall LJ's earlier report, he claimed that it was 'a fundamental principle' that judges do not comment on other judge's decisions outside the appeal process. Thus the family judiciary, under a banner of 'independence' has maintained its unwillingness to participate in, and learn from, reviews into errors and mistakes. While the judiciary continue to impose their views about how the child protection system should be run (*Re M*, 2003[1]; *Re N*, 2015[2]) they refuse to engage in processes designed to respond to failures, even when these focus on learning.

Extrafamilial abuse

As was evident in Table 3.1 mentioned earlier, from the late 1980s public inquiries were not only concerned with errors and mistakes in relation to *intrafamilial abuse* but was also concerned with abuse in institutional settings. High profile police and social services investigations took place across the country, but it was the investigations in north Wales and the north-west of England that proved the most challenging. These led the prime minister, John Major to establish a tribunal of inquiry in 1996 (Waterhouse, 2000).

There have been a growing number of scandals about the physical and sexual abuse of children in a variety of different community and institutional settings including: churches and religious organisations; schools and day-care centres; sports clubs; and a range of other child and youth groups. Increasingly it seemed that any setting where adults had contact with children and young people was a possible site for abuse. By the 1990s it was clear that the abuse of children was an *extrafamilial* as well as an *intrafamilial* problem.

Recent years have also witnessed the emergence of new types of scandal, often historical in nature, and which have included the abusive and exploitative behaviour of a series of high-profile celebrities and a number of members of the 'establishment'. In the process long-established and well-respected institutions such as the BBC (British Broadcasting Corporation), major hospitals and Parliament itself, have come under the spotlight with wide-ranging implications. This led, eventually, in February 2015 to the government setting up the biggest and most expensive public inquiry ever, the Independent Inquiry into Child Sexual Abuse.

This inquiry has established 13 separate investigations covering: accountability and reparation; the Roman Catholic Church; Children Outside the UK; Institutional Responses to Allegations Concerning Lord Janner; the Anglican Church; Lambeth Council; Cambridge House, Knowl View and Rochdale; Nottinghamshire Councils; Westminster investigation; Child Sexual Exploitation by Organised Networks; Residential Schools; Children in Custodial Institutions; Religious Organisations and Settings and the internet. It will take at least five years to complete its work.

Conclusion

Over the last 40 years England has witnessed both a broadening and an increasing complexity in the reach and nature of child protection policy and practice. While local authority children's services continue to play the key role in day-to-day practice and the courts exercise greater influence over the child care system, the 'net of responsibility' has widened considerably with education and health professionals and the police seen to play increasingly key roles. In the process the number of systems operating under the rubric of child protection has multiplied considerably. *Working Together*, the official government guidance, has expanded from 126 pages in 1991 (Home Office et al, 1991), to more than 3,600 pages in 2018 (HM Government, 2018) made up of 109 pages plus more than 3,500 pages of appendices. Responding to errors and mistakes has been a major driver for such changes. Ironically, by trying to ensure that errors and mistakes can be both learned from and thereby avoided, the potential for professionals and others to make mistakes, by failing to follow the increasingly broad, complex and detailed guidance, is thereby increased. When mistakes are made the courts are in the forefront determining responsibility (and sometimes blame) for them but remain beyond the processes for learning from them.

Notes
[1]   *Re M* [2003] 2 FLR 171.
[2]   *Re N* [2015] EWCA Civ. 1112.

References

ADCS (Association of Directors of Children's Services) (2018) *Safeguarding Pressures Project Phase 6.* Available from: http://adcs.org.uk/safeguarding/article/safeguarding-pressures.

Blackstone, W. (1769) *Commentaries on the Laws of England*, Oxford: Clarendon Press.

Bradford Safeguarding Children Board (2013) *A Serious Case Review: Hamzah Khan – The Overview Report*, Bradford: BSCB.

Brandon, M., Bailey, S. and Belderson, P. (2010) *Building on the Learning from Serious Case Reviews: A Two-Year Analysis of Child Protection Database Notifications 2007–2009*, Research Brief DFE-RB040, London: Department for Education.

Brandon, M., Belderson, P., Warren, C., Howe, D., Gardner, R., Dodsworth, J. and Black, J. (2008) *Analysing Child Deaths and Serious Injury Through Abuse and Neglect: What Can We Learn? A Biennial Analysis of Serious Case Reviews 2003–2005*, London: Department for Children, Schools and Families.

Brandon, M., Sidebotham, P., Bailey, S., Belderson, P., Hawley, C., Ellis, C. and Megson, M. (2012) *New Learning from Serious Case Reviews: A Two Year Report for 2009–2011*, London: Department for Education.

Butler, I. and Drakeford, M. (2011) *Social Work on Trial: The Colwell Inquiry and the State of Welfare*, Bristol: Policy Press.

Care Crisis Review (2018) *Care Crisis Review: Options for Change*, London: Family Rights Group.

Children's Commissioner for England (2018) *Annual Study of Childhood Vulnerability in England*. Available from: www.childrenscommissioner.gov.uk/publication/childrens-commissioner-vulnerability-report-2018/.

Corby, B., Doig, A. and Roberts, V. (1998) 'Inquiries into Child Abuse', *Journal of Social Welfare and Family Law*, 20(4): 377–95.

DH (Department of Health) (1991) *Child Abuse: A Study on Inquiry Reports 1980–1989*, London: HM Stationery Office.

DHSS (Department of Health and Social Security) (1974) *Non-Accidental Injury to Children*, LASSL (74)(13), London: DHSS.

DHSS (Department of Health and Social Security) (1976a) *Non-Accidental Injury to Children: Area Review Committees*, LASSL(76)(2), London: DHSS.

DHSS (Department of Health and Social Security) (1976b) *Non-Accidental Injury to Children: The Police and Case Conferences*, LASSL(76)(26), London: DHSS.

DHSS (Department of Health and Social Security) (1978) *Child Abuse: The Register System*, LA/C396/23D, London: DHSS.

DHSS (Department of Health and Social Security) (1980) *Child Abuse: Central Register Systems*, LASSL(80)4, HN(80), London: DHSS.

DHSS (Department of Health and Social Security) (1982) *Child Abuse: A Study of Inquiry Reports 1973–1981*, London: HM Stationery Office.

DHSS (Department of Health and Social Security) (1986) *Child Abuse: Working Together: A Draft Guidance to Arrangements for Inter-Agency Cooperation for the Protection of Children*, London: DHSS.

DHSS (Department of Health and Social Security) (1988) *Working Together: A Guide to Inter-Agency Cooperation for the Protection of Children*, London: HM Stationery Office.

Family Justice Council (2007) *Everybody's Business*, London: Family Justice Council.

Gilbert, N., Parton, N. and Skivenes, M. (Eds.) (2011) *Child Protection Systems: International Trends and Orientations*. New York: Oxford University Press.

Haringey LSCB (2008) *A Serious Case Review 'Child A': The Executive Summary*, November. Available from: www.scie-socialcareonline. org.uk/a-serious-case-review-child-a-the-executive-summary/r/ a11G00000017uvDIAQ.

Haringey LSCB (2009) *Serious Case Review: Baby Peter: Executive Summary*, February. Available from: www.scie-socialcareonline.org. uk/serious-case-review-baby-peter-executive-summary-february-2009/r/a11G00000017slUIAQ.

HM Government (2013) *Working Together to Safeguard Children: A Guide to Inter-Agency Working to Safeguard and Promote the Welfare of Children*, London: Department for Education. Available from: http://www. workingtogetheronline.co.uk/resources.html.

HM Government (2018) *Working Together to Safeguard Children: A Guide to Inter-Agency Working to Safeguard and Promote the Welfare of Children*, London: Department for Education. Available from: www.gov.uk/government/publications/ working-together-to-safeguard-children--2.

HM Treasury (2003) *Every Child Matters*, Cm 5860, London: TSO.

Home Office, Department of Health, Department of Education and Science, and Welsh Office (1991) *Working Together Under the Children Act 1989: A Guide to Arrangements for Inter-Agency Co-operation for the Protection of Children from Abuse*, London: HM Stationery Office.

Jones, R. (2014) *The Story of Baby P: Setting the Record Straight*, Bristol: Policy Press.

Laming Report (2003) *The Victoria Climbié Inquiry: Report of an Inquiry by Lord Laming*, Cm 5730, London: TSO.

London Borough of Brent (1985) *A Child in Trust: Report of the Panel of Inquiry Investigating the Circumstances Surrounding the Death of Jasmine Beckford*, London: Brent Borough Council.

London Borough of Greenwich (1987) *A Child in Mind: Protection in a Responsible Society: Report of the Commission of Inquiry into the Circumstances Surrounding the Death of Kimberley Carlile*, London: Borough of Greenwich Social Services Department.

London Borough of Lambeth (1987) *Whose Child? The Report of the Panel Appointed to Inquire into the Death of Tyra Henry*, London: Borough of Lambeth Social Services Department.

Masson, J. (2006) 'The Climbié Inquiry – Context and Critique', *Journal of Law and Society*, 33(2): 221–43.

Munby, P. (2014) *Transparency: The Next Steps*, consultation paper, London: President of the Family Division. Available from: www. judiciary.uk/wp-content/uploads/2016/05/transparency-the-next-steps-consultation-paper.pdf.

Munby, P. (2017) *President's Guidance: Judicial Cooperation with Serious Case Reviews*, London: President of the Family Division. Available from: www.judiciary.uk/publications/presidents-guidance-judicial-cooperation-with-serious-case-reviews/.

Ofsted (2008) *Learning Lessons, Taking Action: Ofsted's Evaluations of Serious Case Reviews, 1 April 2007 to 31 March 2008*, London: Ofsted. Available from: http://dera.ioe.ac.uk/10562/1/learninglessons_scr.pdf.

Packman, J. (1975) *The Child's Generation: Child Care Policy from Curtis to Houghton*, Oxford: Blackwell.

Parton, N. (1985) *The Politics of Child Abuse*, Basingstoke: Palgrave Macmillan.

Parton, N. (1991) *Governing the Family: Child Care, Child Protection and the State*, Basingstoke: Palgrave Macmillan.

Parton, N. (2004) 'From Maria Colwell to Victoria Climbié: Reflections on Public Inquiries Into Child Abuse a Generation Apart', *Child Abuse Review*, 13(2): 80–94.

Parton, N. (2014) *The Politics of Child Protection: Contemporary Developments and Future Directions*, Basingstoke: Palgrave Macmillan.

Parton, N. (2018) 'The Politics of Child Protection in Contemporary England: Towards the "Authoritarian Neoliberal State"', in S. Dinter and R. Schneider (eds) *Transdisciplinary Perspectives on Childhood in Contemporary Britain: Literature, Media and Society*, London: Routledge, pp 193–211.

Rose, W. and Barnes, J. (2008) *Improving Safeguarding Practice: Study of Serious Case Reviews 2001–2003*, London: Department for Children, Schools and Families.

Saunders, H. (2004) *Twenty-Nine Child Homicides: Lessons Still to Be Learnt on Domestic Violence and Child Protection*, Bristol: Women's Aid. Available from: http://familieslink.co.uk/download/jan07/twenty_nine_child_homicides.pdf.

Secretary of State for Health and Social Security (1974) *Report of Inquiry into the Care and Supervision Provided in Relation to Maria Colwell*, London: HM Stationery Office.

Secretary of State for Social Services (1988) *Report of the Inquiry into Child Abuse in Cleveland*, Cm 413, London: HM Stationery Office.

Shoesmith, S. (2016) *Learning from Baby P: The Politics of Blame, Fear and Denial*, London: Jessica Kingsley.

Sidebotham, P., Brandon, M., Bailey, S., Belderson, P., Dodsworth, J., Garstang, J., Harrison, E., Retzer, A. and Sorensen, P. (2016) *Pathways to Harm, Pathways to Protection: A Triennial Analysis of Serious Case Reviews 2011 to 2014*, London: Department for Education.

Social Work Task Force (2009) *Building a Safe, Confident Future: The Final Report of the Social Work Task Force*, Nottingham: Department for Children, Schools and Families.

Sutton LSCB (2016) *'Child D' Serious Case Review Overview Report*, London: Sutton LSCB.

Wall, N. (2006) *A Report to the President of the Family Division on the Publication by the Women's Aid Federation of England Entitled* Twenty-Nine Child Homicides: Lessons to be Learnt on Domestic Violence and Child Protection *with Particular Reference to the Five Cases in Which There Was Judicial Involvement*, London: Wall LJ. Available from: www.judiciary.uk/wp-content/uploads/JCO/Documents/Reports/report_childhomicides.pdf.

Warner, J. (2015) *The Emotional Politics of Social Work and Child Protection*, Bristol: Policy Press.

Waterhouse, R. (2000) *Lost in Care: Report of the Tribunal of Inquiry into the Abuse of Children in Care in the Former Council Areas of Gwynedd and Clwyd Since 1974*, HC201, London: Stationery Office.

Wood, A. (2016) *Wood Report: Review of the Role and Functions of Local Safeguarding Children Board*, London: Department for Education.

4

The social construction of child abuse in Ireland: public discourse, policy challenges and practice failures

Caroline Shore and Fred Powell

Introduction

This chapter seeks to explore the diverse meanings of child abuse in Ireland, while unpacking the construction, nature and consequences of errors and mistakes in child protection in the state. The contemporary Irish imagination perceives child abuse as a problem of historical memory. The primary reference is the institutionalised child subjected to cruelty and sexual exploitation at the hands of the clergy, with a disengaged state colluding in their misery. Yet there is an accumulating body of evidence that demonstrates beyond doubt that the problem of child abuse is part of present-day social reality in Ireland. There is a shared dynamic between the past and the present. Child abuse is the product of multiple childhoods, differentiating privilege from poverty. Linkages between historic child abuse and contemporary practice in memory and denial, in a society that is rapidly modernising and rejecting its traditionalist past, are the lens used to explore Ireland's understanding of errors and mistakes in child protection.

Ireland: context and orientation

Ireland has a population of almost 4.8 million, with children making up just over a quarter of that total (CSO, 2017) and 40 per cent of Irish households include children (Eurostat, 2018). It now has the highest birth, and lowest mortality, rates of all European Union countries, giving Ireland the largest proportion of children as a percentage of total population in Europe (DCYA, 2016).

55

In global terms, Ireland is a highly developed, safe and prosperous place to live. It has been ranked as eighth in the world on measurements including health, access to education, human rights and standard of living (United Nations Development Programme, 2016), and as the seventh best country in the world in which to raise children (UNICEF, 2016). Despite such glowing accolades, in the same year just over 11 per cent of children in the state were living in consistent poverty and 25 per cent were experiencing deprivation (CSO, 2017).

The 1937 Constitution of Ireland with its clear mandate on the rights of the family unit overrides all legislation in the country. This constitutional obligation has meant that Ireland has traditionally invested greater authority in parents than is explicit in the systems of other countries (Lavan, 1998). This includes child removal and related proceedings governed by the Child Care Act 1991, in which the welfare of the child is paramount but decisions must be made from the initial presumption of children being best nurtured and protected within the family (Coulter, 2015; O'Mahony et al, 2016).

Since 2014, with the creation of a dedicated independent state agency for child welfare, Tusla, the Child and Family Agency, Ireland has had a centralised child protection system structure. Prior to this, statutory responsibility for child welfare and protection rested uncomfortably within the unwieldy Health Service Executive (HSE), an umbrella body responsible for cradle-to-grave health and social services. The new agency provides nationally standardised services, within four geographical regions separated into 17 locally managed areas. Social work is the leading profession with statutory responsibility for child protection in Ireland, having gradually developed into this role alongside the growth in the welfare state over the past four decades. In 2017 1,466 social workers were employed by Tusla (Oireachtas Dáil, 2017). Tusla operates a limited out-of-hours emergency social work service; outside of this provision An Garda Síochána (the police service of Ireland) holds responsibility for emergency child welfare responses (Lamponen et al, 2018).

Ireland's constitutional and legislative provisions have naturally shaped child protection policy and practice on the ground. This can be seen in high thresholds for intervention and a requirement for ongoing consideration of family reunification throughout a child's placement in the care of the state. Ireland's unique guiding framework has also led to a paradox in public discourse whereby, 'there is outrage at the apparent failure of social workers to take action to protect children; yet on the other hand, there is public concern at a perceived over-interference by the State in family life' (Lavan, 1998: 48).

Ireland's child protection system has historically functioned in a risk-oriented manner, with high intervention thresholds and an emphasis on serious circumstances of risk to children (Burns et al, 2017). This is despite government policy and legislation suggesting a more family-service orientation (Buckley and Burns, 2015). Additionally, developments, including a constitutional amendment in 2012 resulting in the inclusion of a specific reference to the rights of the child, indicate a gradual shift towards a child-centric or child-rights approach (Burns et al, 2017).

Errors and mistakes in child protection in Ireland have traditionally been regarded as situations where children have suffered extreme abuse, neglect and/or death at the hands of caregivers. Cases where children and families were known to state services have drawn greatest attention and prompted questions around how such services, and society, could have failed so gravely. The government response has traditionally been to initiate some form of child abuse inquiry, followed by the publication of a report seeking to prevent reoccurrence through policy and practice recommendations. Indeed the child protection and welfare system in Ireland has arguably evolved and reformed in response to a series of incidents and inquiries (Burns et al, forthcoming). The major child abuse inquiries in Ireland have included cases of both inter- and extrafamilial abuse.

The abusive family and historical child abuse and the Catholic Church

The first, and most influential, child abuse inquiry of its kind, the Kilkenny Incest Investigation (McGuinness, 1993) concerned a young woman who was sexually and physically abused by her father over more than a decade, despite repeated contacts with health and social work professionals. That inquiry was followed by a report into the death of Kelly Fitzgerald, a 15-year-old girl whose parents were subsequently convicted of wilful neglect (Joint Commission on the Family, 1996). Two years later, the West of Ireland Farmer report detailed extreme physical and sexual abuse suffered by four siblings at the hands of their father for nearly two decades (Bruton, 1998). Similar to the Kilkenny case, both Kelly Fitzgerald and the McColgan siblings were known to be at risk by child protection services and numerous opportunities to intervene effectively were missed.

In terms of public awareness and mobilising action, 2009 was a seminal year for child protection in Ireland. Both the Commission to Inquire into Child Abuse (known as the Ryan Report), investigating historical abuse of children in state-run institutions, and the Dublin report (Murphy, 2009), which primarily focused on the cover-up of child abuse by the Catholic Church, were published.

The Dublin Report found evidence of widespread sexual abuse of children by members of the Catholic clergy from the mid-1970s to the mid-2000s. Over those 30 years, 320 individual reports of child sexual abuse by the religious were made in the Dublin area. The report identified 46 culpable priests. The breadth of abuse was horrific, as was the secrecy, cover-up and collusion that were at the heart of both Church and state responses to abuse victims who spoke out. The report provided a damning account of the errors of both Church and state in their responses, which became a major public scandal (Powell and Scanlon, 2015).

The reports laid bare to the general public Ireland's child protection failings in a manner unprecedented in the history of the state. They pointed the finger at the clergy who perpetrated the abuse, the state institutions that ignored or buried the evidence presented to them, and at the society of the time, wherein people turned a blind eye to the suffering of this cohort of citizens, regarded by many as 'the other'. These children in the main came from poor and disadvantaged backgrounds, and their rights as human beings were easier to deny as a result (OCO, 2009).

There are varying estimates of the number of children who were incarcerated in Irish industrial and reformatory schools. According to the influential book, *Suffer the Little Children* (Rafferty and O'Sullivan, 1999), 150,000 children were institutionalised in industrial and 15,000 in reformatory schools between 1858 and 1969. The Ryan Report (Ryan, 2009: volume 1, paras 3.01–3.04) estimated that during the period 1936–70 'a total of 170,000 children … entered the gates of the 50 or so industrial schools'. The legitimation of this policy of incarcerating poor and destitute children rested on the myth of religious charity and the monopoly of the Catholic Church over Irish civil society, 'The truest and most pervasive myth was that the children within the system were objects of charity, cared for by the religious of Ireland when no one else would do so' (Rafferty and O'Sullivan, 1999: 11).

The Ryan Report exposed this myth by revealing a Kafkaesque world of abuse, neglect, enforced child labour and sexual exploitation (Powell and Scanlon, 2015), a system of carceral confinement amounting to 'social genetics' (Barnes, 1989: 88). The children confined within these institutions were the subject of vaccine trials, forced adoptions and unexplained child deaths that are currently being considered by public inquiries. The acclaimed film, *Philomena*, the story of a forced adoption, brought into public focus the dark side of Irish family values in a deeply patriarchal society. This was the hidden Ireland further reflected in a series of reports into child abuse in Irish families exposing patriarchal violence, familicide and rudimentary social services.

In 2010, the now infamous Roscommon Child Care Case was published (Gibbons et al, 2010), detailing how six children had suffered chronic neglect, violence and sexual assault by their parents over a 15-year period before being received into state care. These children had been known to the child protection service for most of their lives yet the inquiry noted that their voices were almost completely absent from social work records, and that recommendations of previous inquiries had not been implemented.

Given the revelations of Ryan and Dublin, from which the nation was still reeling, one might have thought that all the taboos around child abuse had finally been exposed. However, the public were now faced with the knowledge that a mother could sexually abuse her child. This became the first time in Irish legal history that a mother was convicted and incarcerated for the crime of incest. The conviction illuminated an anomaly in legislation, reflective of society's misconception about the nature of sexual abuse and abusers, that the maximum sentence for incest by a female perpetrator was seven years, compared to life imprisonment for a male.

A further disquieting element was that social workers had initially sought to remove the children into care many years earlier. The mother, citing the constitutional rights of the married family, applied to the High Court and obtained an injunction. The media reported the belief that the mother's application had been financed by a 'Catholic right wing organisation' (McDonagh, 2009). The interference of religion in matters of the state, leaving children exposed to grave abuse, was again highlighted. Powell and Scanlon (2015) have concluded that the tragedy exposed by this case was the product of traditionalist family rights and cultural disbelief.

Contemporary errors

In most recent years there have been several highly publicised and frequently damning reports into aspects of the operation of the child protection system, including the interaction between different agencies such as Tusla and the police (see, for example, Shannon and Gibbons, 2012; Logan, 2014; Office of the Ombudsman, 2017; Shannon, 2017; HIQA, 2018).

In 2017 a seminal report was published into police use of emergency powers to remove children from their families (Child Care Act 1991, section 12). The report (Shannon, 2017) represented a countrywide audit by the Government's Special Rapporteur on Child Protection, and is understood to be the most comprehensive study into police use of emergency child protection powers internationally. It was commissioned by the Minister for Children and Youth Affairs in response to public outrage expressed at the removal by Gardai of two Roma children from their families in 2013, decisions that were both heavily influenced by the fact that the children did not look like their parents. The removals came just a week after the worldwide coverage of the blonde-haired, blue-eyed little girl, known as 'Maria' found in a Roma camp in Greece.

The cases garnered extensive international media attention, fuelled by fear of child abduction and unfounded suspicions of Roma involvement in child trafficking. The Irish print media labelled An Garda Síochána and the HSE child protection services 'shambolic', 'heavy handed', 'unaccountable' and 'racist' (Marron et al, 2016: 130). The subsequent Ombudsman for Children investigation, while finding no evidence of conscious prejudice by individual Gardai, noted that both cases 'conformed to the definition of ethnic profiling' (Logan, 2014: 56, 94). The resultant national audit found numerous deficits with policy and practice, including inadequate child protection training for Gardai, poor communication between An Garda Síochána and Tusla, and inadequate out-of-hours social work provision (Shannon, 2017).

State responses to changing demographics in modern Ireland have illuminated contemporary child protection failings that have contributed to the creation of a newly stigmatised group within society: immigrant and asylum-seeking children. From the late 1990s asylum seekers from around the globe began arriving in increasing numbers. The government responded by introducing a system of direct provision (DP). Asylum seekers were no longer eligible for state-subsidised accommodation or benefits, but must instead reside in one of a number of institutions dispersed throughout the state, which would provide accommodation and meals. On top of this basic provision, adult residents would receive €19.60 a week for additional needs, with a payment of €9.10 per week for each dependent child. Since 2000, when the policy was first enacted, the adult rate of financial support has remained static, the child rate increasing to €15.60 in 2016. This has effectively ensured that living in poverty is sewn into the asylum-seeker experience.

In 2012, a hard-hitting report, *State Sanctioned Child Poverty and Exclusion* (Arnold, 2012) detailed the experiences of children living in DP. The report was a shocking indictment of childhood in these privately managed, government-funded institutions. Extensive evidence of children living in cramped, overcrowded and often unsanitary conditions was presented. Mass-produced canteen meals were served at set times, with no attention to the child's age, or their religious or nutritional needs. Parents could not invite their children's school friends over to play, leading to social exclusion. The consistent poverty sewn into family life in DP left parents unable to afford school uniforms or excursions, multiplying levels of marginalisation.

Within the communal living spaces, children witnessed adults experiencing mental health difficulties, incidents of aggression and violence, and even sexual acts. The report was unflinching in its attribution of responsibility, noting 'Direct Provision is an example of a government policy which has not only bred discrimination, social exclusion, enforced poverty and neglect, but has placed children at a real risk' (Arnold, 2012: 7).

In 2013, a Northern Irish High Court judgment hit the headlines when the judge overturned a decision to return an asylum-seeking family to the Republic of Ireland, where they had initially sought asylum. Determining that return would be counter to the children's best interests, the judge acknowledged 'a systemic deficiency, known to the United Kingdom, in Ireland's asylum or reception procedures … the asylum seeker would face a real risk of being subjected to inhuman or degrading treatment and a failure to have regard to the need to safeguard and promote the welfare of the children' (Finn, 2013).

A higher rate of child protection referral for children living in DP has been identified. In 2015, 14 per cent of all such children were referred to Tusla, compared to a general population referral rate of just 1.6 per cent. Of DP referrals, 85 per cent met the criteria for assessment, compared with 50 per cent of the total child population cohort (HIQA, 2015). These figures echo earlier findings about children in DP (Shannon, 2012) and the over-representation of African families in childcare proceedings (Coulter, 2013).

Tusla's response to referrals of children in DP was found to be inconsistent across geographical regions, and a lack of adequate, robust data was identified as a deficit in identifying and meeting the needs of this child population (HIQA, 2015). The same year, the newly assigned Minister of State for New Communities, Culture and Equality compared the DP system to the Mother and Baby homes and

Magdalene Laundries of the past, referring to Ireland's 'love affair ... with institutionalising ... and incarcerating people' (O'Connell, 2015).

State reform

The recommendations which attached to the Kilkenny report are acknowledged as the most historically influential in leading to meaningful reform of child protection policy and practice in the state. The inquiry focused its attention on systemic deficits, rather than individual practice issues, resulting in wide-ranging recommendations for whole-system change. After years of delay the Child Care Act 1991 was finally fully implemented, with a significant increase in funding (Buckley and O'Nolan, 2013). The report was the catalyst for health and social service provision to expand considerably, with additional staff employed as well as new disciplines brought onto social work teams such as family support and child care workers (Buckley and Burns, 2015). Many of the inquiry recommendations took form in the introduction of *Children First: National Guidelines for the Protection and Welfare of Children* (Department of Health and Children, 1999), with their emphasis on multidisciplinary working and a holistic approach to child protection.

In the years that followed Kilkenny, and despite the roll-out of reforms, each further inquiry generated more and more predictable recommendations focusing on similar failures. These included the need for better communication between and within agencies, improved recording measures, increased resourcing, strengthened governance, full implementation of policies and guidelines, greater attention given to the voice of the child, and enhanced statutory protection of children's rights. Twenty years after Kilkenny, a government commissioned review identified 29 major inquiries, culminating in 551 recommendations. The authors noted a 'critical mass' of recommendations had now been reached, whereby 'the benefits from inquiries have succumbed to the law of diminishing returns' (Buckley and O'Nolan, 2013: 102).

The Ryan Report had the most influential impact on child protection policy and practice since the Kilkenny Report 16 years before it. Within weeks the government launched a suite of 99 responsive actions, via its *Ryan Report Implementation Plan* (OMCYA, 2009). Two hundred additional front-line social workers were employed. The report was the catalyst for creating the Department of Children and Youth Affairs in 2011 as a stand-alone government department with responsibility for children's welfare, and for removing statutory responsibility for child welfare and protection from the HSE, replacing it with Tusla in 2014. The Health Information and Quality Authority (HIQA), had been established in 2007 to regulate health and social care provision throughout the state. Primarily in response to the identification within the Ryan Report of the lack of adequate inspection or regulation of institutions, the *National Standards for the Protection and Welfare of Children* were launched in 2012 (HIQA, 2012). HIQA carried out its first inspection of child protection services that same year.

Additionally, the government was pushed into action to address the lack of robust information about the deaths of children known to or in the care of child protection services. The Independent Child Death Review Group was established in 2010, with a remit to investigate the circumstances of any child or young person who had died while in the care of the state, or known to child protection or aftercare services since the year 2000.

The ensuing report detailed 196 such deaths and identified poor coordination of communication between agencies, inconsistent risk assessments, inadequate access to assessment and therapeutic services, and insufficient early intervention, noting 'A root and branch reform of the child protection system in Ireland is required' (Shannon and Gibbons, 2012: 24). The National Review Panel was established, and now publishes reports on serious incidents and child deaths, and makes recommendations on child protection policy and practice (Tusla, 2014).

The Ryan Report also led to the 2012 referendum on children's rights, first proposed in 1993 by the Kilkenny Report. The first comprehensive national policy framework for children and young people, *Better Outcomes: Brighter Futures*, was introduced in 2014 (DCYA, 2014). The *Children First* guidelines were finally placed on a statutory footing by the Children First Act 2015, mandating child abuse reporting by professionals, a proposal which had also initially been recommended over 20 years previously in the Kilkenny Report.

The Roscommon Report additionally led to a legislative amendment to redress the sexual abuse inconsistency. The Criminal Law (Sexual Offences) (Amendment) Act 2019, set a maximum custodial sentence of ten years for both men and women convicted of incest.

Reflection and analysis: policy implementation errors

A significant and repeated error in the Irish child protection and welfare landscape of recent decades has been the crafting of copious well-intentioned policies, contrasting sharply with a lack of practical application on the ground. The implementation of the central piece of child care legislation in the state, the Child Care Act 1991, is a cogent example. The ethos of the Act was one of enhancing child welfare through early intervention, family support and preventive measures, with the higher level, statutory mechanisms reserved for the most serious situations of danger to children which could not be ameliorated without intrusive state intervention.

However this ethos was undermined over subsequent years by focusing resources on forensic and investigative practice to identify when abuse was occurring, rather than to intervene earlier (Buckley and Burns, 2015). Such a practice direction was in no small way informed by the string of high-profile child abuse inquiry reports of the 1990s. The Act itself was only eventually fully implemented and financed in response to the revelations of significant deficits in child protection highlighted by the Kilkenny Inquiry report.

Children First: National Guidelines for the Protection and Welfare of Children was introduced in 1999 as a targeted policy to reinforce the welfare and family support orientation of child protection, and to standardise and regulate practice within the complex regional web of service provision at the time. However, commentators noted the paradox that greater practice divergence in fact occurred as each local area developed its own responses to the guidelines (Kemp, 2008).

Eleven years after the introduction of *Children First*, an implementation review was published. Numerous incidents of 'unsound administration' were found, incorporating inconsistencies in practice, poor oversight, and deficient inter-agency collaboration. Importantly, the issues identified could not simply be explained away by a lack of resources: 'Some of the problems identified ... indicate a need for a fundamental change in culture and attitude towards child protection generally' (OCO, 2010). Research in 2014 into this 'policy to practice gap' found greatest attention was given by policy makers to ensuring a robust evidence base, with much less attention to how best policies could be embedded into practice. Front-line child protection workers were described as experiencing 'policy overload' (O'Connell, 2014: 68).

Poor implementation remained a reality by 2016, when the United Nations Committee on the Rights of the Child (CRC) expressed concern about the lack of authority or financial support vested in Tusla to ensure policy compliance (CRC, 2016). The Children's Rights Alliance (2018) has noted that Ireland has the infrastructure to meet the needs of the country's children, but deficits persist in practical service delivery.

A further historical error has been a lack of adequate data collection relating to children's welfare and protection in the state (Buckley,

2012; Kilkelly, 2007). The Ryan Report brought such failings to public attention, highlighting the vacuum in robust knowledge of how the child welfare and protection system was working. In an attempt to fill this void, the National Child Care Information System (NCCIS) Business Process Standardisation model was introduced (HSE, 2009).

The aim of the Business Processes was twofold. First, to create a standard nationwide response to child protection referrals and assessments, and to children in care to ensure consistency. Second, to provide reliable data for a new national computerised information management system. Guidance on procedures and time frames for completing specified tasks was provided. For the first time, Ireland's child protection responses were to be driven and measured by performance indicators and nationally prescribed targets.

While the meticulous recording of standardised procedures and outcomes has undoubtedly resulted in a much greater body of robust data about the workings of the system nationally, the processes themselves, particularly the timelines, have been less successful. Available statistics for 2017 show that only 19 per cent of child protection referrals met the 21-day time frame for initial screening and assessment (Tusla, 2017a).

Ireland's shift towards standardisation as a response to errors and mistakes continues in current child protection policy. The year 2017 saw the launch of a new national practice model, Signs of Safety (SOS) (Turnell and Edwards, 1999). Originating in Western Australia, SOS has been implemented across multiple jurisdictions including parts of the UK, Japan and Sweden (for example see Bunn, 2013; Munro et al, 2016; Baginsky et al, 2017). This will be the first time that a nationally prescribed standard framework of assessment will be used by child welfare and protection social work teams throughout the country.

The announcement of the new model came after the Tusla chief executive officer told the media in late 2016 that the Agency would be looking more to families to share responsibility for child welfare and protection (Hennessy, 2016). Tusla's position is that this new approach marks a shift from the traditionally paternalistic and risk-averse Irish child protection practice, towards an acknowledgement of risk and uncertainty as inevitable, with children's safety best ensured through partnership with families and communities (Tusla, 2017b). Ongoing research into practice implementation has also been announced (Gimpel, 2017), an acknowledgement of the repeated failures to transform past policies into practice realities.

Media and public discourse

Ireland's media has not historically responded to errors and mistakes in child protection by scapegoating individual professionals. When these cases come to light, the focus is more often on systems and management failure, with criticism directed at state bodies. Powell and Scanlon (2015: 49) in their study of media representations of child abuse in Ireland, concluded 'rather than being the vanguard, the media has generally brought up the rear'. That is not to say that critical questions are not asked by the media, but calls for personal accountability tend to be balanced by alternate positions on corporate responsibility, resource limitations and the nature of risk (see for example, O'Connor, 1996; Ferguson, 1998; *The Irish Times*, 2018).

This 'systemic failure' analysis exists within a wider landscape of Irish society traditionally being relieved of responsibility for messy child welfare and protection concerns. Historically responsibility was handed to the Church, along with the subsequent blame and liability for grave and sometimes fatal outcomes. This responsibility, along with its requisite culpability, now rests with the state, in the form of Tusla. The failure of society as a whole to recognise and respond to child abuse and neglect has never received the public critique and analysis that it deserves.

There can be no refuting that Church and state institutions committed often unimaginable horrors against children and vulnerable adults in their care. These bodies and institutions were very much part of the fabric of society, however, and it is credulous to suggest that individuals and communities were unaware of the treatment of people within those walls. Ingrained cultural norms, including a 'look away' attitude and 'othering' of the poor and socially marginalised, contributed to the Irish 'cultures of denial' (Cohen, 2001: 278) which in part allowed the horrors unearthed by the Ryan Report to continue unchallenged in plain sight for so long.

Cultural norms are powerfully pervasive. The Kilkenny Inquiry found a 'degree of ambivalence' from the wider community towards family violence. A number of witnesses to the Commission, including some health and social services staff, regarded domestic violence as 'part of family life' and a hesitation to intervene in a 'family matter' was prevalent in the ethos of the time (McGuiness, 1993: 89). Twenty-five years later, the chief executive officer of the Irish Society for the Prevention of Cruelty to Children has referred to a continuing 'complacency' among the general public towards abuse and neglect of children within their own families (*Today with Sean O'Rourke*, 2018).

Throughout the 1970s and 1980s when the McColgan children were being assaulted by their father, child sexual abuse was barely recognised as a phenomenon and certainly not openly discussed by the general public. Although there is more public and media deliberation of such abuse today, there are still some dominant discourses in Irish society that can militate against adequate protection of some of our most vulnerable citizens. As recently as 2017, the chief executive officer of the children's charity Barnardos referred to an enduring Irish cultural belief 'that children should be seen and not heard' (Oireachtas Joint Committee, 2017: 3).

Conclusion

Given the public shock and horror that greeted revelations of historical child abuse within state and religious institutions, one could be excused for thinking that such incidents define errors and mistakes in child protection in the Irish context. The impact of these scandals on public opinion was profound, leading to a crisis of trust in the Catholic Church and the secularisation of Irish society. The reality, however, is that fairly consistent numbers of children living within our communities continue to experience abuse and neglect, and the state response to this has frequently been found to be lacking. Vulnerable children have been left undetected, or when flagged as at risk, have remained unprotected as a result of lack of coherence between services, gaps in provision, and systemic failures.

Is government policy towards asylum-seeking children and their families, housed in compound-like institutions set apart from the wider community and further isolated by enforced poverty and social stigma, evidence of continued 'othering' of those on the margins of contemporary Irish society? The over-representation of such children in child protection statistics would suggest that there is validity in such questions. The suspicion and panic that led to the removal of two Roma children from their families on the primary basis of physical characteristics was not exclusive to members of An Garda Síochána, and suggests that stereotypes and social prejudices continue to result in errors and mistakes.

Ensuring that children are seen and heard, and that their voices are given due attention, has been a consistent theme of inquiries and reports since the Kilkenny Inquiry in 1993. Yet subsequent investigation and analysis has identified repeated failings in this regard. As recently as 2014, the Ombudsman for Children's report on the Roma children's removal highlighted that throughout her time in foster care, no one had asked the eldest child about who her family were.

'Systems failure' still persists as background commentary to Ireland's mistakes, with inconsistencies in individual practice most frequently presented as structurally and systemically bred. The state's historical pattern of creating new policies each time a mistake is identified, and then failing adequately to support or monitor the subsequent practice implementation, lends credence to this position. More than two decades ago it was recognised that, 'Child protection policy making in Ireland has tended to follow high profile happenings in a political piecemeal fashion' (McGrath cited in Buckley et al, 1997: 20). This situation would not appear to have altered greatly in the subsequent years. The 2017 report into police emergency powers to remove children is just one example, and the repetition of this approach, spanning many years and administrations, can be viewed as an error in its own right.

The 'elaborate systems of governance' (Burns et al, forthcoming: 5) in response to numerous errors and mistakes over the years seek to ensure that child protection policy is no longer a theoretical guideline or ideal, but a blueprint for consistent, uniform practice. There are some welcome indications that Irish child protection is heading in this direction. These include the new stand-alone Tusla, Child and Family Agency, the recently introduced nationally standardised practice approach, 'Signs of Safety', and the injection of considerably increased financial resources to support policy implementation (Oireachtas Dáil, 2018).

Kilkelly's 2012 summary of predominant legislative themes of high profile inquiry reports identified three that stood out – a call for constitutional reform to strengthen the rights of the child, provision for mandatory child abuse reporting, and the need for adequate inspection mechanisms. In 2018, after more than two decades of discussion and debate, all three are finally reflected in Irish legislation.

References

Arnold, S. (2012) *State Sanctioned Child Poverty and Exclusion: The Case of Children in State Accommodation for Asylum Seekers*, Dublin: Irish Refugee Council.

Baginsky, M., Moriarty, J., Manthorpe, J., Beecham, J. and Hickman, B. (2017) *Evaluation of Signs of Safety in 10 Pilots*, research report, London: Department for Education.

Barnes, J. (1989) *Irish Industrial Schools, 1868–1908*, Kildare: Irish Academic Press.

Bruton, M. (1998) *West of Ireland Farmer Case: Report of Review Group, Presented to North Western Health Board, July 1998*, Manorhamilton: North Western Health Board.

Buckley, H. (2012) 'Using Intelligence to Shape Reforms in Child Protection', *Irish Journal of Applied Social Studies*, 12(1): 62–73.

Buckley, H. and Burns, K. (2015) 'Child Welfare and Protection in Ireland: Déjà Vu All Over Again', in A. Christie, B. Featherstone, S. Quin and T. Walsh (eds) *Social Work in Ireland: Continuities and Changes*, Basingstoke: Palgrave Macmillan, pp 51–70.

Buckley, H. and O'Nolan, C. (2013) *An Examination of Recommendations from Inquiries into Events in Families and Their Interactions with State Services, and Their Impact on Policy and Practice*, Dublin: Government Publications.

Buckley, H., Skehill, C. and O'Sullivan, E. (1997) *Child Protection Practices in Ireland: A Case Study*, Dublin: Oak Tree Press.

Bunn, A. (2013) *Signs of Safety in England: An NSPCC Commissioned Report on the Signs of Safety Model in Child Protection*, London: NSPCC.

Burns, K., Devaney, J., Holt, S. and Marshall, G. (forthcoming) 'Child Protection and Welfare on the Island of Ireland: Irish Issues, Global Relevance', in J.D. Berrick, N. Gilbert, and M. Skivenes (eds) *International Handbook of Child Protection Systems*, New York: Oxford University Press.

Burns, K., Pösö, T. and Skivenes, M. (2017) 'Child Welfare Removals by the State: Complex and Controversial Decisions', in K. Burns, T. Pösö and M. Skivenes (eds) *Child Welfare Removals by the State: A Cross-Country Analysis of Decision-Making Systems*, New York: Oxford University Press, pp 1–17.

Children's Rights Alliance (2018) *Report Card 2018: Is Government Keeping its Promises to Children?* Dublin: Children's Rights Alliance. Available from: http://childrensrights.ie/sites/default/files/files/files/report_card_18.pdf.

Cohen, S. (2001) *States of Denial: Knowing About Atrocities and Suffering*, Cambridge: Polity Press.

Coulter, C. (2013) *First Interim Report Child Care Law Reporting Project*, Dublin: Child Care Law Reporting Project. Available from: www.childlawproject.ie/interim-reports/.

Coulter, C. (2015) *Final Report Child Care Law Reporting Project*, Dublin: Child Care Law Reporting Project. Available from: www.childlawproject.ie/interim-reports/.

CRC (United Nations Committee on the Rights of the Child) (2016) *Concluding Observations on the Combined Third and Fourth Periodic Reports of Ireland CRC/C/IRL/CO/3-4*. Available from: www.childrensdatabase.ie/documents/publications/20160504Concludin gObsonCombined3rdand4thPeriodicReportsIreland.pdf.

CSO (Central Statistics Office) (2017) *Census 2016 Summary Results, Part 1*, Dublin: Stationery Office.

DCYA (Department of Children and Youth Affairs) (2014) *Better Outcomes, Brighter Futures: The National Policy Framework for Children and Young People 2014–2020*, Dublin: Government Publications.

DCYA (Department of Children and Youth Affairs) (2016) *State of the Nation's Children: Ireland 2016*, Dublin: Government Publications.

Department of Health and Children (1999) *Children First: National Guidelines for the Protection and Welfare of Children*, Dublin: Stationery Office.

Eurostat (2018) *Eurostat Celebrates Ireland*. Available from: http://ec.europa.eu/eurostat/web/products-eurostat-news/-/EDN-20180317-1.

Ferguson, H. (1998) 'McColgan Case Must Be Judged in Context of Professional Approach of a Different Era', *The Irish Times*, 26 January. Available from: www.irishtimes.com/news/mccolgan-case-must-be-judged-in-context-of-professional-approach-of-a-different-era-1.128272.

Finn, C. (2013) 'Court Won't Send Family Back to Direct Provision Housing in Ireland Due to Child Welfare Concerns' *The Journal.ie*, 15 August. Available from: https://jrnl.ie/1039130/.

Gibbons, N., Harrison, P., Lunny, L. and O'Neill, G. (2010) *Roscommon Child Care Case: Report of the Inquiry Team to the Health Service Executive*, Dublin: HSE.

Gimpel, A. (2017) *Signs of Safety Adopted as National Child Protection Framework for Ireland*. Available from: www.signsofsafety.net/signs-of-safety-adopted-as-national-child-protection-framework-for-ireland/.

Hennessy, M. (2016) '"It's Not the State's problem, It's the Family's": Care System to Adopt Tough Love Approach', *The Journal.ie*, 30 October. Available from: https://jrnl.ie/3046658.

HIQA (Health Information and Quality Authority) (2012) *National Standards for the Protection and Welfare of Children*, Dublin: HIQA.

HIQA (Health Information and Quality Authority) (2015) *Report on Inspection of the Child Protection and Welfare Services Provided to Children Living in Direct Provision Accommodation Under the National Standards for the Protection and Welfare of Children, and Section 8(1) (c) of the Health Act 2007*, Dublin: HIQA.

HIQA (Health Information and Quality Authority) (2018) *Report of the Investigation into the Management of Allegations of Child Sexual Abuse Against Adults of Concern by the Child and Family Agency (Tusla) Upon the Direction of the Minister for Children and Youth Affairs*, Dublin: HIQA.

HSE (Health Service Executive) (2009) *HSE Child Welfare and Protection Social Work Departments Business Processes: Report of the NCCIS Business Process Standardisation Project*, Dublin: HSE.

Joint Committee on the Family (1996) *Kelly – A Child is Dead: Report of a Committee of Inquiry*, Dublin: Government Publications.

Kemp, P. (2008) 'Questioning Quality: A Critical Analysis of the Development and Implementation of the "Quality Agenda" and Its Impact on Child Protection Social Work Practice in Ireland', in K. Burns and D. Lynch (eds), *Child Protection and Welfare Social Work*, Dublin: A. and A. Farmar, pp 97–110.

Kilkelly, U. (2007) *Barriers to the Realisation of Children's Rights in Ireland*, Dublin: Ombudsman for Children.

Kilkelly, U. (2012) 'Learning Lessons From the Past: Legal Issues Arising from Ireland's Child Abuse Reports', *Irish Journal of Applied Social Studies*, 12(1): 8–24.

Lamponen, T., Pösö, T. and Burns, K. (2018) 'Children in Immediate Danger: Emergency Removals in Finnish and Irish Child Protection', *Child & Family Social Work*, ahead of print: DOI: 10.1111/cfs.12628.

Lavan, A. (1998) 'Social Work in Ireland', in S. Shardlow and M. Payne (eds) *Contemporary Issues in Social Work: Western Europe*, Aldershot: Arena.

Logan, E. (2014) *Garda Síochána Act 2005 (Section 42) (Special Inquiries relating to Garda Síochána) Order 2013*, Dublin: Department of Justice.

Marron, A., Joyce, A.M., Carr, J., Devereux, E., Breen, M., Power, M.J. and Haynes, A. (2016) 'Print Media Framings of Those Blonde Roma Children', in A. Haynes, M. Power, E. Devereux, A. Dillane and J. Carr (eds) *Public and Political Discourses of Migration: International Perspectives*, London: Rowman & Littlefield International, pp 117–34.

McDonagh, M. (2009) 'Court Told of Support for Incest Mother by Catholic Group', *The Irish Times*, 22 January. Available from: www.irishtimes.com/news/court-told-of-support-for-incest-mother-by-catholic-group-1.1235901.

McGuinness, C. (1993) *Kilkenny Incest Investigation: Report Presented to Mr. Brendan Howlin T.D. Minister for Health*, Dublin: Stationery Office.

Munro, E., Turnell, A. and Murphy, T. (2016) *'You Can't Grow Roses in Concrete': Organisational Reform to Support High Quality Signs of Safety Practice*, London: MTM Child Protection Consulting.

Murphy, Y. (2009) *Commission of Investigation Report into the Catholic Archdiocese of Dublin*, Dublin: Government Publications.

O'Connell, H. (2015) "'We Have a Love Affair with Incarcerating People in Ireland'", *The Journal.ie*, 3 March. Available from: http://jrnl.ie/1967866.

O'Connell, O. (2014) *Exploring the Policy to Practice Gap: Social Workers' Experience of Embedding Child Protection Policy into Their Practice*, Cork: University College Cork.

O'Connor, A. (1996) 'Board Is Criticised in Report on Kelly Fitzgerald' *The Irish Times*, 18 April. Available from: www.irishtimes.com/news/board-is-criticised-in-report-on-kelly-fitzgerald-1.40519.

OCO (Ombudsman for Children's Office) (2009) *Ombudsman for Children's Office Annual Report 2009*, Dublin: OCO.

OCO (Ombudsman for Children's Office) (2010) *A Report Based on an Investigation into the Implementation of Children First: National Guidelines for the Protection and Welfare of Children*, Dublin: OCO.

Office of the Ombudsman (2017) *Taking Stock: An Investigation by the Ombudsman into Complaint Handling and Issues Identified in Complaints Made about The Child and Family Agency (Tusla)*. Dublin: Office of the Ombudsman.

Oireachtas Dáil (2017) *Child and Family Agency Staff*, debate 17 October. Available from: www.oireachtas.ie/en/debates/question/2017-10-17/32/.

Oireachtas Dáil (2018) *Child and Family Agency Data*, debate 8 March. Available from: www.oireachtas.ie/en/debates/question/2018-03-08/524/.

Oireachtas Joint Committee on Children and Youth Affairs (2017) *General Scheme of Childcare (Amendment) Bill 2017: Discussion*, 8 March. Available from: www.oireachtas.ie/en/debates/debate/joint_committee_on_children_and_youth_affairs/2017-03-08/2/.

O'Mahony, C., Burns, K., Parkes, A. and Shore, C. (2016) 'Representation and Participation in Child Care Proceedings: What About the Voice of the Parents?' *Journal of Social Welfare and Family Law*, 38(3): 302–22.

OMCYA (Office of the Minister for Children and Youth Affairs) (2009) *Report of the Commission to Inquire into Child Abuse, 2009: Implementation Plan*, Dublin: Government Publications.

Powell, F. and Scanlon, M. (2015) *Dark Secrets of Childhood: Media Power, Child Abuse and Public Scandals*, Bristol: Policy Press.

Rafferty, M. and O'Sullivan, E. (1999) *Suffer the Little Children*, Dublin: New Island Books.

Ryan, S. (2009) *Commission to Inquire into Child Abuse Report* (vols i–v), Dublin: Stationery Office.

Shannon, G. (2012) *Fifth Report of the Special Rapporteur on Child Protection*, Dublin: Government Publications.

Shannon, G. (2017) *Audit of the Exercise by An Garda Síochána of the Provisions of Section 12 of the Child Care Act 1991*, Dublin: Government Publications.

Shannon, G. and Gibbons, N. (2012) *Report of the Independent Child Death Review Group*, Dublin: Government Publications.

The Irish Times (2018) *The Irish Times View on Child Protection: A Litany of Failings* (22nd June).

Today with Sean O'Rourke (2018) *RTÉ Radio 1*, 24 May, Dublin.

Turnell, A. and Edwards, S. (1999) *Signs of Safety: A Solution and Safety Oriented Approach to Child Protection Casework*, New York: W.W. Norton.

Tusla, Child and Family Agency (2014) *Guidance for the Child and Family Agency on the Operation of The National Review Panel*. Available from: www.tusla.ie/uploads/content/20141204GuidOperationofationalReviewPanel.pdf.

Tusla, Child and Family Agency (2017a) *Tusla Monthly Management Data Activity Report December 2017 (2)*. Available from: www.tusla.ie/uploads/content/Tusla_Monthly_Management_Data_Activity_Report_December_2016.pdf.

Tusla, Child and Family Agency (2017b) 'Tusla Launches New Child Protection and Welfare Strategy', 22 May. Available from: www.tusla.ie/news/tusla-launches-new-child-protection-and-welfare-strategy/.

UNICEF Office of Research (2016) *Fairness for Children: A League Table of Inequality in Child Well-Being in Rich Countries*, Florence: UNICEF Office of Research.

United Nations Development Programme (2016) *Human Development Report 2016*, New York: UNDP.

5

The level-headed approach on errors and mistakes in Dutch child protection: an individual duty or a shared responsibility?

Kirti Zeijlmans, Tom van Yperen and Mónica López López

Child protection in the Netherlands

Dutch child protection is a family-oriented system (Gilbert et al, 2011), characterised by the recognition of the best interest of the child and a family-friendly approach with an emphasis on supporting families rather than intervening and reporting child abuse (Knijn and Nijnatten, 2011). Child protection policy developments in the Netherlands have been highly influenced by the United Nations Convention on the Rights of the Child and the European Convention on Human Rights. All families must have access to parenting support and family coaching in their municipalities, and great efforts are made to prevent child abuse and neglect, and to detect it at an early stage. Out-of-home placement of a child is considered a last-resort intervention and should be temporary (Harder et al, 2013).

The number of children (0–18 years old) in the Netherlands is estimated at 3,429,193 (CBS, 2015). Research on child abuse shows a prevalence rate of 33.8 children per 1,000 (Euser et al, 2013). Although the prevalence rate appeared relatively stable between 2010 and 2015, the number of victims reported has increased by 67 per cent in this five-year period. Likewise, an increased number of child protection orders has been registered (Netherlands Youth Institute, 2007). This growth has been linked to greater social attention to child abuse and the occurrence of fatal cases.

The Dutch child protection system has undergone important structural changes with the introduction of the Youth Act 2015 (*Jeugdwet* 2015). The main features of this new framework are: the decentralisation of responsibilities for provision and quality of care for children and families to the 393 Dutch municipalities; the aim of reducing the number of children in specialised care by increasing preventive and early intervention measures; and promoting the use of the families' social networks.

Dutch municipalities are responsible for the identification, investigation, intervention and monitoring of child abuse cases. The two key child protection institutions are the Advice and Reporting Centre for Domestic Violence and Child Maltreatment (Advies- en Meldpunt Huiselijk Geweld en Kindermishandeling – AMHK), and the Child Care and Protection Board (Raad voor de Kinderbescherming – RvdK). After a report, the AMHK can investigate a possible situation of child abuse and refer children to voluntary care. The RvdK and the Juvenile Court are involved in investigating and deciding whether compulsory child protection measures are necessary.

This chapter starts by providing some insight into historical child abuse in the Netherlands and a description of fatal cases in child protection. Next, we present the underlying problems that have been identified by the Youth Care Inspectorate and a review of inquiries into critical incidents.

Following these sections, four child protection initiatives, implemented to prevent the occurrence of critical incidents, are discussed. The chapter ends with an analysis of the patterns of handling errors and mistakes and a brief discussion about what we can learn from the Dutch situation.

Historical child abuse in the Netherlands

In the Netherlands, modern child protection started when the Dutch child laws came into effect in 1905 (Bakker et al, 2006). From that date onwards, removal of children from their parents in cases of abuse or neglect became possible, and the government took responsibility for the safety and protection of children (Dekker et al, 2012). The operation of the child laws was not without challenges. Mandatory re-education for problematic children was considered highly distressing and there were critical voices from both practice and policy worlds that claimed youth were hardly better off in protection than they would have been at home. Furthermore, child protection workers revolted against the lack of a minimum age for criminal prosecution that allowed very young children to receive sentences of several years in a reformatory. In the 1930s, increased numbers of parental rights terminations sparked a public fear that parents became indifferent and gave up their parental rights easily (Bakker et al, 2006). However, these issues did not lead to reform of the child protection system until after the Second World War, when the demand for child protection increased and a start was made to professionalise the system. Child protection practice slowly became more critical of its own functioning (Bakker et al, 2006) and the system progressed from a mostly unqualified volunteer-based service to a service with educated child protection workers. Furthermore, from 1947 all organisations dealing with child custody had to submit to standardised regulations and inspection (Dekker et al, 2012).

A legitimacy crisis in child protection followed, triggered by the criticism of the child protection system, as well as the 'de-compartmentalisation' and empowerment revolution from the 1960s. The values of emancipation, participation, empowerment and democracy went against the system of imposing coercive measures on children and families (Bakker et al, 2006; Dekker et al, 2012). There was public criticism and protests against child protection, combined with staffing issues and internal conflicts within the organisations. People became increasingly convinced that child protection had to change (Dekker et al, 2012) and child protection measures decreased, partly due to financial cuts. The legitimacy crisis that started in the 1960s lasted until the 1980s, when trust in the efficacy of interventions was recovered due to increased worries about criminality rates and severe behaviour problems among youth. This motivated a reorganisation, accompanied by the professionalisation of the organisational structure of the child protection system. Child protection became a market with ever-increasing multifunctional players (Dekker et al, 2012).

Fatal cases on child protection: identified errors and mistakes and effects on practice

Our understanding of the terms error and mistake is aligned with the definitions presented by Biesel and Cottier in Chapter 2. Errors and mistakes in child protection systems are socially constructed and develop depending on what a society considers the right or wrong practices in child protection at a particular historical moment.

In the early 2000s, the Netherlands was horrified by child deaths, which made national headlines and had far-reaching consequences for the Dutch child protection system (Baartman, 2011). The Case of 'Rowena Rikkers' and 'Meisje van Nulde' in 2001, the death of six children in Roermond in July 2002, and the case of Savanna in 2004 triggered media attention with gruesome details of the stories, and also by the realisation that their families had been in contact with youth care and/or child protection agencies. Yet child protection workers had been unable to act effectively to protect these children from harm (Baartman, 2011; Dekker et al, 2012). These tragedies were portrayed publicly as mistakes by the child protection agencies to safeguard the well-being of vulnerable children. The case of Savanna is considered to have had the highest impact on the Dutch child protection system and was used to justify several changes in childcare policy and practice (Bruning, 2007). Unique in this case was the prosecution of an individual employee of the child protection agency, who was charged with, but eventually acquitted of, complicity in Savanna's death by failing to take appropriate measures to prevent it (Rechtbank's-Gravenhage, 2007; Kuijvenhoven and Kortleven, 2010). After this case, there was a lingering fear of individual prosecution and a profound belief that cases like Savanna's should never be allowed to happen. This triggered a shift from *compassion* for families in hard times to *control* to make sure that interventions would not be too late (Baartman, 2011). In the subsequent years, there was an increase in the numbers of out-of-home placements, which was explained by child protection professionals taking fewer risks for fear of prosecution (called the Savanna effect). Simultaneously, the improvement of screening instruments for at-risk families and a more widely known system for reporting child abuse could have caused these trends (Berends et al, 2010).

Thus, since the start of modern child protection until now, the general public have not trusted the Dutch child protection system. The dynamic discourses of child protection and the criticism of the system for acting too early or too late at different times in recent history have influenced social work practice with children and families. While the most prevalent discourse in the 20th century focused on the invasive practice of governmental child protection and the early removal of children from homes, the current discourse has changed due to the shock of multiple cases of horrendous child deaths at the beginning of this century (Dekker et al, 2012).

The impact of the Inspectorate for Child and Youth Care and Child Protection

The youth care inspection and supervision system was established at the start of the governmental regulated child protection system (Dekker et al, 2012). However, for a long time these government checks were limited to organisations that received state funding. From 1947, the governmental inspection on youth care broadened to include all organisations providing out-of-home care. Yet, the supervision in those years was described as chaotic (Dekker et al, 2012). Both the government and private organisations supervised child protection organisations, either with a more generic perspective or a case-by-case basis. There was no standardised system for controlling the content and demands on child protection. However, the government tried to get a grip on the details of child protection.

The first Dutch inquiry report dates back to 1988, when the 'Bolderkar' affair took place (Kuijvenhoven and Kortleven, 2010). In the 'Bolderkar' affair, many children from a medical day-care centre were removed from their homes due to alleged sexual abuse by their parents, but further investigations showed that the removal was motivated by wrongful accusations reliant on tests with anatomical dolls and poor professional practice. After this incident, and following the professionalisation of child protection, a national independent inspection agency was established (Dekker et al, 2012). Following that first report, these inquiries became an important instrument for identifying problems in child protection and improving professional practice (Kuijvenhoven and Kortleven, 2010); the inspection of youth care, formalised as a governmental organisation, became progressively better known for their critical role in investigating and acting on potentially flawed social work cases (Dekker et al, 2012).

Until 2005, the Inspectorate for Child and Youth Care and Child Protection (Inspectie Jeugdhulpverlening en Jeugdbescherming) had to rely on the media for notification of serious or fatal abuse of children known to agencies. After a change in the youth law in 2005, organisations became obliged to report cases to the inspectorate (Kuijvenhoven and Kortleven, 2010). However, not all incidents of child death related to child protection are investigated by the inspectorate. The common procedure is to request the organisations involved to conduct a review. When this is deemed insufficient, the incident is considered media sensitive, or they receive a request for an objective investigation, the inspectorate will write their own inquiry report (Kuijvenhoven and Kortleven, 2010; Tielen et al, 2015). These reports are based on case files and other documents together with interviews with stakeholders. Personal information about professionals is not shared in the reports and clients are anonymised as far as possible. These inquiries can become public, with the first report being published in 2000 (Kuijvenhoven and Kortleven, 2010). With the introduction of the new Youth Act in 2015 this became standard practice; all inquiries from the inspectorate are anonymised and published.

Inquiries into critical incidents

Inquiries of critical incidents provide an interesting source of information on the main problems identified in child protection as well as their proposed solutions. Inspectorate inquiries have been subjected to meta-analysis to see overarching trends or repeated patterns of problems (Kuijvenhoven and Kortleven, 2010; De Onderzoeksraad voor Veiligheid, 2011; Samenwerkend Toezicht Jeugd, 2013; Samenwerkend Toezicht Jeugd / Toezicht Sociaal Domein, 2016). These studies are summarised chronologically below.

The article by Kuijvenhoven and Kortleven (2010) examined seven published inquiries that occurred from 2002 to 2007. The main failures and concerns formulated in these inquiries were clustered into seven aspects: coordination, collaboration and responsibilities; information exchange; record-keeping, transparency and accountability; detecting child abuse; cooperating with parents and keeping focus on the child; monitoring and control in child protection services; and resources and staffing capacity. The emphasis in the recommendations of these inquiries was on bureaucratic measures such as regulations, procedures, guidelines and protocols (Kuijvenhoven and Kortleven, 2010). For example, standardised risk assessment has been mentioned more explicitly throughout the analysed inquiries as a means to diminish incidents. There has been criticism that the inquiries are unlikely to contribute much to improvement of child protection, because bureaucratic solutions could only work if attuned to the skills of professionals (Kuijvenhoven and Kortleven, 2010).

The report by the Dutch Safety Board in 2011 (De Onderzoeksraad voor Veiligheid) included 27 fatal or near-fatal incidents between 2004 and 2007. In only five of these cases was an inquiry drafted by the inspectorate. They concluded that the government could not fulfil its responsibility to protect children from parental harm. Professionals were too reticent to take action, especially when parents were unwilling to collaborate; there was a lack of cooperation between organisations; and risk assessments were often not completed. The report recommended learning from incidents and events in a more systematic way (De Onderzoeksraad voor Veiligheid, 2011). Prosecuting individual professionals was not seen as a way of increasing professionalism given the lack of clear guidelines and rules. Rather, supervision and guidance should be central to increasing the quality of child protection work.

The next report focused on eight incident inquiries conducted in 2011/12 (Samenwerkend Toezicht Jeugd, 2013). In four cases, the inquiries focused on the death of a child; two cases concerned sexual abuse; one case was severe child abuse; and a case involved long-term educational neglect of a child with severe behavioural problems. In this report, the concept of a 'duty to act' was presented, meaning that professionals must act on signals of abuse and neglect. The inspectorate concluded that in most cases it could not be substantiated that professionals indeed acted. Recommendations were made to implement explicit measures and to work on adjustments in attitude, behaviour and control. Again, the role of parents was mentioned as a key point for improvement. Professionals were considered to be too focused on parents and, in consequence, failing to assess or safeguard the child. The second problem identified was the lack of seeing, sharing and acting on signals and risks, which indicated that the Reference Index (Verwijsindex Risicojongeren), implemented in 2010, did not work as intended (see also later in this chapter). The report encouraged the use of a standardised reassessment when changes in the family occurred.

The report published in 2016, as a follow-up to that published in 2013, focused on 11 cases from 2013 to 2016 (Samenwerkend Toezicht Jeugd / Toezicht Sociaal Domein, 2016). Three main issues were identified in the inquiries: there was insufficient shift in thinking from parental problems to the potential risk for children; the move to compulsory care happened too late and there was a lack of safety agreements when stepping down care; and chronic problems and risks were underestimated while families' self-reliance was overestimated.

Interestingly, the issues mentioned by Kuijvenhoven and Kortleven (2010) in the first study of critical cases continued to be prevalent in the follow-up inquiries (De Onderzoeksraad voor Veiligheid, 2011; Samenwerkend Toezicht Jeugd, 2013; Samenwerkend Toezicht Jeugd / Toezicht Sociaal Domein, 2016), as well as in the inquiries published after 2016 (Goedegebure and Haan, 2017). In light of these analyses, several initiatives have been introduced over the years to prevent further recurrence.

Child protection initiatives to reduce and to learn from errors and mistakes

In this section, the focus is on the description of four major developments initiated from 1999 onwards, partly in response to the scrutiny of critical incidents, in order to reduce errors and mistakes.

Family Coach

In 2002, a new category of youth care worker was introduced with the main task of supporting multiproblem families by coordinating the help offered to the family by all services or agencies involved. Organisations could choose to implement as part of their services the figure of the Family Coach, who would become responsible for creating an overview of services and arranging an integrated care package for the family.

This initiative came from the state secretary Clemens Ross in response to the turbulence created by the death of the six children in Roermond in 2002 and a general measure to improve the support offered to multiproblem families (Ross – van Dorp, 2002). The goal of this Family Coach is to reduce the lack of communication and coordination in cases, which had been identified as a determining factor in the Roermond case. A pilot was started by the Youth Care Agency (Bureau Jeugdzorg) in Roermond to assess the impact of this initiative. In 2005, the Family Coach was enshrined in the Youth Care Act (Wet op de Jeugdzorg).

Although the Province of Limburg, responsible for the pilot, reported positive practitioner experiences with the Family Coach (Provincie Limburg, 2005), the media were critical, arguing that the coaches had no formal authority to act if providers failed to cooperate, and that a new professional category had the risk of becoming just another worker added to the bureaucrats in contact with the family (Van Enennaam, 2005; Volkskrant, 2005). Almost ten years later, there was a new pilot, again in the Province of Limburg, to evaluate the figure of the Family Coach. This qualitative study showed that the Family Coach had very limited value; effects were predominantly reported in motivated families with single problems (Bureau Onderzoek & Statistiek Heerlen, 2014). Virtually no effects were found in the complex cases, the situations in which calamities were most likely to occur.

Reference Index for high-risk youngsters

A second initiative is the implementation of the Reference Index (Verwijsindex Risicojongeren) in 2010. This national electronic system aims to inform all professionals that are involved in the support of a child of other professionals engaged in the case. As mentioned earlier in this chapter, the critical incidents in the early 2000s showed that in nearly all cases there was a lack of coordination, information exchange, and cooperation between services and officials, which led to a lack of detecting, sharing and acting on signs of risk. The Reference Index is a tool for sharing information on involvement in cases of suspected risk of abuse, neglect or other concerns. When a professional indicates concerns about a child, this should produce a 'match', a signal that tells the professional that there is a shared concern. The purpose is not to exchange the details of this concern, but to create an overview and to stimulate cooperation between the professionals involved.

From 2010, every municipality was responsible by law for arranging that services report their involvement in a case using the Reference Index, or a local variant (Article 2j, Amendment Youth Care Act, 2009). The system includes information from schools, child and youth care, healthcare, the justice offices and social security. A special website provides criteria for when to report involvement in a case.[1]

Two studies have been undertaken to evaluate the use of the Reference Index. Lecluijze et al (2015) were mostly negative about its value. In their ethnographic study, they noted that in most cases the shared involvement of the professionals was already known; the criteria for reporting vague, leading to professionals assessing risk in cases quite differently; and professionals tended to over-report cases in order to avoid negative consequences if they failed to detect risks early enough. Lecluijze et al (2015) concluded that the system puts an over-reliance on a large-scale technical solution for a problem that is mostly personal: how to use this Index as a learning tool for professionals in order to increase their self-efficacy and competence in handling complex cases.

The research by Abraham and Van Dijk (2015) produced a more nuanced picture, showing that in the period 2011–14 the number of reports using the Index had doubled (from about 55,000 to 111,000), and the number of participating organisations had quadrupled (from about 450 to 1,700). About 25 per cent of the matches led to new contacts between professionals and in about 40 per cent the matches led to contacts between professionals at an earlier stage. The system was most beneficial for cases from different local systems, identifying concerns with multiproblem families that have moved from one region to another, and with young adolescents who lived and attended school in different regions. However, the use of the Index was undermined by anonymous reports and the poor technical fits between different local systems, which made it more difficult to match at risk cases.

Assessment procedures LIRIK and ORBA

The third initiative represents an attempt to structure professional assessment and decision-making by using protocols and diagnostic tools with the aim of guiding professional consideration of factors relevant for identifying child abuse and neglect, increasing the transparency of decision-making and enhancing agreement between professionals about risk assessments. Two well-researched examples of these tools, widely implemented in the Netherlands, are the ORBA (Onderzoek Risicotaxatie Besluitvorming AM(H)Ks [Investigation Risk Assessment Decision Making AM(H)Ks])[2] and the LIRIK (Licht Instrument Risicotaxatie Kindveiligheid [Light Instrument Risk Assessment Child Safety]). The ORBA is a decision-making method with guidelines, criteria and checklists, which aims to support professionals in collecting relevant information, making judgements about children's safety and deciding whether to report the case for child protection. The LIRIK is an instrument designed to guide professionals in their assessment of signs, risk factors and protective factors for a child's safety. It aims to check systematically the relevant factors and helps professionals to conclude, based on these factors, whether or not children's safety is endangered or at risk.

The initial response was that these instruments could indeed support decision-making about safety and risks (Ten Berge and Van Rossum, 2009; Ten Berge and Meuwissen, 2013). However, later studies had disappointing results. As to the ORBA, a study of De Kwaadsteniet et al (2013) showed that professionals' decision-making processes had become more systematic and transparent in the period 2005–10, when the ORBA was implemented. However, in most cases the decisions continued to lack reasons. Moreover, a second study by Bartelink et al (2014) revealed that practitioners not trained in the ORBA showed little agreement on their decisions, but trained practitioners did not perform any better. The authors concluded that there was no convincing evidence that structured decision-making led to more agreement on decisions about child abuse and neglect.

The LIRIK has been studied by Bartelink et al (2017) who analysed the interrater agreement and predictive validity of professionals' judgements made with the instrument. Their finding was that the instrument did not improve agreement between professionals. Using the LIRIK did not result in better predictive validity compared with professionals who did not use the instrument. The authors concluded that the LIRIK could help professionals to assess systematically relevant factors related to the child's safety; yet, it seemed cognitively too demanding to consider all relevant cues consciously, while simultaneously expecting that agreement and predictive validity would improve.

Innovative methods of family guardianship

If child protection services are needed, the Dutch Juvenile Court can impose a supervision order and assign a family guardian for the child. About 20 years ago, there was a great deal of dissatisfaction with the quality of this guardianship, fuelled by the calamities mentioned previously. The Association of Child Protection Agencies (Stichting Vedivo) observed that there was a lack of a systematic and transparent approach to family guardianship: goals and means were unclear, there were difficulties in dealing with parents, and a focus on the child's safety was absent. This led the Association to formulate an innovative vision, called Leading Change (Stichting Vedivo, 2000), followed by the publication of a handbook on family guardianship (Van Hout and Spinder, 2001). However, studies by Slot et al (2002) and the Inspectorate for Child and Youth Care and Child Protection (Inspectie jeugdhulpverlening en jeugdbescherming, 2003) showed that guardians had to support too many cases, the goals of this support were still unclear, the number of out-of-home placements was exceedingly high, and in more than 70 per cent of the families the situation showed no improvement or even deteriorated.

In that same period, the child protection agencies started pilots to develop a new version of their handbook, now called the 'Delta Method' (*Deltamethode*), which is aimed at reducing caseloads and improving the quality of support by family guardians. This method was characterised by an unequivocal focus on the safety of the child, an approach led by the needs of the family, the formulation of a clear support plan together with the family, and the activation of the family's social network. This development was adopted by the Ministry of Justice as part of a large-scale improvement programme 'Better Protected' (*Beter Beschermd*; Ministerie van Justitie, 2004). In 2004, these pilots resulted in a first draft of the Delta Method, developed by researchers and practitioners (Van Wijk, 2004).

The pilots were evaluated in a quasi-experimental study by Slot et al (2004), and Lunenburg et al (2006). These studies showed promising results: the pilot families were more satisfied with their guardians and the support received than the control group; the family guardians themselves were more satisfied about their work and the results achieved; the goals formulated in support plans were clearer; the pilot group showed more improvement compared with the control group; and caseloads were significantly lower. However, there was no difference between the pilot group and the control group in the time needed to restore the children's safety and the number and duration of out-of-home placements. The evaluation also revealed wide variations in the application of the Delta Method. Furthermore, the guardians stated that they needed more detailed instructions on how to use the general principles of the method in their daily work with families.

These detailed instructions were offered in an extended version of the *Handboek Deltamethode*, again developed in close cooperation with practitioners (Slot and Van Montfoort, 2009). A study by Stams et al (2010) evaluated the effects of working with the Delta Method which had been implemented nationwide in 2007. By analysing the degree of adherence to the method and the results attained, they were able to show that working according to this method had significant positive effects. Close cooperation between the family guardian and the parents led to an eight-month reduction in the duration of the guardianship needed. Furthermore, working with a clear support plan reduced the chance of a child's out-of-home placement in 50 per cent of cases and, if this support plan was guided by concrete goals, the duration of out-of-home placement could be shortened by 14 months on average. The duration of an out-of-home-placement was 17 months previously, with a standard deviation of 30 months (Stams et al, 2010).

After the implementation of the Delta Method, the professional community has continued to improve its work. The current improvements incorporate elements of solution-focused therapy and Signs of Safety (Turnell and Edwards, 1999), which aim to improve the cooperation between parents, their social network and the professionals involved, and to diminish the use of supervision orders. As yet there has been no large-scale evaluation of these initiatives but the developments are considered promising by participants (for an overview of developments, see Addink et al, 2017).

Conclusion

The main focus of concern in the Netherlands is identifying children in complex and dangerous environments. Cases where multiple organisations are involved and problems are numerous (the so-called multiproblem families) can be identified as challenges for the Dutch child protection system. Multiproblem families, who often show care-avoidant behaviour, are seen as the group with the highest risks and the greatest dangers for children.

The same causes of errors and mistakes have repeatedly been identified in the Dutch inquiries over recent decades: lack of collaboration between professionals, poor exchange of information between organisations, and the challenges of detecting child abuse in complex cases. In this sense, the Netherlands, as other countries analysed in this book, has clearly moved from a traditional inquiry approach, focused on human errors, to a more systemic approach characterised by the emphasis on analysing the whole context in which the professional makes decisions in order to understand the various sources of errors (Biesel and Cottier, Chapter 2 in this volume).

Overall, the liability for any critical incident is not tied to a single professional but explained by the (lack of) collaboration between professionals. After the case of Savanna, where an individual professional was prosecuted, there has been no naming and shaming or personalised blame. Furthermore, use of disciplinary law against individual workers has not been viewed as a suitable way to increase the professionalism among child protection workers (De Onderzoeksraad voor Veiligheid, 2011). Review reports are anonymous, and the media does not report names of individual workers. However, the initiatives to reduce errors and mistakes, such as the Family Coach and the innovative methods for family guardianship, are intended to make one person responsible for coordinating the care provided. The Dutch child protection system seems to be faced with the challenge of finding a balance between the obligation of each individual to oversee the safety of the child and the shared responsibility of fragmented organisations to collaborate in order to really provide this safety net.

Two initiatives introduced to improve collaboration between professionals and organisations, the Family Coach and the Reference Index, have had little impact. This is understandable from the perspective of what is required to bring about a high degree of integration of services and care (see, for instance, Heath et al, 2013). Strictly speaking, for example, every practitioner involved can continue to focus on their own profession, while the Reference Index tells each of them that they are not acting alone, and the Family Coach tries – and may or may not succeed – to tie everything together. A high degree of integration requires much more frequent mutual communication between practitioners and the organisations involved, the use of a common language, and a fundamental understanding and appreciation of everyone's role and so on. The Family Coach and Reference Index may facilitate this, but they are worthless unless those involved are really encouraged to collaborate.

Overall, the initiatives to reduce errors and mistakes show an interesting pattern: initiatives that started from the field of practice work better than those initiatives that were imposed from higher up. Both the Family Coach and the methods for family guardianship aimed to provide a key person at the centre of complex cases; while the Family

Coach introduced by the State Secretary showed limited value, the innovative methods for family guardianship have had significant positive effects. This is in line with the current approach of the Inspectorate, where the common procedure is to request the organisations involved to conduct an inquiry and identify their own solutions in order to prevent future incidents from occurring. Furthermore, when cases are very high profile, the results are published anonymously. The focus is not on blaming organisations or individuals, but on learning from mistakes.

In conclusion, many efforts have been devoted to providing child protection workers in the Netherlands with a series of tools in order to minimise their professional autonomy and individual judgement, and hence to reduce human error. However, 'tools do not always have the intended effect' (Munro, 2005: 376) and no important advances have been made through their introduction. Moreover, an understanding has developed that incidents are not completely preventable, and that the death of a child might not always be tied to avoidable human failure. This aligns with the perception of Dutch public opinion on calamities in youth care investigated by Helsloot et al (2014), who concluded that Dutch citizens recognise that calamities are unavoidable. Their study uncovers a paradox: errors and mistakes are considered unavoidable but they should be prevented as far as possible.

Notes

[1] See www.handreikingmelden.nl.

[2] AM(H)K = Advies-en Meldpunt Huiselijk geweld en Kindermishandeling [Advice and Report Center Domestic Violence and Child Abuse].

References

Abraham, M. and Van Dijk, B. (2015) *Evaluatie verwijsindex risicojongeren. Onderzoek naar het gebruik, het nut en de noodzaak van de verwijsindex risicojongeren: de VIR* [*Evaluation Reference Index for High-Risk Youngsters. Research into the Use, Value and Necessity of the Reference Index for High-Risk Youngsters: The VIR*], Amsterdam: DSP-Groep.

Addink, A., Van den Bosch, H., Holdorp, J. and Prakken, J. (2017) *Samen werken aan jeugdbescherming. Verslag van het SWING-programma nieuwe jeugdbescherming 2015–2017* [*Working Together on Child Protection: Report of the SWING Programme New Child Protection 2015–2017*], Utrecht: Netherlands Youth Institute.

Baartman, H. (2011) 'Compassie en controle in de Jeugdzorg' ['Compassion and Control in Youth Care'], *Ouderschapskennis*, 13: 63–81.

Bakker, N., Noordman, J. and Rietveld-Van Wingerden, M. (2006) *Vijf eeuwen opvoeden in Nederland: idee en praktijk, 1500–2000* [*Five Centuries of Child Rearing in the Netherlands: Idea and Practice, 1500–2000*], Assen: Koninklijke Van Gorcum.

Bartelink, C., De Kwaadsteniet, L., Ten Berge, I.J. and Witteman, C.L.M. (2017) 'Is It Safe? Reliability and Validity of Structured Versus Unstructured Child Safety Judgments', *Child & Youth Care Forum*, 46(5): 745–68.

Bartelink, C., Van Yperen, T.A., Ten Berge, I.J., De Kwaadsteniet, L. and Witteman, C.L.M. (2014) 'Agreement on Child Maltreatment Decisions: A Nonrandomised Study on the Effects of Structured Decision-Making', *Child & Youth Care Forum*, 43(5): 639–54.

Berends, I.E., Campbell, E.E., Wijgergangs, E. and Bijl, B. (2010) *Bescherming bekeken: een onderzoek naar ontwikkelingen en regionale verschillen in het aantal ondertoezichtstellingen en machtigingen uithuisplaatsingen* [*Protection Examined: A Study into the Developments and Regional Differences in the Number of Supervision Orders and Out-of-Home Placements*], Duivendrecht: PI Research.

Bruning, M.R. (2007) 'Risico's in de jeugdzorg: Over veiligheid en controle' ['Risks in Child Welfare: On Safety and Ccontrol'], *Proces*, 6: 239–47.

Bureau Onderzoek & Statistiek Heerlen (2014) *Onderzoeksrapport Evaluatie Pilot Gezinscoaching. Een kwalitatief onderzoek naar gezinscoaching in de gemeente Heerlen* [*Research Report Evaluation Pilot Family Coaching: A Qualitative Study of Family Coaching in the Municipality of Heerlen*], Heerlen: Gemeente Heerlen.

CBS (Centraal Bureau voor Statistiek [Statistics Netherlands]) (2015) *Jeugdbeschermingstrajecten* [*Young Protection Trajectories*]. Available from: http://statline.cbs.nl/Statweb/publication/?DM=SLNL&PA=82974NED.

De Kwaadsteniet, L., Bartelink, C., Witteman, C., Ten Berge, I. and Van Yperen, T. (2013) 'Improved Decision Making About Suspected Child Maltreatment: Results of Structuring the Decision Process', *Children and Youth Services Review*, 35(2): 347–52.

De Onderzoeksraad voor Veiligheid (2011) *Over de fysieke veiligheid van het jonge kind. Themastudie: voorvallen van kindermishandeling met fatale of bijna fatale afloop* [*On the Physical Safety of the Young Child. Thematic Study: Incidents of Child Abuse with Fatal or Near-Fatal Ending*], The Hague: De Onderzoeksraad voor Veiligheid.

Dekker, J.J.H., Amsing, M., Van der Bij, I., Dekker, M., Grietens, H.W.E., Harder, A., Koedijk, P.C.M., Parlevliet, P., Schreuder, P., Talhout, M. and Timmerman, M.C. (2012) *Jeugdzorg in Nederland, 1945–2010: Resultaten van deelonderzoek 1 van de Commissie-Samson: Historische schets van de institutionele ontwikkeling van de jeugdsector vanuit het perspectief van het kind en de aan hem/haar verleende zorg* [*Youth Care in the Netherlands, 1945–2010: Results of Subproject 1 of the Samson Commission: Historical Sketch of the Institutional Developments of the Youth Sector from the Perspective of the Child and the Care Provided to Him/Her*], Groningen: Rijksuniversiteit.

Euser, S., Alink, L.R.A., Pannebakker, F., Vogels, T., Bakermans-Kranenburg, M. and Van IJzendoorn, M.H. (2013) 'The Prevalence of Child Maltreatment in the Netherlands Across a 5-Year Period', *Child Abuse & Neglect*, 37(10): 841–51.

Gilbert, N., Parton, N. and Skivenes, M. (eds) (2011) *Child Protection Systems: International Trends and Orientations*, New York: Oxford University Press.

Goedegebure, S.C. and Haan, I.C.C. (2017) *Calamities in Child Protection: What Can Be Learned from Them?* Groningen: University of Groningen.

Harder, A.T., Zeller, M., López, M., Köngeter, S. and Knorth, E.J. (2013) 'Different Sizes, Similar Challenges: Out-of-Home Care for Youth in Germany and the Netherlands', *Psychosocial Intervention*, 22(3): 203–13.

Heath, B., Wise Romero, P. and Reynolds, K. (2013) *A Standard Framework for Levels of Integrated Healthcare*, Washington DC: SAMHSA-HRSA Center for Integrated Health Solutions. Available from: www.integration.samhsa.gov/integrated-care-models/A_Standard_Framework_for_Levels_of_Integrated_Healthcare.pdf.

Helsloot, I., Scholtens, A. and Melssen, N. (2014) *Risico's en incidenten in de jeugdzorg. Hoe kijken burgers daar tegenaan?* [*Risks and Incidents in Young Care: How Do Civilians View Those?*], Renswoude: Crisislab.

Inspectie jeugdhulpverlening en jeugdbescherming (2003) *Jeugdigen onder voogdij* [*Youth in Custody*], Zwolle: IJJ.

Knijn, T. and Van Nijnatten, C.H.C.J. (2011) 'Child Welfare in the Netherlands: Between Privacy and Protection', in N. Gilbert, N. Parton and M. Skivenes (eds), *Child Protection Systems: International Trends and Orientations*, New York: Oxford University Press, pp 223–40.

Kuijvenhoven, T. and Kortleven, W.J. (2010) 'Inquiries into Fatal Child Abuse in the Netherlands: A Source of Improvement?' *British Journal of Social Work*, 40(4): 1152–73.

Lecluijze, I., Penders, B., Feron, F.J. and Horstman, K. (2015) 'Co-production of ICT and Children at Risk: The Introduction of the Child Index in Dutch Child Welfare', *Children and Youth Services Review*, 56: 161–8.

Lunenburg, P., Bijl, B. and Slot, W. (2006) *Bescherming in ontwikkeling: het vervolg. Vervolgonderzoek in het kader van het 'Deltaplan Kwaliteitsverbetering Gezinsvoogdij'* [*Protection in Development: The Sequel. Follow-Up Research in the Framework of the 'Delta Plan Quality Improvement Family Guardianship'*], Duivendrecht: PI Research.

Ministerie van Justitie (2004) *Brief van de minister van Justitie aan de Voorzitter van de Tweede Kamer der Staten-Generaal, 30 juni 2004, vergaderjaar 2003–2004, 28 606 en 29 200 VI, nr. 19* [*Letter of the Minister of Justice to the Chairman of the House of Representatives, Parliamentary Year 2003–2004, 28 606 and 29 200 VI, No. 19*], https://zoek.officielebekendmakingen.nl/kst-28606-19.html, Den Haag: Ministerie van Justitie.

Munro, E. (2005) 'Improving Practice: Child Protection as a Systems Approach', *Child and Youth Services Review*, 27(4): 375–91.

Netherlands Youth Institute (2007) *Youth Policy in the Netherlands: An Overview of Policies, Structures and Provisions Concerning Children and Young People Living in the Netherlands*, Utrecht: Netherlands Youth Institute.

Provincie Limburg (2005) *Gezinscoaching. Coördinatie van zorg aan multiprobleemgezinnen. De oogst van twee jaar experimenteren in Limburg* [*Family Coaching: Coordination of Care for Multiproblem Families – The Harvest of Two Years of Experiments in Limburg*], Maastricht: Provincie Limburg.

Rechtbank's-Gravenhage (2007) *ECLI:NL:RBSGR:2007:BB8016*, court ruling. Available from: https://uitspraken.rechtspraak.nl/inziendocument?id=ECLI:NL:RBSGR:2007:BB8016.

Ross – van Dorp C. (2002) *Verbeteringen werking jeugdzorg in relatie tot Wet op de jeugdzorg: Brief aan de Tweede Kamer, DJB/JHV-2331221, 11 november 2002* [*Improvements in the Functioning of Youth Care in Relation to the Youth Care Act: Letter to the Lower House, DJB/JHV-2331221, 11 November 2002*], The Hague: Ministerie van Volksgezondheid, Welzijn en Sport.

Samenwerkend Toezicht Jeugd (2013) *Leren van Calamiteiten* [*Learning from Calamities*], Utrecht: Samenwerkend Toezicht Jeugd.

Samenwerkend Toezicht Jeugd / Toezicht Sociaal Domein (2016) *Leren van Calamiteiten 2: Veiligheid van kinderen in kwetsbare gezinnen* [*Learning from Calamities 2: Safety of Children in Vulnerable Families*], Utrecht: Samenwerkend Toezicht Jeugd / Toezicht Sociaal Domein.

Slot, N.W. and Van Montfoort, A. (2009) *Handboek Deltamethode Gezinsvoogdij: De nieuwe methode voor de uitvoering van de ondertoezichtstelling [Handbook Delta Method Family Guardianship: The New Method for the Implementation of the Supervision Order]*, Woerden/ Duivendrecht: Adviesbureau Van Montfoort / PI Research.

Slot, N.W., Theunissen, A., Esmeijer, F.J. and Duivenvoorden, Y. (2002) *909 Zorgen. Een onderzoek naar de doelmatigheid van de ondertoezichtstelling [909 Worries: A Study on the Effectiveness of the Supervision Order]*, Amsterdam: Vrije Universiteit.

Slot, N.W., Van Tooren, A. and Bijl, B. (2004) *Bescherming in ontwikkeling: De evaluatie van de methodische vernieuwing in het kader van het Deltaplan kwaliteitsverbetering gezinsvoogdij [Protection in Development: The Evaluation of the Methodical Renewal Within the Framework of the Delta Plan on Quality Improvement of Family Guardianship]*, Duivendrecht: PI Research.

Stams, G.J.J.M., Top – Van der Eem, M., Limburg, S., Van Vugt, E.S. and Van der Laan, P.H. (2010) *Implementatie en doelmatigheid van de Deltamethode Gezinsvoogdij. Onderzoek naar de invloed van de Deltamethode Gezinsvoogdij op het verloop van de ondertoezichtstelling [Implementation and Efficiency of the Delta Method Family Guardianship: Investigation into the Influence of the Delta Method Family Guardianship on the Course of the Supervision]*, Amsterdam / The Hague: Universiteit van Amsterdam / WODC, Ministerie van Justitie.

Stichting Vedivo (2000) *Leiding geven aan verandering [Leading Change]*, Utrecht: Vedivo.

Ten Berge, I. and Meuwissen, I. (2013) *Bruikbaarheid en mogelijke aanpassingen van de LIRIK voor de toepassing in de (L)VB-sector: Bevindingen van de pilot augustus 2012 – oktober 2013 [Utility and Possible Adaptations to the LIRIK for the Use in the (Mild) Mental Disabilities Field: Findings from the Pilot August 2012–October 2013]*, Utrecht: Nederlands Jeugdinstituut.

Ten Berge, I. and Van Rossum, J. (2009) *Evaluatie en bijstelling GCT en LIRIK. Samenvatting resultaten en aanpassingen [Evaluation and Adaptation GCT and LIRIK: Summary Results and Adaptations]*, Utrecht: Nederlands Jeugdinstituut.

Tielen, G.E.M., De Vries, J.F. and Bos, J.G. (2015) *Leidraad meldingen jeugd [Guidelines Reports Youth]*. Available from: https://www.igj.nl/ binaries/igj/documenten/publicaties/2015/10/20/inspectiebrief-meldplicht-leidraad-en-meldformulier.pdf-pdf-321.449-bytes/ Inspectiebrief-over-Meldplicht-leidraad-en-meldformulier.pdf.

Turnell, A. and Edwards, S. (1999) *Signs of Safety: A Safety and Solution Oriented Approach to Child Protection Casework*, New York: W.W. Norton.

Van Enennaam, A. (2005) *Beoogde invoering van gezinscoach loopt averij op: Huiverig voor gezinsdrama's* [*The Planned Introduction of a Family Coach Is Damaged: Fearing Family Dramas*]. Available from: www. zorgwelzijn.nl/beoogde-invoering-van-gezinscoach-loopt-averij-op-huiverig-voor-gezinsdramas-zwz013032w/.

Van Hout, A. and Spinder, S. (2001) *De (gezins)voogd als jongleur: Een methodisch handboek voor het gezinswerk* [*The (Family) Guardian as a Juggler: A Methodical Manual for Family Work*], Houten: Bohn Stafleu en Van Loghum.

Van Wijk, P.J.T. (2004) *'Leiding geven aan verandering': Een methodiek voor het handelen van gezinsvoogdijwerkers in het Bureau Jeugdzorg (versie 3.0)* [*'Leading Change': A Method for the Work of Family Guardians in the Youth Care Agency (Version 3.0)*], Driebergen: WWRG & Partners.

Volkskrant (2005) *Coach voor probleemgezin biedt families geen soelaas* [*Coach for Problem Family Offers Families No Solution*]. Available from: www.volkskrant.nl/nieuws-achtergrond/-coach-voor-probleemgezin-biedt-families-geen-soelaas-~be3f3714/.

I

6

The Finnish approach to errors and mistakes in child protection: trust in practitioners and service users?

Essi Julin and Tarja Pösö

Introduction

The topic of errors and mistakes only exists as a vague category in child protection policy, practice or research in Finland. This is not to say that errors and mistakes do not take place. Rather, it is to say that they have not been established (yet) as a distinctive and clear-cut conceptual category that goes beyond a few scandals presented in the media. Therefore, very much from scratch, the chapter searches for – or even constructs – an understanding of the existing and emerging definitions of errors and mistakes, and the practices for recognising and responding to errors.[1] As there is no body of research on errors and mistakes in Finnish child protection, this chapter is based on our reading of legislation, policy programmes and related research examining child protection.

We claim that while tragic incidents, some of them even leading to a child's death, have been brought to public awareness by a critical media, the responses overall have aimed to improve the system, in a variety of ways, to abolish the 'deficiencies' of the system rather than pointing out the errors and mistakes of individual practitioners. Therefore, one should acknowledge the proactive and reactive approaches to errors and mistakes that are embedded in the Finnish custom of treating child protection as a social service provided by public administration, as well as the deficiency-driven view of system failures; both views are represented in this chapter after a short overview of Finnish child protection. In the final part of the chapter we speculate about the strengths and weaknesses of the present approaches to errors and mistakes and also speculate about the controversial tendencies that shape errors and mistakes.

Finnish child protection in brief

The present rationale of Finnish child protection was introduced in the 1980s. The ethos of the welfare state, universal social policy services and benefits to families in particular was reflected in new child protection legislation introduced at that time: child protection was seen as being on the continuum of services to families with children (Valjakka, 2016: 194). Child protection services were needed to support parents in their task of bringing up children when universal services were not sufficient. Like other social services, child protection services were to be provided with a low threshold, on a voluntary basis for service-users, and from the point of view of the child's best interest. Involuntary measures were to be implemented only as a last resort, which was fundamentally different from child protection as defined by the very first Child Welfare Act in 1936. This emphasis on voluntary and low threshold services provided by the Child Welfare Act 1983 and now the current Child Welfare Act 2007 has indeed positioned Finnish child protection with a 'family services' orientation in international comparisons (Gilbert et al, 2011). The present Act also puts a lot of emphasis on children's rights in general and on their participation right in particular.

It is the task of municipalities to implement the Child Welfare Act. As there are 311 municipalities in a country with 5.5 million inhabitants and about 1 million children below the age of 18 in Finland, the implementation of legislation may vary to some extent among the municipalities due to their political, social and cultural characteristics (see, for example, Harrikari, 2014). The Act specifies social workers as those practitioners who have the right and obligation to make a variety of decisions concerning children and families according the Child Welfare Act. They may even make a decision to take a child into care (Pösö and Huhtanen, 2017) or into emergency care (Lamponen et al, 2018), which both restrict parents' and children's rights considerably. Courts are only involved in care order decisions which include an objection ('involuntary care orders') or which result from an appeal made by parents or children. These examples reflect the wide discretion given to social workers in Finland (Berrick et al, 2015) and the role given to professionals, social workers in particular, in child protection decision-making, which is claimed to be stronger than in other Nordic countries (the professionalised decision-making model) (Hultman et al, 2018). Although social work is a strong profession in child protection,[2] other professionals and their understanding of family troubles are included either in multi-professional teams supporting social workers or in services, such as family support work or family rehabilitation, which are provided to families as part of child protection services. In addition, children and families are served by a number of healthcare and education professionals as part of the universal welfare state service provision.

Child protection services work with a substantial proportion of children. In 2017, 4.4 per cent of children below the age of 18 received in-home services. This number showed a dramatic decline since the implementation of the new Social Welfare Act in 2014. Before this Act, the number was more than 7 per cent of all children. In 2017, 1 per cent of children had been taken into care (Terveyden ja hyvinvoinnin laitos, 2017: Figures 5 and 13).

The emphasis of child protection on aiming to be a consensus-based service for families and children may, for its part, explain why errors and mistakes have not impacted heavily on child protection policy and debate in Finland. The philosophy of seeing child protection as a 'service' reflects some deep cultural views of the role of the state and administrative power. State and society are not categorically contrasted in the Finnish way of thinking of the role of the state (Kettunen, 2014) and, thus, the authorities are seen more as 'servants' for citizens, rather than as adversaries who restrict their fundamental rights and liberties, as they are known to be viewed in some countries (see, for example, Pelton, 2016). The coercive nature attached to child protection may invite a more critical sensitivity towards errors and mistakes than the image of child protection within voluntary services. Also, as child protection is a part of public administration in Finland, the laws, norms and rules of public administration have shaped the protocols which define and deal with any deviation from 'good service'.

Errors and mistakes at first glance

When writing this chapter in 2018, the understanding of errors was influenced by the death of a young girl called Vilja Eerika and the investigation of abuse in out-of-home care in the past. Such cases should, accordingly, also be given attention here.

When the girl, who was already known to the child protection services long before the events leading to her death, died as a result of violence by her father and stepmother in 2012, the media became very active in examining the case and pointing out errors. In the extensive media publicity, the coverage especially pointed out that the child had been well known to statutory child protection services and several other professionals had been involved in her life. A large number of practitioners in child protection, healthcare and elsewhere were prosecuted for their failures in practice, but only a couple of them were sanctioned in the end. The death was examined in national and local case reviews, resulting in an overall review of the state of Finnish child protection by a committee appointed by the Ministry of Social Affairs and Health (Sosiaali- ja terveysministeriö, 2013). The committee presented more than 50 recommendations for changes in practice. Interagency information exchange and cooperation, as well as the recognition of the child and her or his views and needs, were among the suggested changes (Sosiaali- ja terveysministeriö, 2013). In fact, the notion of a 'child protection crisis' became a common way to refer to child protection and the nature of its deficiencies at that time. To solve the crisis, the committee wished to strengthen preventive services and early intervention, which were seen to form the most important policies for the future.

It also became obvious that the responses to reviewing and examining such cases were not sufficient. The investigation team set up by the Ministry of Justice reached the following conclusion:

> By Western standards, Finland shows high levels of domestic violence that end in fatalities. However, insufficient lessons have been learned from violent incidents, because there is no obligatory systematic multi-professional inquiry, only criminal investigations. A system should be adopted for gathering information on all cases of serious domestic violence, including regular reporting on such cases and the presentation of any conclusions that can be drawn.
> (Oikeusministeriö, 2013: 10)

This extract highlights that the existing pattern for investigating errors and mistakes related to such cases focuses on criminal investigations to find out the culpabilities of those involved. Indeed, the Safety Investigation Authority examines the course of events related to accidents and incidents in order to prevent any new ones from occurring, but so far the cases investigated have mainly been related to road accidents and fires. The case of Vilja Eerika is one of the rare 'exceptional events' investigated by this authority (Safety Investigation Authority, 2018). The investigation team set up by the Ministry of Justice further stated that the existing practice of investigations was inadequate: there should be a standard system in which the serious domestic violence cases are examined in a multi-professional manner in order to learn from any failures. Its view on the high levels of domestic violence that end in fatalities is further supported by research findings that child mortality from accidents and violence is at a higher level in Finland than in most other countries in Western Europe, and that accidents and other non-natural causes of death also constitute a major public health problem in Finland (Onnettomuustutkintakeskus, 2014). A study focusing on the deaths of children in the period of 2009–11 found out that 13 children (aged 0–17) died due to homicide. Five of those children were known to child protection authorities (Onnettomuustutkintakeskus , 2014: 36). Yet only the girl Vilja Eerika became known to the wider public, only her case was examined by (non-criminal) investigation teams[3] and only her case initiated major policy concerns.

A different view on errors and mistakes in child protection is currently provided by the reports examining the experiences of the ex-residents of residential and foster care (Hytönen et al, 2016; Laitala and Puuronen, 2016). The first cited of these reports focused on abuse in care during the period 1937–83, that is to say, the period covered by the first Child Welfare Act. The study was encouraged by other similar studies both in the Nordic countries and elsewhere, and was commissioned by the Ministry of Social Affairs and Health. The interviews with 300 ex-residents highlight serious shortcomings in the care provided by child protection authorities and experiences of physical, emotional and sexual abuse among ex-residents in substitute care during the study period. The other study, by Laitala and Puuronen (2016), had similar findings. Although the studies demonstrated very dramatic failures in substitute care and suggested requirements for change, very little is done to monitor the quality of present substitute care as a result. The shortcomings of substitute care and residential care in particular were highlighted again in late 2018 when the Parliamentary Ombudsman presented his investigations (Eduskunnan oikeusasiamies: tarkastukset, 2018) Consequently, the shortcomings were viewed from the legal point of view and that of the Convention on the Rights of the Child in particular.

At first glance, these two examples of errors and mistakes echo the tragic events also recognised as errors in other countries represented in this book. They would, however, give a narrow and rather scandalised view of the errors and mistakes in Finnish child protection. The mainstream view tackles errors and mistakes using an approach more or less grounded in the systems approach (see Chapter 2 by Biesel and Cotter), which we call here a 'deficiency-driven view' of errors and mistakes.

The deficiency-driven view of errors and mistakes

Deficiencies of service provision are commonly understood and addressed in Finnish child protection rather than the errors and mistakes of individual practitioners. Like the errors and mistakes of individual practitioners, they deviate from 'good practice'. The recognition of deficiencies initiated major changes in child protection legislation, policy and practice. One example from the 1990s will be presented as having been very influential. The Finns remember it well by the name of the child in question (Niko), making the case close and human.

In the 1990s, a need to develop treatment of children experiencing abuse arose from a case about a five-year-old boy, Niko. He was taken into care and stayed there for almost four years because his father was suspected of having sexually abused him. Eventually, the father was found not guilty. However, the methods used to interview the boy were examined and were regarded as questionable (Korkman et al, 2017). Afterwards, it was not only the interview techniques in this boy's case but also the interview techniques with children in criminal investigations in general that seemed to need improvement. Their deficiencies received attention both in the media and also from researchers (Korkman et al, 2017).

Researchers from different disciplinary backgrounds demonstrated that practitioners interviewing children in abuse situations did not have enough skills or supervision to carry out investigative interviews properly (Korkman, 2006). Psychiatrists, psychologists and social workers working with children were also shown to have prejudices towards child sexual abuse and its investigation methods, leading to a practice which did not recognise then-current scientific knowledge (Finnilä-Tuohimaa, 2009). The practices for investigating child sexual abuse were incoherent, the quality of investigations varied considerably and, in addition, Finnish legislation had gaps in regard to meeting this issue properly (Hirvelä, 2006). The researchers suggested that there should be a centralised and inter-organisational model with which to investigate children who we were thought to have been exposed to violence, including sexual violence, in order to overcome these deficiencies.

Accordingly, recognition of those deficiencies inspired a new model and related methods to investigate child abuse, a kind of a Finnish application of the 'Barnahus model' (Korkman et al, 2017). Specialised, multidisciplinary forensic units were established at university hospitals to support police investigations (Julin, 2018). Since 2003 there has been guidance for practitioners in order to harmonise practice (Taskinen,

2003; Duodecim, 2013). There is also inter-organisational education for authorities who meet and investigate child abuse. However, the changes introduced were not only about professional approaches, they also marked the role of the state in these matters in a new way: the legislation introduced in 2009 and 2014 specified that the costs of investigations of all forms of child abuse should be paid by the state (instead of the municipalities), underlining the national importance of the quality of these investigations (Julin, 2018). Also, the mandatory reporting system was expanded so that practitioners working with children and families now had an obligation to notify both the police and the child protection authorities when suspecting child sexual or physical abuse. This duty was first introduced in 2012 to cover sexual abuse and in 2015 extended to cover all forms of physical abuse, including disciplinary violence. The latter change resulted from the death of Vilja Eerika in 2012, mentioned earlier, which was seen to be related to deficiencies in cooperation between different authorities.

This ambition to solve the deficiencies of practice and service provision by providing practitioners with specific guidelines, skills and procedures, as well as by expanding the notification obligations, may have had some unintended consequences. The Niko case was built strongly on the frame of criminal justice, approaching different actors as suspects, victims, witnesses, bystanders or perpetrators when met by professionals in healthcare and child protection. However, children, mothers, fathers and others have other positions in their everyday lives as family members. Children, in particular, may not expect procedures to be conducted in a way that treats them as 'victims' or 'witnesses'; instead, they might expect to be looked after and protected and to have a say in the matters concerning them. They might not want their family relations to be regulated only by the investigative process and roles allocated to them accordingly. Indeed, there are empirical findings suggesting that the investigative procedures and their norms are given the first priority when abuse is suspected and that children's and parents' other positions, needs and rights are meanwhile ignored (Julin, forthcoming). Some researchers argue that the changes in legislation and policy mean increased regulation intensifying criminal control over parents as part of a new punitive culture (Satka and Harrikari, 2008).

In the 2010s, the deficiencies of child protection were also pointed out by the committee investigating the death of Vilja Eerika, as described earlier. Furthermore, this deficiency-driven view of child protection has been supported by research findings about the outcome of children in the care system. These studies use the population register data and compare those who have been in out-of-home care with their peers who have not been in out-of-home care regarding education, employment, health and similar issues, demonstrating poorer outcomes for care leavers in Finland (as in Cameron et al, 2018). The claims of the deficits in the system also refer to the costs of child protection services, which are high, and initiate debates about cost-effectiveness (Sipilä and Österbacka, 2013). In addition, the deficiency-driven view of child protection has been supported by the studies highlighting that social workers struggle to meet the good standards of practice due to their heavy caseloads (Alhanen, 2014; Mänttäri-van der Kuip, 2016; Tiitinen and Silén, 2016). The fundamental changes required now are being put into practice by the Government Key Reform Programme of the Ministry of Social Affairs and Health for 2016–18 (as at the time of writing). This programme emphasises that services in general should be given at the right time – as early as possible – and child protection services should be regarded as last-resort services. Regarding child protection in particular, the reform programme aims to introduce an interactive, participatory, child-centric, family-therapeutic, solution-focused, relationship-based and multi-professional systemic approach to child protection (Lahtinen et al, 2017). Relations between social workers, children and parents are hoped to be more like 'therapeutic alliances'. The model is a Finnish implementation of the English Hackney model, which is seen as having solved the problems with which the Finnish child protection system struggles (Lahtinen et al, 2017). This emphasis is about to be put in practice at the same time as the obligations of practitioners to report and exchange information are strengthened, suggesting that there will be conflicting approaches to guide practitioners and service-users. How errors and mistakes will be viewed in the future remains to be seen.

The proactive and reactive approaches to tackling errors

Legislation is a critical reference point for understanding how errors and mistakes are defined and responded to because legislation and legalism have been important elements in Finnish society throughout its history and remain important elements now (Nylund, 2017). Its importance and acceptance may be grounded in the fact that the law has guaranteed equal rights for all citizens, and according to Nylund (2017), legislation enhancing the rights of the poor has been used several times to unite – not separate – the people. Regarding errors and mistakes, it is not only the criminal law which is relevant for this chapter but all the legislation that regulates service provision and the role and obligations of public authorities. As child protection is part of public administration, the legislation on good public administration and the rights of service-users, among similar pieces of legislation, regulates child protection and identifies deviations from 'good practice'. The Child Welfare Act (417/2007) itself approaches errors indirectly as it addresses the obligations of the municipalities and social workers, as well as the rights of children and parents in child protection matters. It also defines the duties to monitor the quality of services and the criteria for practising child protection work, as well as the rights of parents and children to make complaints and appeals about the decisions made concerning them. We will look at these duties and rights in more detail, separating proactive and reactive approaches.

Proactive approaches to errors and mistakes

Proactive approaches rest on an understanding that the regulation of practitioners and service providers improves the quality of child protection and thereby prevents errors and mistakes from happening. Licensing and registering practitioners and service providers and monitoring the quality of services are examples of this approach.

Since 2016, qualified social workers should also be registered social workers. Through registration, the quality of qualifications and the minimum standard of professional competence and knowledge of social workers and social counsellors working in child protection (as well in social welfare in general) is monitored. The ambition is to improve customer safety, which is presented on the website of the National Supervisory Authority for Welfare and Health (which is in charge of the registrations) as follows: 'The purpose of the new act is to improve customer safety and the right to good quality social welfare services for social welfare customers. In addition, the act clarifies the rights and obligations of social welfare professionals' (National Supervisory Authority for Welfare and Health, 2018). The argument is that the registration of professionals is necessary to improve the rights and safety of service-users. The reverse message is that the rights and safety of service-users would be threatened without certain qualifications of the staff. Also, that the wide area of discretion given to social workers in statutory social work is regulated by the qualification standards of social workers.

The right to provide child protection services is restricted. Municipalities are obliged to provide child protection services according to the Child Welfare Act. Certain tasks may only be carried out by authorities employed by the local government. Such tasks include several decisions made about the assessment of the need for services (such as eligibility criteria) and the provision of services (taking a child into care, for example) whereas some in-home and out-of-home care services (such as family support, assessment of parental skills, family rehabilitation, foster family support and training, residential care) can be outsourced. As a result, the majority of residential care, for example, is outsourced to agencies which mainly include profit-making private enterprises (Porko et al, 2018). However, the services must meet certain criteria and the service providers must be given the right to provide services to the municipalities. The licensing and registration of service providers is done by Regional State Administrative Agencies which, together with the municipalities, should also have oversight of the quality of the child protection services.

The efficiency of the present monitoring system for the outsourced service providers has been a critical concern of the state and the national non-governmental child welfare associations (Valtion tarkastusvirasto, 2012: 85; Hoikkala and Lavikainen, 2015). In particular, the recent emphasis on self-monitoring has raised concerns as it is not seen as sufficient to protect the rights of vulnerable children. In addition, auditing by the public bodies has been criticised as being too fragmentary due to the limited resources available (Valtion tarkastusvirasto, 2012). From the point of view of errors and mistakes, the criticism highlights that the licensing of service providers and obligations for oversight over the quality of services do not necessarily guarantee high quality of services if the proactive practices and their quality control are not adequately resourced.

Reactive approaches to errors and mistakes

The reactive approaches to errors and mistakes include, on the one hand, the rights given to parents and children as service-users to appeal decisions concerning them and make complaints about the quality of services they receive. On the other hand, they also include obligations on practitioners to report failures and shortcomings in service provision, and the tasks of certain public authorities in examining the reports of errors in the national context, which is our focus here, as well as in the European context (such as in the European Court of Human Rights).

According to the Child Welfare Act, parents and children aged 12 years old or older can appeal decisions that they consider unjust to the Administrative Court and further to the Supreme Administrative Court. Information about the process of making an appeal is included in writing with decisions, which should always be shared and sent to the family. Parents and children also have the right to make complaints about the services and their quality, and there are local, regional and national bodies whose task is to examine these complaints. At the national level, the Parliamentary Ombudsman of Finland is responsible for ensuring that public authorities obey the law and contribute to good administration; people may submit complaints to the Ombudsman. In addition, complaints may be filed with the government's Chancellor of Justice if it is thought that a civil servant or an authority has acted unlawfully or not fulfilled their duties (Nylund, 2017). According to Nylund, decisions made by those bodies are often discussed in public and the authorities often modify their practice and sometimes individuals get some kind of a remedy (Nylund, 2017: 301). Decisions related to child protection are also included in a web-based handbook of child protection, accessible for anyone interested to read.

The mechanisms for appeals and complaints tend to serve adults better than children. The Parliamentary Ombudsman has included a special route for children to make complaints via the internet. The instructions include the following description related to child protection: 'Did a reform school punish you for something that other people had done? Did a children's home treat you in a way that was humiliating? Did a social worker not listen to your worries? Or did some other public servant or authority treat you unfairly?' (Eduskunnan Oikeusasiamies, 2018). This extract suggests that this high authority that deals with the complaints has reason to assume that children in the child protection system have to be especially encouraged to make their experiences of unfair treatment known. This may suggest that practitioners working closely with the child – social workers in particular – do not necessarily inform the children about their right to make complaints.

Unfortunately, very little is known about these appeals and complaints, although studies highlight shortcomings regarding the rights of children and parents in child protection decision-making (de Godzinsky, 2014; Pösö and Huhtanen, 2017). Even more unfortunate is that national statistics are no longer published of the numbers of appeals and related judgments. When such statistics were still published –up to 2013– the number of appeals relating to care order decisions was very low considering the number of decisions about care orders (Pösö and Huhtanen, 2017). In an ongoing study examining the child protection appeals to three (out of six) administrative courts, the appeals are generally made by parents and their legal representatives. Children have not made any use of this legal opportunity to make their experiences of unfair decisions known (Pösö et al, 2019). Only 34 appeals out of 351 were accepted by the courts, which suggests that the appeal system is not very productive as a means of error correction for those who use it.

Even less is known about the complaints. The local or regional Social Ombudsmen include an overview of complaints in their annual reports, to the municipal boards, and these reports are public as they are part of local government activities. The most recent report to the municipal board in Tampere, for example, indicated that child protection issues made up roughly one third of the complaints in the Tampere region (Mehtonen and Helovuo, 2018). Social Ombudsmen do not make any decisions about individual matters but give guidance and information to individuals and instruct the public authorities about the shortcomings experienced in their services.

The role of the public authorities in their reactive responses to errors and mistakes is changing. The move towards self-monitoring means that agencies, whether municipal or outsourced, should monitor their quality themselves, and that the supervisory national body only focuses on selected matters. There is an obvious trust placed in both the sincerity of service providers in assessing the quality of the services they provide and in the skills and competence of service-users when asking for changes in matters that concern them. Indeed, these reactive approaches follow the pattern of 'enforced self-regulation' pointed out by Power (2007: 37–40) as an internal control system in which uncertainty is managed by cooperative relationships between regulator and regulated. It includes specific moral technologies (Power, 2007).

From the point of view of enforced self-regulation, practitioners in social welfare, including child protection, are now also obliged to report the failures and shortcomings that they come across in their work. The *Sosiaalihuoltolaki* (Social Welfare Act 2014, § 47 and 48) defines how these reports should be dealt with. This is a new regulation in Finnish child protection where mandatory reporting used only to relate to concerns about a child's welfare. According to a survey of social workers ($N = 183$) in 2016, roughly two years after the law was established, 88 per cent of practitioners reported that they had observed at least one shortcoming in their work environment of social welfare during the previous year (Tiitinen and Silén, 2016). The shortcomings referred to in that study related to procedures which are illegal, unethical or do not meet the objectives of the agency. More than half of the practitioners reported that the agency had no shared protocols for reporting these observations, and many felt insecure about the implications of the new practice for the practitioner reporting shortcomings (Tiitinen and Silén, 2016).

Balancing trust and doubt

At the beginning of the chapter we mentioned that the authorities have been traditionally seen as 'serving people' in Finland, suggesting that the relations between authorities and service-users are not based on conflict but rather on giving and receiving services. This might be an oversimplification of the complex and power-intermediated relations that exist between people and the state. Nevertheless, it is also an empirical finding that the Finns are reported to express a lot of trust in authorities and public institutions in society in general. This trust is demonstrated in European Union–wide surveys of public opinion towards public administration, and regional and local authorities in which, respectively, 77 per cent and 72 per cent of Finns reported trust in late 2017, both numbers being much higher than in the European Union in general (European Commission, 2018). The surveys do not examine trust in social workers but they include trust in the police, which is exceptionally high in Finland (Kääriäinen et al, 2016). If you trust authorities, doubts of misuse of authoritative power and errors in service provision colour the relations less than when you do not trust them. Indeed, when service providers and service-users are given the primary rights and duties to have an oversight of the quality of services and when external control is limited, trust plays an important part. Trust colours the emotional politics of child welfare very differently from mistrust and adversity (Warner, 2015).

Trust can, however, also be a sign of naivety. The tradition of trusting child protection authorities and their 'right' decisions is reflected in the lack of oversight of services and critical analysis of their quality, as well as in the lack of systematic procedures for investigating errors and mistakes. We have already seen that the proactive and reactive approaches have their limitations and that, in particular, their implementation is overshadowed by a shortage of human and organisational resources. Due to the limited scope of national and regional statistics, systematic investigations, reports and academic research, it is difficult to estimate whether there are, for example, any biases towards children and families from certain ethnic backgrounds, which might lead to under- or overuse of child protection measures, or whether certain decisions are especially error sensitive. Most importantly, learning from mistakes is not supported.

Moreover, the Finnish Ombudsman for Children has, in recent years, expressed his concerns about the legal protection of children (see, for example, Lapsiasia, 2017). These concerns address child protection decision-making as well, and include statements claiming that children are taken into care on false grounds. Furthermore, social workers express their concerns about the moral distress, among other similar issues, that they experience in their practice. This is to say that they cannot practise social work according to the legislation and professional ideals (Mänttäri-van der Kuip, 2016). Due to the heavy workloads and high staff turnover, the indirect message given by social workers is that it is likely that mistakes and errors do and will happen. Also indirectly, insiders in child protection, social workers, say that in the present conditions of child protection, you should not trust the authorities.

Doubts and criticisms about the present mechanisms for recognising and responding to errors and mistakes in the child protection system are expressed more loudly outside the formal protective and reactive approaches, government programmes and research. Social media and advocacy groups actively point out mistakes and errors in child protection. They share experiences of misuse on equal bases and give advice about how to deal with practitioners. One of the most powerful advocacy groups – Lokakuun liike [the October Movement] – profiles itself as a human rights organisation which is involved in structural social work and investigative journalism (Lokakuun liike, 2018). It consists of parents whose children have been taken into care or are otherwise using child protection services. The public websites inform about the errors practitioners make in their decision making, with some of them being identified by their names and organisations. Indeed, the advocacy group, as well as some public social media sites, claim that errors and mistakes take place. Also, groups of children and young adults who have had care experiences (experts by experience) have expressed their poor experiences of child protection particularly the recognition of their rights of participation (Pösö, 2018).

Conclusion

In the Finnish child protection system and its decentralised and professionalised practice the approach to errors and mistakes is coloured by trust in practitioners and in service-users and their skills, competences and good intentions when tackling errors, mistakes and shortcomings in practice. Trust in self-regulation may, however, preclude a critical examination of – and learning from – errors and mistakes. There are several weak points in the present child protection system and its approaches to tackling errors and mistakes which should invite a more systematic policy, practice and research analysis of errors and mistakes and the methods used to respond to them. Analysis and methods should be adapted to the Finnish tradition of child protection, which deviates from the countries in which errors and mistakes have been more clearly on the agenda of policy and research. The platform of 'trust' should provide opportunities to support practices in which learning from errors and mistakes is possible. The precondition is that the conceptualisation of errors and mistakes should not be too narrow (such as only focusing on individual failures or the legal recognition of errors) nor too wide (only focusing on system features, for example) but rather it should be a complex and multi-voiced one.

However, as the very organisation of social and healthcare services is rapidly changing, the future of child protection might include both the tendency for more regulated and investigative as well as more therapeutic child protection as presented in this chapter. The future will show what kind of understandings of errors and mistakes these tendencies will introduce.

Notes

[1] This chapter has been written as part of the project 'Consent and Objection in Child Welfare Decision-Making: A Socio-legal Analysis' funded by the Academy of Finland (Decision 308402).

[2] Although social workers make a variety of decisions, some of which restrict human rights, the practices of decision making have not been paid much attention in research. The existing studies on child protection decision-making focus on the court decisions (for example, de Godzinsky, 2014; Hiitola, 2015) and only fragmentally focus on decision making in the child protection agencies (see, for instance, Hietamäki, 2015; Pösö et al, 2018; Pösö and Laakso, 2016).

[3] There may have been some local, organisation-based investigations, but their findings are not publicly available.

References

Alhanen, K. (2014) *Vaarantunut suojeluvalta – Tutkimus lastensuojelujärjestelmän uhkatekijöistä* [*The Compromised Power of Protection: A Study of Threats to the Child Welfare Service System*], Helsinki: Terveyden ja hyvinvoinnin laitos.

Berrick, J., Peckover, S., Pösö, T. and Skivenes, M. (2015) 'The Formalized Framework for Decision Making in Child Protection Care Orders: A Cross-Country Comparison', *Journal of European Social Policy*, 25(4): 366–78.

Cameron, C., Hollingworth, K., Schoon, I., van Santen, E., Schröer, W., Ristikari, T., Heino, T. and Pekkarinen, E. (2018) 'Care Leavers in Early Adulthood: How Do They Fare in Britain, Finland and Germany?', *Children and Youth Services Review*, 87: 163–72.

De Godzinsky, V.-M. (2014) *Lapsen etu ja osallisuus hallinto-oikeuksien päätöksissä* [*The Best Interests of the Child and the Child's Right to Participate in Administrative Court Proceedings*], Helsinki: Oikeuspoliittinen tutkimuslaitos.

Duodecim (2013) Lapsen seksuaalisen hyväksikäytön epäilyn tutkiminen. Käypä hoito –suositus. *Suomalaisen Lääkäriseura Duodecimin ja Suomen Lastenpsykiatriyhdistyksen asettama työryhmä [Evaluation of a suspected child sexual abuse. Current Care Guideline: 2013'.* Working group set by the Finnish Medical Society Duodecim and the Finnish Society for the Child and Adolescent Psychiatry], available from: http://www.kaypahoito.fi/web/kh/suositukset/suositus?id=hoi34040

Eduskunnan Oikeusasiamies (2018) *Oikeusasiamies – Lasten ja nuorten sivut 2018* [*Ombudsman – The Pages for Children and Young People 2018*]. Available from: www.oikeusasiamies.fi/en/web/lasten-ja-nuorten-sivut/home.

Eduskunnan oikeusasiamies: tarkastukset 2018 [Parliamentary Ombudsman: Inspections 2018]. Available from https://www.oikeusasiamies.fi/fi/web/guest/tarkastukset-tarkea-osa-tyota.

European Commission (2018) 'Public Opinion: Trust in Media and Institutions'. Available from: http://ec.europa.eu/commfrontoffice/publicopinion/index.cfm/Chart/getChart/themeKy/18/groupKy/92 and http://ec.europa.eu/commfrontoffice/publicopinion/index.cfm/Chart/getChart/themeKy/18/groupKy/317.

Finnilä-Tuohimaa, K. (2009) *Expertise and Decision Making Among Clinicians in Investigating Alleged Child Sexual Abuse*, Turku: Annales Universitatis Turkuensis.

Gilbert, N., Parton, N. and Skivenes, M. (eds) (2011) *Child Protection Systems: International Trends and Orientations*, New York: Oxford University Press.

Harrikari, T. (2014) 'Social Disorganization and the Profile of Child Welfare: Explaining Child Welfare Activity by the Community-Level Factors', *Child Abuse & Neglect*, 38(10): 1671–82.

Hietamäki, J. (2015) *Lastensuojelun alkuarvioinnin vaikutukset vanhempien näkökulmasta* [*The Outcomes of the Assessment in Child Welfare from the Parents' Perspective*], Jyväskylä: Jyväskylän yliopisto.

Hiitola, J. (2015) *Hallittu vanhemmuus. Sukupuoli, luokka ja etnisyys huostaanottoasiakirjoissa* [*Governed Parenthood: Out-of-Home Placements and Gender, Class and Ethnicity*], Tampere: Tampere University Press.

Hirvelä, P. (2006) *Rikosprosessi lapsiin kohdistuvissa seksuaalirikoksissa* [*Criminal Process in Child Sexual Abuse Cases*], Helsinki: Helsingin yliopisto.

Hoikkala, S. and Lavikainen, V. (2015) *Sattumuksia vai suunnitelmallisuutta? Selvitys sijaishuollon laadusta* [*Coincidences or a Plan? A Report on the Quality of Substitute Care*], Helsinki: Lastensuojelun keskusliitto.

Hultman, E., Forkby, T. and Höjer, S. (2018) 'Professionalised, Hybrid, and Layperson Models in Nordic Child Protection: Actors in Decision-Making in Out of Home Placements', *Nordic Social Work Research*, ahead of print: https://doi.org/10.1080/2156857X.2018.1538897.

Hytönen, K., Malinen, A., Salenius, P., Haikari, J., Markkola, P., Kuronen M. and Koivisto, J. (2016) *Lastensuojelun sijaishuollon epäkohdat ja lasten kaltoinkohtelu 1937–1983* [*The Failures and Abuse of Children in Substitute Care 1937–1983*], Helsinki: Sosiaali- ja terveysministeriö.

Julin, E. (2018) *Lapsiin kohdistuvien väkivaltarikosten selvittäminen terveydenhuollossa. Selvitys lasten oikeuspsykiatrian yksiköiden toiminnasta* [*Health Services' Investigations of Violent Crimes Against Children: A Report on the Activities of Forensic Child Psychiatry Units in Finland*], Helsinki: Sosiaali-ja terveysministeriö.

Julin, E. (forthcoming) 'Lapsiin kohdistuva väkivaltarikostutkinta: Vanhempien näkökulma' ['Child Abuse Investigations: A Parent Perspective'], doctoral thesis, Tampere: Tampere University.

Kääriäinen, J., Isotalus, P. and Thomassen, G. (2016) 'Does Public Criticism Erode Trust in Police? The Case of Jari Aarnio in the Finnish News Media and Its Effects on the Public's Attitudes Towards the Police', *Journal of Scandinavian Studies in Criminology and Crime Prevention*, 17(1): 70–85.

Kettunen, P. (2014) 'The Language of Social Politics in Finland', in D. Béland and K. Petersen (eds) *Analysing Social Policy Concepts and Language*, Bristol: Policy Press, pp 157–76.

Korkman, J. (2006) 'How (Not) to Interview Children: Interviews with Young Children in Sexual Abuse Investigations in Finland', thesis, Turku: Åbo Akademi University. Available from: www.doria. fi/handle/10024/88732.

Korkman, J., Pakkanen, T. and Laajasalo, T. (2017) 'Child Forensic Interviewing in Finland: Investigating Suspected Child Abuse at the Forensic Psychology Unit for Children and Adolescents', in S. Johansson, K. Stefansen, E. Bakketeig and A. Kaldal (eds) *Collaborating Against Child Abuse: Exploring the Nordic Barnahus Model*, London: Palgrave Macmillan, pp 145–64.

Lahtinen, P., Männistö, L. and Raivio, M. (2017) *Kohti suomalaista systeemistä lastensuojelun toimintamallia* [*Towards a Finnish Systemic Child Protection Practice Model*], Helsinki: THL.

Laitala, M. and Puuronen, V. (2016) *Yhteiskunnan tahra? Koulukotien kasvattien vaietut kokemukset* [*The Stain of Society? The Silenced Experiences of Reform School Residents*], Tampere: Vastapaino.

Lamponen, T., Pösö, T. and Burns, K. (2018) 'Children in Immediate Danger: Emergency Removals in Finnish and Irish Child Protection', *Child & Family Social Work*, ahead of print: DOI: 10.1111/cfs.12628.

Lapsiasia (2017) Onko lapsella oikeusturvaa? [*Do Children Have Legal Protection?*] Lapsiasiavaltuutetun vuosikirja 2017. Available from: http://lapsiasia.fi/wp-content/uploads/2017/04/LA_vuosikirja_2017_.pdf.

Onnettomuustutkintakeskus (2014) *Lasten kuolemat* [*Deaths Among Children*] Tutkintaselostus Y2102-S1. Helsinki: Onnettomuustutkintakeskus.

Lokakuun liike [The October Movement] (2018) 'Lokakuun liike on ihmisoikeusliike, joka tekee rakenteellista sosiaalityötä ja tutkivaa journalismia' ['The October Movement Is a Human Rights Movement that Does Structural Social Work and Investigative Journalism']. Available from: www.lokakuunliike.com/lokakuun-liike.html.

Mänttäri-van der Kuip, M. (2016) 'Moral Distress Among Social Workers: The Role of Insufficient Resources', *International Journal of Social Welfare*, 25(1): 86–97.

Mehtonen, T. and Helovuo, L. (2018) *Asiakkaan asema ja oikeudet 2017, Sosiaaliasiamiehen selvitys kunnanhallitukselle* [*The Position and Rights of Service Users 2017: Report by the Social Ombudsman to the Municipal Board*]. Available from: www.tampere.fi/tiedostot/a/XbqPS59JV/Tampereen_seutukunnan_sosiaaliasiamiehen_selvitys2017.pdf.

National Supervisory Authority for Welfare and Health (2018) *Professional Practice Rights for Social Welfare Professionals*. Available from: www.valvira.fi/web/en/social_welfare/professional-practice-rights-for-social-welfare-professionals.

Nylund, A. (2017) 'An Introduction to Finnish Legal Culture', in S. Koch, K.E. Skodvin and J.Ø. Sunde (eds) *Comparing Legal Cultures*, Bergen: Fagbokforlaget, pp 285–316.

Oikeusministeriö (2013) *8-vuotiaan lapsen kuolemaan johtaneet tapahtumat* [*The Events Leading to the Death of an Eight-Year-Old Child in Helsinki in May 2012*], Helsinki: Oikeusministeriö.

Pelton, L. (2016) 'Separating Coercion from Provision in Child Welfare: Preventive Supports Should Be Accessible Without Conditions Attached', *Child Abuse & Neglect*, 51: 427–34.

Porko, P., Heino, T. and Eriksson, P. (2018) *Selvitys yksityisistä lastensuojelun yksiköistä* [*Report About the Private Child Protection Units*]. Available from: http://urn.fi/URN:ISBN:978-952-343-131-7.

Pösö, T. (2018) 'Experts by Experience Infusing Professional Practices in Child Protection', in A. Falch-Eriksen and E. Backe-Hansen (eds) *Human Rights in Child Protection: Implications for Professional Practice and Policy*, London: Palgrave Macmillan, pp 111–28.

Pösö, T. and Huhtanen, R. (2017) 'Removals of Children in Finland: A Mix of Voluntary and Involuntary Decisions', in K. Burns, T. Pösö and M. Skivenes (eds) *Child Welfare Removals by the State: A Cross-country Analysis of Decision-making Systems*, New York: Oxford University Press, pp 18–39.

Pösö, T. and Laakso, R. (2016) 'Matching Children and Substitute Homes: Some Theoretical and Empirical Notions', *Child & Family Social Work*, 21(3): 307–16.

Pösö, T., Pekkarinen, E., Helavirta, S. and Laakso, R. (2018) "Voluntary" and "Involuntary" Child Welfare: Challenging the Distinction', *Journal of Social Work*, 18(3): 253–72.

Pösö, T., Toivonen, V. and Kalliomaa-Puha, L. (2019) "Haluaa kotiin äidin luo" Erimielisyydet ja lapsen etu huostaanoton jatkamista koskevissa valituksissa ja hallinto-oikeuden ratkaisuissa ["Wants to be with her mother". Disagreement and the best interest of the child in appeals and administrative court decisions], *Oikeus* 48:3.

Power, M. (2007) *Organized Uncertainty: Designing a World of Risk Management*, New York: Oxford University Press.

Safety Investigation Authority (2018) 'Exceptional Events'. Available from: www.turvallisuustutkinta.fi/en/index/tutkintaselostukset/poikkeuksellisettapahtumat.html.

Satka, M. and Harrikari, T. (2008) 'The Present Finnish Formation of Child Welfare and History', *British Journal of Social Work*, 38(4): 645–61.

Sipilä, J. and Österbacka E. (2013) *Enemmän ongelmien ehkäisyä, vähemmän korjailua? [More Prevention, Fewer Corrective Measures?]*, Helsinki: Valtiovarainministeriö.

Sosiaali- ja terveyministeriö (2013) *Toimiva lastensuojelu [Functioning Child Welfare]*. Report 19. Helsinki: Ministry of Social Affairs and Health.

Taskinen, S. (2003) *Lapsen seksuaalisen hyväksikäytön ja pahoinpitelyn selvittäminen: Asiantuntijaryhmän suositukset sosiaali- ja terveydenhuollon henkilöstölle [Investigating Abuse and Sexual Abuse of Children: The Recommendation Given by an Expert Group to Practitioners in Social Welfare and Health]*, Helsinki: Stakes.

Terveyden ja hyvinvoinnin laitos (2018) Lastensuojelu 2017 [*Child Welfare in 2017*], Tilastoraportti [statistical report] 17. Available from: http://urn.fi/URN:NBN:fi-fe2018052524627.

Tiitinen, L. and Silén, M. (2016) *Sosiaalialan epäkohdat ja niiden käsittely −kyselyraportti* [*Shortcomings and Handling Them in Social Welfare: A Report on a Survey*]. Available from: www.luc.fi/loader. aspx?id=2641402d-5a35-4f8c-84b0-88c107f5eb1e.

Valtion tarkastusvirasto (2012) *Tuloksellisuuskertomus. Lastensuojelu* [*Performance Management Report: Child Welfare*] Report 6. Helsinki: National Audit Office of Finland.

Valjakka, E. (2016) *Vain lakiko suojelee lasta?* [*Is it Only Law That Protects the Child?*], Turku: Turun yliopisto.

Warner, J. (2015) *The Emotional Politics of Social Work and Child Protection*, Bristol: Policy Press.

7

Errors and mistakes in the Norwegian child protection system

Marit Skivenes and Øyvind Tefre[1]

Introduction

While there is no clear explanation, 'Norwegian child protection' has become infamous around the world, with the local word for child protection, *barnevern*, said to be the most commonly known Norwegian word. Possibly because of this, the European Court of Human Rights (ECtHR) has in recent years selected numerous Norwegian child protection cases to be heard before the court.[2] Criticism, either from international sources, such as the foreign mass media and religious organisations, or domestically, from various professional groups[3] or concerned parties, provides a good reason to examine how this system works in terms of detecting errors and mistakes. A key insight from the organisational research literature is that there must be structures for learning and improvement. This is to ensure not only that the system can adjust and improve, but also to secure accountability and oversight. Importantly, a system that has the power to make intrusive interventions into private lives must account for and justify its decisions. In this chapter, we examine the structures for detecting and communicating errors and mistakes in the Norwegian child protection system at three levels: the state, the court and locally. To establish an overview of the discourse on errors and mistakes, we have examined national audits and reports by regulatory agencies.

The various regulatory agencies in Norway employ two main types of oversight: first, centrally planned, countrywide audits that examine predefined areas of child protection practice within a sample of agencies, and second, local incident-based audits and inspections that address individual agencies or specific cases. It is then up to the regulatory authorities themselves to decide which cases they consider necessary to investigate further. However, unlike England, Norway does not have a system for serious case reviews of cases that lead to the death or serious injury of a child, although such a system was proposed by an expert committee a few years ago, and may still be implemented (NOU, 2017:12). Generally, the Norwegian system is revised incrementally (Hestbæk et al, 2020), and so we use the centrally planned countrywide audits and reports by regulatory agencies and expert panels to provide a window into errors and mistakes in Norwegian child protection. The data for our analysis consist of eight audit reports over the period 2010–19. We also examine a sample of Norwegian press coverage of child welfare over a four-year period.

In what follows, we present a brief overview of the accountability mechanisms followed by an outline of the Norwegian child protection system. Thereafter, we examine the three levels of accountability structures, followed by a critical discussion of the system. We end the chapter with a few concluding remarks.

The structures for identifying error and mistakes

The child protection system is a part of, and organised according to, the same principles and structures as most other public administration in Norway. The governmental system is based on the principle of the separation of powers, meaning that the responsibilities for governing, judging and legislating are divided into three separate branches. The purpose of this is to prevent any misuse of power, and to ensure there are adequate checks and balances. The executive is responsible for administrative tasks in the child protection systems, and the judiciary for all court decisions. In Norway, all serious child protection interventions are decided by the County Social Welfare Boards (County Boards). Although the County Boards are independent and apply court-like procedures, formally they are an administrative bodies and their decisions may be appealed to courts. Different forms of accountability arrangements and standards for responsible conduct accompany the checks and balances embedded in constitutional democracies. The terms error and mistake are defined in this book by Biesel and Cottier (Chapter 2). We address whether and how the Norwegian system secures accountability and learning with a specific focus on the decision-making processes and service provision. There are at least five main arenas demanding justifications and responses from public organisations (Bovens, 2007: 454–6):

1 'Political Accountability: Elected Representatives, Political Parties, Voters, Media' captures the ministerial and political responsibility

for the performance of the administrative system and the welfare state. This pinpoints how the welfare state provides for its citizens (Rothstein, 2011), and emphasises the responsibility that front-line staff have to elected representatives. Public discourse, via the media, provides a channel for discussion and is useful for shedding light on practice and eliciting critique.

2 'Legal Accountability: Courts' includes the court system and the decision-making power assigned solely to it. This is a legalistic system following the logic of the law and determines what decisions are legally valid and how they can be contested. The courts have a prominent role in the child protection system.

3 'Administrative Accountability: Auditors, Inspectors and Controllers' covers a range of established organisations whose main purpose is to supervise and control public spending, compliance with the law, efficient use of resources and ethical conduct. The auditing organisations regularly review public organisations, and the child protection system is no exception.

4 'Professional Accountability: Professional Peers' includes the professional and ethical standards of the profession that the public employee belongs to. This community consists of peers, the education system and the professional association, and thus may set demands for work conduct and the treatment of service-users/ patients/clients/customers.

5 'Social Accountability: Interest Groups, Charities and Other Stakeholders' covers non-governmental organisations and the more or less organised interest groups. This is an accountability forum that overlaps somewhat with arena 1, as the public sphere is the main platform for voicing criticism and mobilising action. However, this is also an arena driven by social media, which both complements and competes with the mainstream media.

Our primary focus in this chapter on errors and mistakes in the child protection system lies in administrative accountability through examination audit and oversight reports. Different types of external auditing are important parts of the Norwegian system of administrative accountability.[4] In this regard, external auditing has at least three intended functions. First, auditing aims to protect the legal rights of citizens against state encroachment and ensure their access to the services to which they are entitled. Audits thus exert a control function against the arbitrary exercise of state power. Second, there is the important element of maintaining public trust in the system and its legitimacy. Holding public institutions to account should increase public confidence that local services comply with legally binding decisions. Finally, audits should reveal errors and enable learning to improve the quality of the system. Without the capacity for learning and development in response to errors revealed in audits, audits have limited practical value.

The Norwegian child protection system[5]

Norway has a population of 5.2 million, of which about 1.13 million are children. Roughly 3 per cent of these children are involved in child protection, with about 2 per cent receiving services while remaining with their families.[6] Child protection systems in most modern states are typically categorised into risk- and service-oriented systems (Gilbert, 1997; Gilbert et al, 2011). For its part, Norway has a service-oriented child protection system, prioritising in-home measures to prevent harmful care and more intrusive interventions. In service-oriented systems, the aim is to promote healthy childhoods and prevent harm, in addition to mitigating serious risks (Skivenes, 2011). The overall ideology of Norwegian child and family politics is based on the premise that parents carry the ultimate responsibility for child-rearing and childcare. Different services within the system are then to a certain extent only complementary to the role of parents. The service norm should be the least intrusive intervention, which implies that, even where the child's living conditions are quite adverse, voluntary, in-home services are the preferred choice and reflect the reality. In fact, 85 per cent of children in the child welfare system receive voluntary services. In some cases, in-home measures can also include placement outside the parental home, with parental consent. It is only in situations where in-home services do not work or are considered ineffective that compulsory intervention removing the child would be used.

Front-line services in the 422 Norwegian municipalities bear the primary responsibility for providing services to the families; the child protection services (CPS) are typically staffed with social workers and child welfare workers with a bachelor's degree. As of 2019, there are about 5,200 front-line staff employed in Norway. Typically, smaller municipalities form inter-municipal collaborations, and child protection agencies organise their work according to either a specialist or generalist model. The specialist model differentiates aspects of casework and allocates specialised tasks to its workforce. The generalist model provides a single caseworker to follow a child and its family through child protection services – from referrals to the decision to intervene and through to service provision, follow up and case closure.

The Norwegian system demands that all intrusive interventions be decided by County Boards, a court-like decision-making body consisting of three decision makers: a lawyer, an expert on children's upbringing and needs, and a layperson (for details: Skivenes and Søvig, 2017). The County Board operates according to due process and the principles of court proceedings and, compared with other systems, scores highly on adhering to the rule of law (Burns et al, 2017). All decisions by the County Board can be appealed to the district courts, and under some conditions, even to the Norwegian appeal and supreme courts. The Norwegian system is also characterised as child-centric; the United Nations Convention on the Rights of the Child (UNCRC) is incorporated in national legislation and the Norwegian state seeks to fulfil the obligations set in that Convention (Skivenes, 2011). Legal accountability is also high. The legal system in Norway is considered to uphold all relevant standards of due process and the rule of law. Proceedings in child protection also operate similarly with access to justice for private parties so that all cases can be fully heard in the County Board, and thereafter appealed. Decisions are fully reasoned in judgments and many are made publicly available in an anonymised form.

The municipalities and the state are together accountable for the detection and correction of errors and mistakes in child protection. The municipalities are responsible for maintaining a Child Welfare Service and are accountable for securing services that operate according to the law. They are also required to have state-approved systems of internal control to ensure that child welfare practices comply with the law (Child Welfare Act [CWA] § 2-1). Lastly, the municipalities are responsible for approving and supervising foster homes, as well as training and guiding foster care supervisors (CWA § 4-22). At the state level, responsibility for child welfare is divided between the Ministry of Children and Equality, the County Governors, the Board of Health Supervision (BHS) and the Office of Children, Youth and Family Affairs (Bufetat). The Ministry has overarching responsibility for supervising the correct operation of all law (CWA § 2-3 (1a)). Bufetat is responsible for running state residential care units and for aiding municipalities to find foster homes, the recruitment and allocation of foster homes, and for training and guiding foster parents (CWA § 2-3 (2)). Like the municipal services, Bufetat is also required to have an approved system of internal control to ensure work follows legal regulations (CWA § 2-3 (3)).

The BHS has a primary and supervisory responsibility for all municipal and state child welfare services (CWA § 2-3 b (1)). Their mandate is carried out in close cooperation with the County Governors. The

BHS undertakes planned countrywide audits of selected areas of child welfare. It is also responsible for developing methods for audit and control as well as the tools and guidance used by the County Governors in their supervisory role. The County Governors are the state representatives in Norway's 19 counties. They supervise municipal child welfare services within their jurisdiction (CWA §§ 2-3 (4), 2-3 b (2)), as well as state and private residential care centres for children and parents (CWA § 2-3 b (3-4)). Their mandate is to ensure that services are performed in compliance with the CWA. The County Governors also function as an appellate administrative body for decisions made by child welfare services that are not subject to the authority of the County Boards and the courts. The County Governors also advise and guide municipal child welfare services (CWA § 2-3 (4)); this function is independent from their supervisory role.

Together, the BHS and the County Governors form the most important mechanisms for administrative accountability in Norwegian child welfare system. However, other regulatory bodies also have oversight of decisions and activities in the child protection system. First, the Parliamentary Ombudsman for Public Administration (Parliamentary Ombudsman) is tasked with monitoring and preventing injustice to individual citizens by the public administration and ensuring respect for human rights (Constitution, § 75 (l); Sivilombudsmannsloven § 3). The Parliamentary Ombudsman is a final step for those cannot appeal to a higher authority within the public administration or the courts (Instruks for Sivilombudsmannen § 5). Anyone who feels that they have been treated unjustly by the public administration can file a complaint with the Parliamentary Ombudsman (Sivilombudsmannsloven § 6). The Parliamentary Ombudsman occasionally publishes written statements on specific cases, which have wider implications. Second, the Ombudsman for Children (Barneombudet) is an independent body that advocates for children's and youth rights and is tasked with ensuring that Norwegian authorities comply with the UNCRC. However, the Ombudsman for Children only works at the system level and does not handle individual cases. Children may contact the Ombudsman directly for advice about their rights or to facilitate contact with people or authorities who can assist. Third, the Office of the Auditor General of Norway (OAG), the independent audit agency of the Norwegian parliament, monitors the performance of public administration and, through audits and guidance, contributes to uncovering and preventing errors, mistakes and default (Riksrevisjonsloven § 9). The OAG has wide discretion to decide where and how to perform its duties and has conducted several audits in child welfare. Fourth, Norway is a member of the European Convention of Human Rights; as elsewhere in Europe, cases alleging breach of the Convention by Norway can be brought to the ECtHR.

Errors from the system perspective: controllers and auditors

We examined planned external audits by regulatory agencies to gain a broader perspective on what the supervisory authorities themselves perceive as errors and mistakes in Norwegian child protection. These audits are in place both to uncover errors and mistakes in child welfare and to assist agencies to identify areas where they need to address any shortcomings.

In 2010, the responsibility for supervision of child welfare, which had hitherto rested with the 19 County Governors, was handed to the BHS. The goal was to strengthen coordination and state oversight of public welfare provision (Ot.prp. nr. 69 (2008–09): 70). Since then, the BHS has published several countrywide reports based on audits of municipal and state child welfare.

There are two main types of audit system audits and case reviews. System audits focus on whether service provision in specified areas complies with the law and assesses whether the organisation's steering and internal control systems can ensure adequate and safe services within a specified service area (BHS, 2018b). These focus on many agencies and a large number of observations within a narrow field of activity. In contrast, case reviews focus on a limited selection of child welfare cases where the auditing bodies examine all documentation for each case, often covering a range of different service providers. This gives a deeper insight into the different aspects of case handling, but over a smaller number of cases. Both types of audit rely on the examination of case files and interviews with agency managers and employees.

The publication of reports, a practice they had already established within their other areas of supervision based on countrywide child welfare audits, began when the BHS took over responsibility for supervision in 2010. While the County Governors audited agencies before 2010, they did not systematically publish reports. This restricts our review to after 2010. We examined all national reports from the BHS on child welfare and have included five reports of national audits that examine possible sources of errors and mistakes in child welfare. We also included two audits by the OAG and a recent expert commission report ordered by the Ministry of Children and Equality on failures to protect children from maltreatment, eight reports overall (Table 7.1).

Table 7.1: Public audits and reports on the child protection system 2010–19

Year	Controller	Controlee	Method(s)	Sample	Topic
2012	OAG	Municipal CPS	Register data Interviews Questionnaire Case files	7 agencies (155 children)	Early intervention Availability of services Follow-up in foster care
2012	BHS	Municipal CPS	Systems Audit	44 agencies	Investigation and evaluation of services
2015	BHS	Municipal CPS	Systems Audit	94 agencies (151 municipalities)	Follow-up of children in foster care
2017	BHS	Municipal CPS	Systems Audit Self-evaluation	57 agencies (76 municipalities) 114 agencies (149 municipalities)	Reporting – Reception and follow-up
2017	NOU 2017: 12	Broad range of state and municipal services	Case Review	Case files from 20 cases 57 children where CPS failed to protect	Could cases of serious abuse and neglect have been prevented or uncovered at an earlier stage?
2018	OAG	State CPS	Register data Interviews Questionnaire Documents	Bufetat	Emergency placement support for Municipal CPS
2018	BHS	State CPS	Systems Audit	Bufetat	Placement support for Municipal CPS
2019	BHS	Municipal CPS	Case Review	Case files from 106 cases	Review quality of assessment and decision processes in CPS

We have also included four written statements by the Parliamentary Ombudsman where violations of individual rights were found to have public interest (Table 7.2).

Each of these reports directed strong criticism at important areas of child welfare performance both by the state and by municipalities. We examined the audits and reports to identify key themes concerning the errors and mistakes in current Norwegian child protection. All the reports uncovered errors and mistakes that resulted in children remaining in high-risk families without necessary intervention, or

Table 7.2: Public statements by the Parliamentary Ombudsman

Case number	Topic	Conclusion
2008/1080	CPS responsibility for providing services to parents following care order	Parents have a right to services even if the care order is not yet finalised
2008/2663	Child's right to access information case files	Children aged 15 and above have a right to access their own case files, even if their case was closed before they turned 15
2016/1353	Foster parents' right to submit complaints	An individual assessment is necessary to determine if foster parents have a right to submit complaints about CPS decisions, based on their knowledge of the child and insight into the child's best interests
2016/1152	Children's rights to participate in CPS decisions	The basis of Article 12 in the UNCRC is that the child's right to participate in decisions affecting them is absolute. The CPS cannot refuse a child's participation by reference to the child's best interests

with an intervention that was not appropriate to the situation and the child's needs. All these reports focus on systemic rather than individual errors or mistakes. Importantly, criticism is not always directed at the child welfare agencies but at a broader range of agencies with a role in the lives of the children and their families.

Three main types of errors were repeatedly identified in these eight audit reports: failure to involve the child and speak to him or her in a manner that allows free expression of their views; failure by child welfare agencies to follow procedures and record casework actions sufficiently; and both state and municipal agencies have poor internal control, managers often fail to address known errors and to establish or follow necessary routines. In addition, studies on public confidence in the child protection system are discussed.

Child perspective errors

Studies of children's participation in child protection cases in Norway show the difficulties and barriers in realising children's rights to participate in matters concerning them (such as Archard and Skivenes, 2009; Vis and Fossum, 2013; Magnussen and Skivenes, 2015). The expert by experience group, Barnevernsproffene, has repeatedly raised this issue.[7] The child perspective errors we identified in our review of audit reports included failures to identify, consider, acknowledge or act on the child's interests and viewpoints, for example by not taking the child's views properly into account in decisions, not considering child's needs or by prioritising a good working relationship with adults above the needs of the child.

Despite the fact that the CWA (§§ 4-1 and 6-3) clearly asserts children's right to participate and be heard, the failure to consider the child's views and perspective is common. Six out of seven reports criticised agencies involved with the child and families for failing to ensure that children were heard (OAG, 2011–12; BHS, 2012, 2015, 2017, 2018a NOU, 2017:12). Indeed, the BHS (2012: 17) found that the majority of municipal agencies did not comply with the requirements for children's participation during investigations. Other agencies did not have protocols for interviewing children; some did but did not follow them. Some carried out interviews but failed to document them. Managers did not require interviews with children, and caseworkers lacked competence in direct work with children. The Board's conclusion was that it may be chance whether the child is heard or not, and that failure to document coupled with high staff turnover means that critical information can be lost, and the child forced to tell his or her story repeatedly.

Audits also identified failure to speak to children throughout all stages of casework. Three reports found that agencies dismissed reports of maltreatment without first interviewing the child, in some cases even when it was based on things the child had actually said (BHS, 2012, 2017; NOU, 2017:12). Interviews with children were also missing from investigations of maltreatment. The expert report (NOU, 2017: 50) provides examples of how even when interviews did take place, the child's voice was not necessarily heard because of the way interviews were arranged. Caseworkers did not ask children about their family or home situation or did not probe into what caused a child's behaviour. Instead, the focus was on trying to help the child with social or school-related issues. In other cases, children's views were not given sufficient weight, or the children were simply not believed, even when they reported neglect or being abused physically or sexually (BHS, 2019). The Parliamentary Ombudsman also stresses that a child's right to participate according to Article 12 of the UNCRC is absolute and cannot be set aside simply by reference to the child's best interests. Furthermore, the Parliamentary Ombudsman highlights the general challenge involved in many areas of the system and that measures need to be taken to ensure child participation (Sivilombudsmannen, 2016). In a report from the Ombudsman for Children (2018), experts by experience reported that they were not understood or believed when attempting to tell caseworkers, teachers, public health nurses or mental health professionals about their experiences of abuse or neglect. Some even reported that professionals contacted their parents to tell them about what the children had said.

Procedural errors

Procedural errors arise when caseworkers fail to follow established regulations and procedures in their casework. Such errors include: (1) the failure to provide proper documentation and keep records; (2) the failure to perform the necessary investigations before making assessments and decisions; and (3) the failure to comply with legal requirements.

1 Nationwide audits have found that both municipal and state child welfare agencies often fail to comply with the requirements to document casework (BHS, 2012, 2015, 2017, 2018a, 2019; NOU, 2017:12). A recurrent finding is that case files lack information about what was done to investigate a case, what information was gathered, what professional assessments were made and the central conclusions of assessments. Moreover, recording failures seem to occur at all stages of casework, at referral, investigation, assessment, decision making and in evaluating the service provision. Consequently, in many cases, it is impossible to tell from a child's record what matters the child welfare agency considered before deciding on an action, and whether the action taken was appropriate for the child. This criticism of errors arising from poor or missing documentation has also been raised by parents' groups who criticise the child welfare system (email correspondence with Skivenes).

2 Several reports also highlight inadequate investigation before making assessments and decisions, or that conclusions lack a proper analysis to justify decisions (BHS, 2012, 2015, 2017, 2018a, 2019; NOU, 2017:12). This includes: assessments without home visits, observation of the child and parents together, conversations with the child, investigation of symptoms that indicate possible child maltreatment, and expert reports based on insufficient investigation (NOU, 2017: 12, 53–4). The OAG noted that less than 20 per cent of investigations used a case plan and argued that child welfare investigations generally lacked a systematic approach (OAG, 2011–12: 70). The BHS also found several cases where reports of sexual and physical abuse were dismissed without investigation, despite the obvious severity of the reports. The Board also found that in many cases agencies had not assessed the need for emergency services (BHS, 2017: 13). A recent

review of 106 case files found that conclusions and decisions commonly lacked an analytical approach to justify the decisions made. Although investigations gathered the relevant data, the material was often not structured or analysed in the conclusions, which resulted in important information being overlooked in decisions about future action, even though it was there. In particular, caseworkers sometimes got caught up in certain aspects of a case (such as proving drug abuse), but failed to include a thorough consideration of what the home conditions meant for the child's care. Consequently, children and families were frequently provided with services that reviewers considered inappropriate or ineffective (BHS, 2019).

3   The third type of procedural error concerns the lack of compliance with routines for case handling. The BHS (2017) found that many agencies failed to provide feedback to those reporting concerns, as required by law. For its part, the OAG identified that many agencies failed to follow up case plans for children in care or receiving services; as a result, many families were receiving services over a long period without any knowledge of their effect on the child's situation (OAG, 2011–12). The BHS (2019) made similar findings, and similarly argued that families were given services that were inappropriate over extended periods because analysis of the child's needs had not been properly conducted.

Organisational errors

The types of organisational errors identified here include a lack of internal control or oversight and failure by administrators to address errors that are uncovered and to support and monitor caseworker decision-making (OAG, 2011–12; BHS, 2017, 2019). The lack of support for caseworkers was also evident in a recent review, which found no trace of any internal deliberation between colleagues or leadership support in decision making in just under half of the 106 cases examined (BHS, 2019).

Errors of cooperation and oversight concern those in relationships with external agencies and services that are important to child protection work, including errors in coordinating the necessary mental health services for children in the system and failures to share information between different service providers. This leaves service providers with a fragmented image of the child's situation, where a more complete picture might have led to earlier action. Agencies with reporting duties often fail to comply with them and, for their part, child welfare agencies often fail to provide the required feedback to reporters. Also, auditing and supervisory bodies typically lack the necessary resources and competence to provide oversight and guidance to the child welfare system (NOU, 2017:12; BHS, 2009).

Public opinion and confidence in the system

It is unclear whether the increased criticism and the enormous negative attention that Norwegian child protection has received is due to the public's lack of trust in the system and its decision makers. What we do know, however, is that the level of trust is a well-established factor in measuring legitimacy in a democracy. As evidence, a study based on a 2014 survey ($N = 4,003$) of public confidence in the child protection system across four countries: England, Finland, Norway and the US (California) (Juhasz and Skivenes, 2016) showed that Norwegians were more confident of their child protection system than respondents in England and the US. About 50 per cent of the Norwegians surveyed stated that they had 'quite a lot or a great deal' of confidence in front-line staff, judges and the child welfare agency. Nevertheless, the study only related to general impressions of a system, and not substantial knowledge or experience with this system.

A similar study was undertaken in Norway among immigrants (or born to immigrant parents) from Poland, Somalia, Pakistan, Iraq, Vietnam and Bosnia-Herzegovina ($N = 977$), including a random comparison with a group of non-immigrants ($N = 618$) (IPSOS, 2017). The report examined perceptions of trust in the child protection system in these two groups. The findings showed that a significantly lower proportion of immigrants displayed a high trust in the system (41 per cent), compared with the 55 per cent in the general population. This accords with findings by Juhasz and Skivenes (2016), that expressed distrust was more evident among immigrants, with 30 per cent of immigrants reporting 'low or no trust' in the system, compared with only 19 per cent in the comparison group. In a survey commissioned by the Directorate for Children, Youth and Family Affairs of persons aged 15 years or over ($N = 4,000$), 62 per cent of respondents had high levels of confidence in the child protection system, although 36 per cent reported having a negative perception of how the child protection system explained and justified its actions in public (Sentio, 2018). Interestingly, given the aim of this chapter, that study also showed that 53 per cent of the sample believed that child protection interventions were undertaken in serious cases, but only 37 per cent responded they had confidence in how children were followed up subsequently. Of course, we cannot expect that the population as a whole has sufficient knowledge about how the system operates and how interventions are followed up, and thus such results must be interpreted with some caution.

Mass media scrutiny

An analysis of media coverage of the child protection system in recent years was undertaken as a means to identify the issues and themes raised and discussed in public discourse. The media have an obligation to act ethically in their work, as expressed in the *Be Careful Poster* 'Ethical norms for the press (printed press, radio, television and online publications)'.[8] Under point 4.8, it is explicitly stated that: '[w]hen children are mentioned, it is good practice to consider the consequences that the media coverage can have for the child. This also applies when guardians have given their consent to exposure. Children's identity should as a rule not be disclosed in family disputes, child welfare cases or court cases' (authors' translation).

Our sample included media critique[9] of the system or its processes from five major Norwegian newspapers (*VG, Dagbladet, Bergen Tidende, Aftenposten, Nordlys*) in the period 2015–18 when international protest against Norwegian child protection was at its height. Our initial search identified a large number of articles that included the terms 'flaws', 'errors' and 'mistakes' in combination with child protection system. However, reviewing the content of the articles, only 165 articles addressed the specific topic of concern in this chapter – errors and mistakes – representing some 41 articles a year, which is much lower than we expected given the international criticism. Most articles adopted a predominantly critical perspective, and only a few have positive messages about the system. Many articles ($n = 52$) addressed various types of deficits within the system, such as a lack of staff competence, the poor quality of child welfare services, criticism of case processing or of experts, and a lack of sufficient follow-up in the system. Some articles ($n = 18$) highlighted the poor supervision of residential units and the use of force and involuntary measures against adolescents ($n = 13$), while others expressed concern with issues addressed in the courts ($n = 8$), regarding migrants and culture ($n = 8$), or recounted or supported the views of parents ($n = 14$). Only a few articles ($n = 5$) criticised privatised service provision in the child protection system.

However, many of these 165 articles ($n = 47$) came into none of these categories, but addressed broader concerns about data security breaches, the level of state/municipality responsibility, and accusations that the child protection system removes children from their homes simply because they are fed unhealthy food, like pizza. This brief media analysis reflects findings by Stang (2018) in an analysis of international and domestic Facebook groups protesting the Norwegian child protection system. One of Stang's findings was that 'the international groups protest the fact that the state has the authority to remove children from their families, while the Norwegian groups are protesting abuse of power, injustice and unethical professional conduct' (2018: 273). A surprising finding from our media analysis may be the relatively low number of articles in the Norwegian press, suggesting that it is not a major issue in the domestic mainstream mass media debate, despite the pronounced international interest.

Conclusion

In this chapter, we distinguished between five accountability mechanisms and reviewed recent public reports and audits by Norwegian regulatory agencies to provide an overview of the central themes of errors and mistakes in Norwegian child protection. We identified the most important discourses in the last ten years focusing on reports based on nationwide audits by the BHS and the OAG. Norway approaches change to the child protection system in an incremental way, including through amendment to the law which is regularly supplemented by more global reforms focusing on, for example, involvement and continuity (Hestbæk et al, forthcoming). So far, discussions about establishing a system of 'serious case reviews' have not become part of the political discourse, but this may change following an incident of severe failure. In this chapter, we have focused predominantly on administrative and social accountability mechanisms. The findings from our review and analysis identify three main types of errors that are consistently repeated over time: (1) the lack of involvement of children, and not treating children in a manner that allows them to express their views freely; (2) the repeated criticism of child welfare agencies for their failure to follow procedures and provide sufficient documentation in casework; and (3) that both state and municipal agencies have poor internal control and leadership, fail to address known errors, and are slow to establish or follow necessary routines. Albeit limited, our media analysis primarily concurs with finding 2.

It seems clear to us that the Norwegian child protection system is not driven by incidents and crisis, and that the errors and mistakes identified have not created pressure for immediate reforms. It appears that Norwegian developments focused more on a critique of the system than on individual errors and mistakes. We also question the value of learning provided by the system of audits when the same errors are repeatedly identified. This may be the reason why some long-standing issues, for example, children's participation, remain unaddressed. Although there have been many changes with regard to children's rights to participate, with legal provisions and child-centric programmes (Hestbæk et al, forthcoming), progress is being made only slowly. One indication of this incremental approach to child protection is that between 1997 and 2018, various governments have put at least 20 propositions concerning changes to the Child Welfare Act to the Norwegian parliament. On average, the CWA is amended in some way at least once a year. While some of these changes may have resulted in important shifts in child welfare practice, the policy shifts and processes leading to these amendments appear to be characterised by continuity and gradual development. Thus, for Norway, we would not be able to identify any defined turning point in child welfare practice, although this might be possible from a longer-term historical perspective over the past century.

Notes

[1] The authors would like to thank the editors for their constructive feedback. Thanks also to Barbara Ruiken for researching the media articles and assisting with the references and chapter layout. This project has received funding from the Research Council of Norway under the Independent Projects – Humanities and Social Science programme (grant no. 262773).

[2] Five cases have been decided, and over thirty cases are pending.

[3] www.kibnorge.no.

[4] The Norwegian *tilsyn* (supervision) is used both as a way of naming the authorities tasked with providing supervision and the act of making inspections or audits. It is difficult to find a good English translation and so in this chapter we mainly use 'audit' to describe the systematic inspection of casework performed by an external party, both planned and incident-based. We use 'supervision' or 'oversight' to describe the more general control functions.

[5] Falch-Eriksen and Skivenes (2019) provide a detailed overview of the Norwegian child protection system.

[6] Measured at end of year.

[7] www.forandringsfabrikken.no/#

[8] In Norwegian, *Vær Varsom Plakaten*. Available from: https://presse.no/pfu/etiske-regler/vaer-varsom-plakaten/.

[9] We searched child protection in combination with errors, nonconformities, failure, abuse of power, coercion, criticism, complaint, notice, legal protection (in Norwegian: *feil, avvik, svikt, maktmisbruk, tvang, kritikk, klage, varsel, rettssikkerhet*).

References

Archard, D. and Skivenes, M. (2009) 'Hearing the Child', *Child & Family Social Work*, 14(4): 391–9.

BHS (Board of Health Supervision) (2009) *Rapport 5/2009, Utsatte barn og unge – behov for bedre samarbeid: Oppsummering av landsomfattende tilsyn i 2008 med kommunale helse-, sosial- og barneverntjenester til utsatte barn* [Report 5/2009, Exposed children and infants – the necessity for better collaboration: Conclusionary remarks from country-wide supervision in 2008 of municipal health-, social- and child welfare-oriented services to exposed children], Oslo: Statens Helsetilsyn.

BHS (Board of Health Supervision) (2012) *Rapport 2/2012, Oppsummering av landsomfattende tilsyn i 2011 med kommunalt barnevern – undersøkelse og evaluering* [Report 2/2012, Conclusionary remarks from country-wide supervisions in 2011 of municipal child protection agencies – examination and evaluation], Oslo: Statens Helsetilsyn.

BHS (Board of Health Supervision) (2015) *Rapport 1/2015, 'Bare en ekstra tallerken på bordet?' Oppsummering av landsomfattende tilsyn i 2013 og 2014 med kommunenes arbeid med oppfølging av barn som bor i fosterhjem* [Report 1/2015, 'Only one more plate on the table?' – Conclusionary remarks of country-wide supervisions in 2013 and 2014 of municipal efforts to follow up children in foster care], Oslo: Statens Helsetilsyn.

BHS (Board of Health Supervision) (2017) *Rapport 1/2017, Bekymring i skuffen. Oppsummering av landsomfattende tilsyn i 2015 og 2016 med barnevernets arbeid med meldinger og tilbakemelding til den som har meldt* [Report 1/2017, Concerns hidden in the drawer – Conclusionary remarks of country-wide supervisions in 2015 and 2016 of child protection services' processing of reported concerns and following up those who reported], Oslo: Statens Helsetilsyn.

BHS (Board of Health Supervision) (2018a) *Rapport 3/2018, Barnets synspunkt når ikke frem: Oppsummering etter landsomfattende tilsyn med Bufetat 2017* [Report 3/2018: The child's perspective does not reach forward: Conclusionary remarks from country-wide supervision of the Norwegian Directorate for Children, Youth and Family Affairs], Oslo: Statens Helsetilsyn.

BHS (Board of Health Supervision) (2018b) *Internserien 4/2018, Veileder for tilsyn utført som systemrevisjon* [Internal series 4/2018, Supervisor for the supervision as a systematic audit], Oslo: Statens Helsetilsyn.

BHS (Board of Health Supervision) (2019) *Det å reise vasker øynene. Gjennomgang av 106 barnevernsaker* [Travelling clears the eyes. Review of 106 child protection cases], Oslo: Statens helsetilsyn.

Bovens, M. (2007) 'Analysing and Assessing Accountability: A Conceptual Framework', *European Law Journal*, 13(4): 447–68.

Burns, K., Pösö. T. and Skivenes, M. (eds) (2017) *Child Welfare Removals by the State: A Cross-Country Analysis of Decision-Making Systems*, New York: Oxford University Press.

Falch-Eriksen, A. and Skivenes, M. (2019) 'Right to Protection', in Langford, M., Skivenes, M. and Søvig, K. (eds) *Children's Rights in Norway. An Implementation Paradox*, Oslo, Universitetsforlaget.

Gilbert, N. (1997) *Welfare Justice: Restoring Social Equity*, New Haven, CT: Yale University Press.

Gilbert, N., Parton, N. and Skivenes, M. (eds) (2011) *Child Protection Systems: International Trends and Orientations*, New York: Oxford University Press.

Hestbæk, A.-D. Skivenes M., Falch-Eriksen, A., Leth-Svendsen, I. and Backe-Hansen, E. (2020) 'Norwegian and Danish Child Protection Policies and Practice', in J.D. Berrick, N. Gilbert and M. Skivenes (eds) *International Handbook of Child Protection Systems*, New York: Oxford University Press.

IPSOS (2017) *Holdninger til innvandring og integrering* [Attitudes toward immigration and integration], Available from: www.ipsos.com/sites/default/files/2017-05/Ipsos_Rapport_Innvandring.pdf.

Juhasz I. and Skivenes M. (2016) 'The Population's Confidence in the Child Protection System: A Survey Study of England, Finland, Norway and the United States (California)', *Social Policy & Administration*, 51(7): 1330–47.

Magnussen A.M. and Skivenes M. (2015) 'The Child's Opinion and Position in Care Order Proceedings: An Analysis of Judicial Discretion in the County Boards' Decision-Making', *International Journal of Children's Rights*, 23(4): 705–23.

NOU 2017:12 (2017) *Svikt og svik. Gjennomgang av saker hvor barn har vært utsatt for vold, seksuelle overgrep og omsorgssvikt* [Norwegian Official Report: Failure and betrayal. Review of cases where children have been exposed to violence, sexual abuse and neglect], Oslo: Barne- og likestillingsdepartementet.

OAG (Office of the Auditor General) (2011–12) *Riksrevisjonens undersøkelse om det kommunale barnevernets og bruken av statlige virkemidler* [The Auditor General's audit of municipal child protection agencies and the use of public funds], Dokument 3:15.

Ombudsman for Children (2018) *'Hadde vi fått hjelp tidligere, hadde alt vært annerledes' Erfaringer fra barn og unge utsatt for vold og overgrep* [On the law on changes in the child protection service: Ministry for Children and Equality].

Ot.prp. nr. 69 (2008–09) *Om lov om endringer i barnevernloven : Barne- og likestillingsdepartementet.* [On the Act on amendments to the Child Welfare Law] Available from: www.regjeringen.no/no/dokumenter/ otprp-nr-69-2008-2009-/id556260/sec1.

Rothstein, B. (2011) *The Quality of Government: Corruption, Social Trust and Inequality in International Perspective*, Chicago: University of Chicago Press.

Sentio (2018) *Befolkningens holdninger til barnevernet* [The population's attitude toward the (Norwegian) child protection services], Available from: https://www.bufdir.no/globalassets/global/befolkningenes_ holdninger_til_barnevernet.pdf.

Sivilombudsmannen (2016) *Barns rettigheter ved barnevernstjenestens avgjørelser* [The child's rights in decisions by the child protection service], Available from: www.sivilombudsmannen.no/uttalelser/ barns-rettigheter-ved-barnevernstjenestens-avgjorelser/.

Skivenes M. (2011) 'Norway: Toward a Child-Centric Perspective' in N. Gilbert, N. Parton and M. Skivenes (eds) *Child Protection Systems: International Trends and Orientations*, New York: Oxford University Press, pp 154–79.

Skivenes, M. and Søvig, K.H. (2017) 'Norway: Child Welfare Decision-Making in Cases of Removals of Children', in K. Burns, T. Pösö and M. Skivenes (eds), *Child Welfare Removals by the State: A Cross-Country Analysis of Decision-Making Systems*, New York: Oxford University Press, pp 40–64.

Stang E. (2018) 'Resistance and Protest Against Norwegian Child Welfare Services on Facebook: Different Perceptions of Child-Centring', *Nordic Social Work Research*, 8(3): 273–86.

Vis, S.A. and Fossum, S. (2013) 'Representation of Children's Views in Court Hearings About Custody and Parental Visitations: A Comparison Between What Children Wanted and What the Courts Ruled', *Children and Youth Services Review*, 35(12): 2101–9.

8

The political-administrative and the professional approach to errors and mistakes in Swedish child protection

Inger Kjellberg and Staffan Höjer

Introduction

The discussions and debates on errors and mistakes in child protection in Sweden concern issues of different degree and extent. Only a few years ago the Swedish state both gave recognition and apologies to persons who had been maltreated in the Swedish child protection system historically and up to 1980. The role of Social Services in these cases has been depicted as faulty. The failure to strengthen children's rights in relation to the decision-making system in child protection, as well as in the Social Services' day-to-day work. For instance, the large number of unaccompanied children in Sweden over recent years raise other issues, which have been much discussed and debated. For example, arbitrary age assessment of young asylum seekers has aroused anger and conflict within professional groups working with unaccompanied children (Hjern et al, 2012). Other debates focus on creating better services and developing professional expertise in order to reduce errors and mistakes. The most serious cases of maltreatment resulting in the death of children evoke great distress in Social Services in general and these cases are also a matter of public concern. Questions of whether Social Services could have acted differently and averted the tragedy are at the forefront of the discussions in these instances and have resulted in more demands for investigations when children have died as a result of crime.

Child protection in Sweden

The population of Sweden was 2017 just over 10.1 million, of whom 2.1 million, approximately 21 per cent, were aged 0–17 years (SCB, 2019). Child protection in Sweden is handled at municipality level by professional social workers employed by Social Services in each of the 290 municipalities. The larger municipalities often have a decentralised organisation with a Social Service organisation in each district. Social work is not a formally protected profession, meaning that the municipality could employ people without a social work degree, but in today's social work practice professional social workers undertake investigations, build relations with children and families, and propose the decisions in child protection cases (Höjer et al, 2012).

The child protection system in Sweden has an explicit family service orientation. Within a family service orientation the various problems found among parents and families are considered central to the understanding of the child's situation. Therefore, risk situations, abuse and neglect are generally approached as resulting from dysfunctional relationships (Leviner, 2014; Burns et al, 2017; Heimer et al, 2018). Social Services work primarily with support and change through consensus and voluntariness where trust between social worker and parents is fundamental. Coercive interventions and the removal of a child from her or his family interfere with such relationships. Swedish Social Services resort to coercive interventions at a much later stage in social investigations than, for example, in England, Australia and the US (Gilbert et al, 2011). In Sweden, 9 out of 1,000 children were placed in care (2014), in a ratio of 2.4 involuntary and 6.6 voluntary (with consent from parents). The comparable figures for UK in 2013 with 6.6 per 1,000 in care, were 4.3 involuntary and 1.8 on voluntary grounds (Burns et al, 2017). Many scholars have pointed at distinctive elements of hidden coercion behind these high voluntary figures (Svensson and Höjer, 2017). There has also been substantial criticism of the Swedish child protection system from different, somewhat contradictory, perspectives; children exposed to violence within the family do not receive sufficient care and support but very many children are removed from their families (CRC, 2009).

Social welfare boards

Sweden is, as far as we know, the only country in Europe where lay persons have a determining influence in decision-making bodies in child protection. All voluntary decisions about placement in care, as well as all applications for care orders in the administrative courts are taken by local social welfare boards. The members of these boards are politically appointed, but they are not supposed to act according to their political ideology; instead they are instructed to follow the law and make decisions in the child's best interests. They are supposed to act as 'good citizens' and use their judgement, based on Social Services' social workers' assessments and their common sense (Forkby et al, 2015; Svensson and Höjer, 2017). In the past this system was used also in the other Nordic countries but over the last 20 years Sweden has changed its system in response to criticisms about problems in complying with the rule of law as well as safeguarding the best interests of children (Hultman et al, 2018).

Mandatory reports of concern

The majority of child protection cases are initiated by mandatory reports about concerns (Leviner, 2014). All social institutions which have contact with children: schools, health, dental and social care facilities must report concerns about children to the Social Services (Social Services Act [SSA] § 14:1). All safeguarding concerns should be reported, including unverified information, suspicions and so on. Where the concern relates to a child who has (or may have) been subject to physical violence or sexual abuse, or has witnessed abuse by a close relative, the Social Services must immediately start an investigation. Any other person (such as a neighbour, friend or family member) may report such concerns about children to the Social Services, which gives the Social Services much information about children in need of protection, but also requires substantial work of critical investigation.

Involuntary actions can only be taken when a child is at serious risk for harm. Such interventions are set out in the Care of Young Persons Act (CYPA) and require a court order. The municipal welfare board applies for a court order and if this is refused, the Social Services can only offer voluntary support. Parents do not have to accept voluntary support and can withdraw from such services at any time. Where involuntary care is used, care orders are reviewed by the board every six months; the aim of Swedish child protection practice is to work for reunification (Leviner, 2014). In most cases the parents remain the child's legal guardians (Mattson, 2010), and adoptions are unusual.

Understanding of errors and mistakes

We follow the definitions of errors and mistakes (see Chapter 2) as social constructions, where 'error' indicates a deviation from standards or rules, and 'mistakes' denote when things go wrong due to misunderstandings. Child protection is a complex area and when things go wrong there may be a mixture of errors and mistakes leading to serious and unwanted consequences for children's safety. These incidents can also be the result of failures, unjust actions or violations of legal norms by a number of different people. A much-used term in social care in Sweden is 'mistreatment' which is defined to include positive acts, as well as neglect, which cause or risk a threat to an individual's life, personal safety and physical or psychological health (SOSFS, 2011). Mistreatment can occur because of errors and mistakes. Another term often used in the Swedish context is 'irregularities' which is synonymous with errors, something that deviates from standards.

What 'errors and mistakes' are is usually understood in retrospect, after decisions and measures have been taken. When tragic events occur in child care the public response to the professional practice and their legal mandate to protect children can be threefold (Braye and Preston-Shoot, 2006). First, social workers may be accused of having done too little too late, by not using their legal mandate. That is, by not intervening in time or not acting on information about children being abused. Second, the practitioners may be seen as doing too much too soon, by using their legal mandate but misinterpreting or misunderstanding the situation or their mandate. An example is the removal of children from their families without sufficient evidence of a problematic home environment. Third, the management of the welfare system and/or the administrative and supervisory systems can be understood as flawed, resulting in more regulation, surveillance and control measures with the intention that social workers get it just right. However, as Braye and Preston-Shoot (2006) point out, such measures can also undermine both children's and parents' human rights. Nonetheless, when things go wrong professional practice or organisational management are perceived as being at fault leading to solutions geared to more law and regulations (Braye and Preston-Shoot, 2006). This is also the case in Sweden.

Errors and mistakes in the history of child protection

Text books on Swedish social work usually describe the pre-professional history of social work where measures were applied within a context of charity and philanthropy (for example, Meeuwisse et al, 2000). Until the beginning of the 1900s, the Swedish state took little responsibility for social affairs. Studies on how vulnerable children were treated depict a precarious situation (Lundström, 2017). It was, for instance, common to arrange auctions in foster care, where the family who agreed to take care of a child for the lowest payment was chosen by the local municipality. Statistics from that time show a higher mortality rate for children born out of wedlock, and many blamed the foster care system of that time. A new law was enacted in 1902 where foster parents, who received children in their home for payment, had to report to the authorities. Child auctions where banned by law from 1918, but by then there had not been any child auctions in the bigger cities for more than 20 years, only in the coastal areas and smaller villages in the north of Sweden (Söderlind and Sköld, 2018). At the beginning of the 20th century there was a common belief that public engagement in and responsibility for these issues would create higher standards, equal opportunities and a better situation for the children. Still, at that time child protection was underdeveloped in Sweden and many children, particularly from poor families were exploited and abused (Lundström, 2017).

During the 20th century a slow professionalisation of child protection took place. In the first half of the century, specific boards were created, made up of lay persons and professionals, to make decisions in child protection cases; the vicar was the chair, and a local doctor and teacher were members, with at least one woman. This period is described as moralising and paternalistic. Later when more social workers were educated, as well as other welfare professions, the boards where reconstructed with only lay persons but with the intention of basing decisions on expertise from outside.

The Swedish Inquiry on Child Abuse and Neglect in Institutions and Foster Homes and claims for redress

Sweden, like other countries, has held inquiries on abuse and neglect in institutions and foster homes. The Swedish Inquiry on Child Abuse and Neglect in Institutions and Foster Homes (Swedish Government, 2011a) was initiated following the broadcast of a TV documentary (*Stolen Childhood*) in November 2005. As in other countries it was the stories told by people who had experienced abuse and neglect in institutions and foster homes that led to the inquiry. The governmental report covers a long period, from the 1920s until the 2000s. It is based on archive documents and 866 individual interviews, although the inquiry was in touch with some 2,000 people. There are also written accounts of memories and experiences in childhood. It is indeed heartbreaking reading. Physical abuse was routine and sexual abuse was common. Of 798 young people placed in foster homes, 763

(96 per cent) reported abuse or neglect; of 665 placed in institutions 462 (69 per cent) reported abuse or neglect (Swedish Government, 2011a: 45). The inquiry also includes accounts of what happened to interviewees later in their adult lives. The conclusion in the inquiry is very clear: the childhood experiences from institutions and foster homes limited the interviewees' opportunities for their future quality of life, severely.

In the aftermath of the inquiry there were claims for redress from those who had experienced inadequate or abusive care. Another governmental report, the Inquiry on Redress for Past Abuse (Swedish Government, 2011b) proposed a three-part process in response: recognition and apology, compensation, and prevention. Although it followed the example of other countries in recognising and making official apologies to people suffering from abuse while in the care of the authorities, the way in which the Swedish government managed the question of compensation has evoked anger and further calls for justice. The main reason for criticism was the limited possibility of compensation for those who had been mistreated in the years 1920–80. Anyone mistreated after 1980 could not obtain financial redress (Government Bill 2011/12:160). However, these inquiries have had some positive effects: people's stories have been told; they have been listened to; and abusive behaviour in institutions and foster homes has been recognised. As far as preventive measures are concerned, the situation regarding foster homes and institutions today is quite different although there is more to be done. Despite knowledge of the history and of preventive measures, only 23 per cent of Swedish municipalities have implemented guidelines for how to act when mistreatment in foster homes or institutional care for children is disclosed (Children's Ombudsman, 2011).

Two central approaches to errors and mistakes

Since the early 1990s, the governing of the welfare state in Sweden has been highly influenced by economic management ideas and New Public Management (Johansson et al, 2015). With this influence, quality assurance and quality control have increasingly been addressed in social and health care. However, the development of the welfare state has proceeded hand in hand with the development of welfare professions where educated persons with a specific knowledge have been given a monopoly on the areas and occupational activities they can handle best (Macdonald, 1995). In child protection in Sweden these are social workers with a specific university education. When errors and mistakes are made by professionals, the whole profession's legitimacy is challenged. The political and administrative authorities in Swedish child protection respond to errors and mistakes with calls for more law to control the professional practice and the implementation of quality assurance mechanisms. Professionals working within child protection organise their own control system to meet criticism when things go wrong. In this section we first discuss these legal and quality assurance responses and then the professional approach.

The political-administrative approach

In Sweden, policy makers have followed the path of 'more law' in response to the public reaction to failures in child protection. Another strong influence is the increased call for the inclusion of the children's own perspective in legislation. As has been concluded, when children are invited to make their own statements in Social Services' investigations and are listened to, the result better reflects the child's perspective (Heimer et al, 2018). However, Swedish Social Services still focus on the partnership with parents to a very high degree, which undermines their compliance with the United Nations Convention on the Rights of the Child (UNCRC) (Heimer et al, 2018). The call for more law has mainly arisen in the context of child abuse deaths (Munro, 2005). Incidents where children die from neglect or abuse are fortunately quite rare in Sweden, but on average six children a year die because of violence perpetrated by someone with whom they have a close relationship (Statskontoret, 2014). However, when such tragic events happen the public response is usually very strong.

Other examples of the call for 'more law' is the incorporation of the UNCRC in Swedish law, effective from 2020, and changes in CYPA. Neither the incorporation of the UNCRC nor the changes in CYPA have passed without criticism. The two main arguments against incorporation are that several laws already reflect the Convention, and the difficulties of applying its provisions to individual cases because it is drafted in general terms (Council of Law, 2017). The changes in CYPA have in general been received more positively because they include a stronger focus on children's perspectives, increased rights for children to appeal decisions and a wider range of placements for compulsory care (Children's Ombudsman, 2015).

It has been pointed out that the application of law to child protection is problematic in more than one way (Leviner, 2014; Linell, 2017). There is not enough guidance for the Social Services, for example, regarding the use of involuntary measures, how to take account for the best interest of the child and to apply the UNCRC, resulting in individual social workers having extensive discretion. Sanctions against professionals who misuse their discretion, or who make errors or mistakes are quite rare in Sweden. They can be convicted for misfeasance and approximately 15 persons a year (Brå, 2013) in all of Sweden (and all governmental agencies) are prosecuted for such offences. However, during the last few years there has been more focus on social workers' working conditions, as victims of threats and violence, than on their misbehaviour (SWEA, 2018).

Quality assurance

Quality assurance has become a central discourse in social work because it carries with it not only a set of evidence-based methods but also specific vocabulary and ways of talking about social work that influence social work practice and child protection. Although, the word 'quality' is ambiguous, it is usually associated with services carried out according to a standard. The Children's Ombudsman (2015) stated that 'good quality' was closely related to the competence and knowledge of social workers working with children at risk and suggested that staff should also have specific knowledge of the UNCRC.

One example of the increasing implementation of quality assurance systems in child protection is the mandatory reporting of mistreatment in Social Services. After the disclosure of severe abuse in a nursing home in 1997, a new obligation was added to the SSA requiring staff to report mistreatment. From 2011, the provision in Swedish referred to as Lex Sarah applied to all the social services, including support for disabled people, children and families, and the Swedish National Board of Institutional Care (NBIC). All social services must report all kinds of mistreatment and errors that occur within their own facility and which have consequences for service-users' (including children's) well-being. These reports are investigated by the facility itself (SSA § 14, 3–7). The aim is to protect vulnerable service-users, change and improve services, and enable staff to report all errors and mistreatments without risk of reprisal and thereby to increase quality. The key concern behind the provision was to make visible any abuse and shortcomings in order to learn from mistakes. Thus, it is in line with a systems approach in the protection of service-users. The idea of learning from mistakes is mainly transferred to social care from the healthcare sector, and these ideas of safety and quality improvement were originally adopted from accident investigations in the aircraft industry (Kjellberg, 2012). The legislation has been tainted with a certain 'blaming and shaming' attitude which has discouraged staff from reporting incidents. There have also been misunderstandings concerning the threshold of seriousness for making reports and who has responsibility to make these judgements. If staff do not report mistreatments of which they are aware there are no sanctions in the legislation, despite the matter of sanctions having been actively discussed. The reasoning behind this reflects thinking from the system approach: errors and mistakes are inevitable; it is essential to learn from them and this requires maintaining an open and non-blaming organisational culture. Staff should be encouraged to report and to discuss errors and mistakes openly without blaming. Consequently, the provision in the SSA provides the possibility of discovering errors and preventing further mistakes if the Social Services play their part by making and circulating their reports and incorporating the lessons learned in their activities. Still, evidence from other areas of social work indicates a lack of feedback to staff and service-users, which suggests that more work has to be done (Kjellberg, 2012; Rytterström et al, 2012).

Professional approach

The autonomy some professional groups have managed to achieve is dependent on the legitimacy they can build in relation to their activities. In many countries a licensing system is used as a way to assure the link between society and professions. In the US, social workers describe their licensing system as a way to assure the public that social work will follow standards for the safe professional practice of social work, 'the paramount reason for licensure is to protect people, who often represent the most vulnerable in society, from mistakes and ethical misconduct that may occur in the provision of Social Services' (Donaldson et al, 2014: 52). In Sweden, social workers are not as yet licensed, although there has been much discussion and debate about this. The basis of a licensing system for social workers is that practitioners need appropriate, formal education and proof (normally a test) that they are competent to qualify for a licence. With the licence comes obligations, such as following certain ethical rules, and various forms of sanction if these rules are broken, the ultimate one being loss of the right to practise as licensed social worker. The possibility of removing the right to practise from social workers who misbehave is a key argument in favour of a licensing system.

Another professional system linked to the licensing system is the construction of a social work register. Only persons who have completed a social work education and have the right to call themselves social workers would be included on the register, and social work practice would become a protected area. In the US both systems apply to social work, but Italy and the UK have only a register. Sweden currently has neither system (Frost et al, 2018).

In Sweden, the social work profession has failed to get a general licensing system (Wingfors, 2004; Sjöström, 2013). One reason for this is that social workers' discretion is limited by a strong political governance so others (social welfare boards) make decisions in individual cases, for instance in child protection (Höjer et al, 2014). Further arguments come back to issues of jurisdiction. Social work is not a protected professional area and others apart from those with a social work education may be employed in social work jobs. Municipalities have the discretion to organise and comply with national legislation on social issues as they see fit. This has been an issue for the professional group, which has used different strategies to overcome it. There have been calls for both a national register of social workers and different forms of licensing system, but so far without success.

Strategies to identify and prevent errors and mistakes

In this section we will give a few examples of strategies pertaining to the political-administrative approach in new legislation and the quality assurance system as well as the professionals' strategies to avoid errors and mistakes.

There are two recent examples of new legislation initiated as a result of the deaths of children. A new Act on investigations regarding children who have died as a consequence of crime was adopted in year 2007 after a boy was killed by his stepfather. The National Board of Health and Welfare (NBHW) is responsible for these investigations and their analysis shows that 46 children have died as a consequence of crime during the ten years the law has been in force, and in 18 cases (40 per cent) the Social Services had information about risk to the child (NBHW, 2018). However, an investigation was only started in six cases, half of those reported. In addition, the NBHW found that the children were not recognised by the health services as family members when parents had severe problems, and many different people with knowledge of the child's situation did not notify Social Services. In none of the six cases investigated during year 2016–17 did the Social Services receive any concerns about the child's situation in the year before the child's death (NBHW, 2018). The second new regulation is the mandatory general guidelines about violence in close relationships (SOSFS, 2014). These were adopted after the death of an eight-year-old girl, who was killed by a relative with whom she lived. Before these guidelines, Social Services could make a preliminary assessment of a reported concern without starting an investigation. This is no longer possible: an investigation must be initiated promptly if there are any concerns about abuse or violence where children are present or subject to the abuse. This limits the discretion of social workers because they cannot use their own judgement in cases where they believe the concerns do not warrant an investigation.

Nevertheless, the NBHW's investigations of child deaths as a consequence of crime have had little or no significance for those involved as they do not lead to any new knowledge on the matter (Statskontoret, 2014). Rather, the investigations work as a reminder of the complex of problems related to child abuse. This is also in line with the conclusions of the Inquiry on Child Abuse and Neglect (Swedish Government, 2011a). It was not a lack of laws or regulations that resulted in serious neglect and abuse of children but the practitioners' failure to comply with laws.

Mandatory reports of mistreatment in Social Services are a tool for quality assurance. Since 2013, the Health and Social Care Inspectorate has monitored the reports that the local municipal boards considered serious. The number of reports from the children and family Social Services has increased from 109 in 2013 to 349 in 2017 (HSCI Statistics, 2013–17). The most commonly reported type of mistreatment concerning children and family Social Services during this period was failure to respect the legal rights of individual family members (HSCI Statistics, 2013–17). Most of these cases refer to the excessive time taken by social workers to investigate and remedy concerns about children and to find housing for newly arrived unaccompanied children. The reports present a picture of the most conspicuous problems within the Social Services' child protection work: too heavy a workload and very many children with refugee status, a rather 'new' issue for Sweden. The NBHW (2016) has also compiled the results of 66 serious reports of mistreatment within social child and youth care and interviewed social workers in the municipalities. This indicates that there is a high risk that concerns from the public and from social institutions, such as schools, are not dealt with promptly because of a shortage of social workers with the right skills and competence. The situation for planning and arranging the placement of children and youth in foster homes and in residential care homes is described as alarming.

The NBIC provides compulsory care and treatment for young persons under the age of 18 years under the terms of the CYPA. The NBIC also runs special residential homes for young people with psychosocial problems, substance abuse or criminal behaviour. The most commonly reported mistreatment in these settings also concerned individuals' legal rights followed by the misuse of coercive measures (NBHW, 2016). The staff can use certain coercive measures in threatening situations, for example locking up and isolating young residents for a period of time or applying physical restraint. The threshold for using coercive interventions, and how much and for how long, is indeed disputable. There are different perspectives and interpretations of the need for coercion. As yet there has been no evaluation to establish whether errors and mistakes are openly discussed nor how the agencies are learning from mistakes as a result of the reporting system.

In anticipation of social work licences, the Swedish social work professional organisations have introduced an authorisation system, aiming at ensuring that authorised social workers have the theoretical competence, practice experience and aptitude to work as a social worker in direct contact with patients and clients. In order to be authorised you need to have completed social work education and have 100 hours of supervision and support documents from managers and supervisors; social workers must also adhere to the ethical code for social work. So far, this system has not been successful, either in terms of encouraging many social workers become authorised (less than 15 per cent) or in terms of controlling bad practice (Dellgran and Höjer, 2005). As far as is known, nobody has been de-authorised nor been given any warnings because of their errors and mistakes despite the fact that these occur. Consequently, the professional organisations do not currently have their own system to sanction individual social workers who commit errors and mistakes.

Instead, the professional organisations and the universities work on a proactive basis, providing the best possible education and support for social workers to limit the risk of their making errors and mistakes. There are many examples of this within the professional discourse. The most evident is in social work education. Social workers learn the laws, learn and discuss ethical, professional practice, and students are tested on their own ethical behaviour in practice as well as their ability to function as a good social worker. Formal education as well as research in and about social work also has this as an underlying logic. According to this logic the result will be more educated and specialised social workers, who better understand both the situations of children and families as well as law and policy and commit fewer mistakes. However, a social work degree cannot be a guarantee that social workers will not commit errors and mistakes, whether due to the complexities inherent in child protection work, the sometimes very pressured situation within the Social Services or because of personal reasons and limitations in social workers themselves.

Besides social work education, perhaps the most noted action to prevent errors and mistakes in social work practice is the introduction of supervision and other forms of support. Supervision has, since its inception, always been described as having three main functions: administrative, supportive and educative (Bradley et al, 2010). The focus on these functions may vary in different contexts, but the underlying logic relates to issues of accountability and sustainability. Social workers should do the right thing and should be able to survive the complex and difficult activities inherent in child protection (Frost et al, 2018). In Sweden, the call for supervision by an external supervisor focusing on providing support has been high since the 1980s; the number of child protection social workers receiving supervision is around 90 per cent, and most of them report positive outcomes from supervision (Dellgran and Höjer, 2005; Bradley and Höjer, 2009). However, whether more supervision leads to fewer errors and mistakes in social work practice has yet to be examined.

Conclusion

In this chapter we have described and discussed how errors and mistakes are understood and responded to in Swedish child protection within a political-administrative approach where law, regulation and quality assurance are central, and highlighted the aspiration to introduce a licence for social workers. Examples of errors and mistakes have been given from reports of mistreatment and governmental reports. These reports show that there are some serious challenges with child protection in Sweden: there is a shortage of competent social workers and new legislation has not yet produced any improvements regarding errors and mistakes. Moreover, there is a need for a more pertinent discussion about what can be expected in relation to preventing errors and mistakes.

When child protection fails, the general understanding in Sweden is that the welfare, administrative and supervisory systems need to be adjusted with additional laws and regulations, including stronger quality assurance systems. New legislation has followed child homicides. Attention has also been given to the professionals and their organisations; that is, social workers who have the legal mandate to work with child protection. There is little discussion about social workers who deliberately use their powers illegally and the number of professionals convicted of wrongdoing is negligible. Other factors that shape child protection in Sweden is its family orientation and the potential breach of the rights of parents and children where parents are led to believe they are being supported when they are actually being investigated and monitored in the grey zone between voluntariness and coercion (for a longer discussion on this see Leviner, 2014).

The aims of mandatory reporting within Social Services and child protection are to protect the most vulnerable service-users, enable staff to report mistreatment and encourage staff to speak openly about errors and mistakes without the risk of reprisal. Learning by mistakes is paramount and, at least in theory, mandatory reporting comes within what has been described as a system approach. However, there is still not enough evidence of the results of reporting in child protection. Criticism has also been raised against the reporting procedure because it only leads to an internal investigation and because the administrative workload is increasing (Kjellberg, 2012).

It is, perhaps, within the professional approach that making claims about best practice in child protection is most evident. Any profession will claim they are the best to undertake certain tasks on the basis of their education, experience and professional culture. In social work it is, however, hard to examine the outcome of different measures. For example, listening to children's voices in cases of child protection may indeed seem necessary but the decision making may still be circumscribed by organisational or political limitations, leading to children feeling disappointed and deceived. There are still many knowledge gaps concerning how to better prevent errors and mistakes and to develop social work practice.

References

Brå (2013) *Statistics*. Available from: www.bra.se/statistik/kriminalstatistik/personer-lagforda-for-brott.html.

Bradley, G. and Höjer, S. (2009) 'Supervision Reviewed: Reflections on Two Different Social Work Models in England and Sweden', *European Journal of Social Work*, 12(1): 71–85.

Bradley, G., Engelbrecht, L. and Höjer, S. (2010) 'Supervision: A Force for Change? Three Stories Told', *International Social Work*, 53(6): 773–90.

Braye, S. and Preston-Shoot, M. (2006) 'The Role of Law in Welfare Reform: Critical Perspectives on the Relationship Between Law and Social Work Practice', *International Journal of Social Welfare*, 15(1): 19–26.

Burns, K., Pösö, T. and Skivenes, M. (eds) (2017) *Child Removals by the State: A Cross-Country Analysis of Decision-Making Systems*, New York: Oxford University Press.

Children's Ombudsman (2011) *Barnen som samhället svek – åtgärder med anledning av övergrepp och allvarliga försummelser i samhällsvården* [*Comment on Swedish Governmental Report 2011:9: The Children that Society Let Down – Measures Due to Abuse and Serious Neglect in Social Care*] (SOU 2011:9), Stockholm: Socialdepartementet.

Children's Ombudsman (2015) *Slutbetänkandet: Barns och ungas rätt vid tvångsvård. Förslag till ny LVU* [*The Rights of Children and Youth: Proposition to a New Act on Care for Young People*] (SOU, 2015:71), Stockholm: Socialdepartementet.

Council of Law (2017) *Lagrådsremiss 2017 – om barnkonventionen som blir lag* [*Comment from the Council of Law on child convention as legislation in Sweden*], Stockholm: Lagrådet.

Dellgran, P. and Höjer, S. (2005) 'Rörelser i tiden. Professionalisering och Privatisering i socialt arbete' ['Motions in Time: Professionalisation and Privatisation in Social Work'], *Socialvetenskaplig tidskrift*, 12(2/3): 246–67.

Donaldson, L.P., Hill, K., Ferguson, S. Fogel, S. and Erickson, C. (2014) 'Contemporary Social Work Licensure: Implications for Macro Social Work Practice and Education', *Social Work*, 59(1): 52–61.

Forkby, T., Höjer, S. and Liljegren, A. (2015) 'Questions of Control in Child Protection Decision Making: Laypersons' Monitoring and Governance in Child Protection Committees in Sweden', *Journal of Social Work*, 15(5): 537–57.

Frost, E., Höjer, S., Campanini, A., Sicora, A. and Kullberg, K. (2018) 'Why Do They Stay? A Study of Resilient Child Protection Workers in Three European Countries', *European Journal for Social Work*, 21(4): 485–97.

Gilbert, N., Parton, N. and Skivenes, M. (eds) (2011) *Child Protection Systems: International Trends and Orientations*, New York: Oxford University Press.

Heimer, M., Näsman, E. and Palme, J. (2018) 'Vulnerable Children's Rights to Participation, Protection, and Provision: The Process of Defining the Problem in Swedish Child and Family Welfare', *Child & Family Social Work*, 23(2): 316–23.

Hjern, A., Brendler-Lindqvist, M. and Norredam, M. (2012) 'Age Assessment of Young Asylum Seekers', *Acta Paediatrica*, 101(1): 4–7.

Höjer, I., Sallnäs, M. and Sjöblom, Y. (2012) *När samhället träder in – barn, föräldrar och social barnavård* [*When Society Steps In – Children, Parents and Social Care of Children*], Lund: Studentlitteratur.

Höjer, S., Liljegren, A. and Forkby, T. (2014) 'Lekmän inom den sociala barnavården' ['The Layperson Within Social Care of Children'], *Socionomens forskningssupplement*, 2(35): 42–54.

HSCI (Health and Social Care Inspectorate) Statistics (2013–17) *Lex Maria och lex Sarah [Maria's Law and Sarah's Law]*. Available from: www.ivo.se/om-ivo/statistik/lex-maria-och-lex-sarah/.

Hultman, E., Forkby, T. and Höjer, S. (2018) 'Professionalised, Hybrid, and Layperson Models in Nordic Child Protection: Actors in Decision-Making in Out of Home Placements', *Nordic Social Work Research*, ahead of print: https://doi.org/10.1080/2156857X.2018.1538897.

Johansson, S., Dellgran, P. and Höjer, S. (eds) (2015) *Människobehandlande organisationer. Villkor för ledning, styrning och professionellt välfärdsarbete [Human Service Organizations: Conditions for Management, Governance and Professional Welfare Work]*, Stockholm: Natur & Kultur.

Kjellberg, I. (2012) 'Klagomålshantering och lex Sarah-anmälningar i äldreomsorgen. En institutionell etnografisk studie' ['Complaints Procedures and Mandatory Report in Swedish Elder Care: An Institutional Ethnography'], doctoral thesis, University of Gothenburg.

Leviner, P. (2014) 'Child Protection Under Swedish Law: Legal Duality and Uncertainty', *European Journal of Social Work*, 17(2): 206–20.

Linell, H. (2017) 'The Characteristics and Extent of Child Abuse: Findings from a Study of the Swedish Social Services Child Protection', *European Journal of Social Work*, 20(2): 231–41.

Lundström, T. (2017) 'Från sedlig försummelse till brister i omsorgen, om barnavårdslagstiftningens historia' ['From Moral Neglect to Lack of Care: The History of Childcare Legislation'], in P. Leviner and T. Lundström (eds) *Tvångsvård av barn och unga: rättigheter, utmaningar och gränszoner [Custodial Care for Children and Youth: Rights, Challenges and Borders]*, Stockholm: Wolters Kluwer, pp 43–58.

Macdonald, K.M. (1995) *The Sociology of the Professions*, London: Sage.

Mattson, T. (2010) *Rätten till familj inom barn- och ungdomsvården [The Right to Family Within the Social Child and Youth Care System]*, Malmö: Liber.

Meeuwisse, A., Sunesson, S. and Swärd, H. (2000) *Grundbok i socialt arbete [Basic Book of Social Work]*, Stockholm: Natur & Kultur.

Munro, E. (2005) 'A Systems Approach to Investigating Child Abuse Deaths', *British Journal of Social Work*, 35(4): 531–46.

National Board of Health and Welfare (2016) *Lägesbild av socialtjänsten [Situational Picture of the Social Services]*, Stockholm: Socialstyrelsen.

National Board of Health and Welfare (2018) *Dödsfallsutredningar 2016–2017 [Investigations of Deaths 2016–2017]*, Stockholm: Socialstyrelsen.

Rytterström, P., Unosson, M. and Arman, M. (2012) 'Care Culture as a Meaning-Making Process: A Study of a Mistreatment Investigation', *Qualitative Health Research*, 23(9): 1179–87.

SCB (2019) *Befolkningsstatistik i sammandrag 1960–2017* [*Summary of Population Statistics 1960–2017*]. Available from: www.scb.se/hitta-statistik/statistik-efter-amne/befolkning/befolkningens-sammansattning/befolkningsstatistik/pong/tabell-och-diagram/helarsstatistik--riket/befolkningsstatistik-i-sammandrag.

Sjöström, M. (2013) *To Blend In or Stand Out? Hospital Social Workers' Jurisdictional Work in Sweden and Germany*, Skriftserien [Writing Series] 2013:2, University of Gothenburg.

Söderlind, I. and Sköld, J. (2018) 'Privata utförare av social barnavård. En affär under flera sekel' ['Private Providers of Child Protection: A Business over Decades'] in M. Sallnäs and S. Wiklund (eds) *Socialtjänstmarknaden: om marknadsorientering och konkurrensutsättning av individ och familjeomsorgen* [*The Market of Social Services: Market Orientation and Exposure for Competition of Child and Family Social Services*], Stockholm: Liber, pp 30–60.

SOSFS (2011) *Ledningssystem för systematiskt kvalitetsarbete* [*Management System for Systematic Quality Work*], SOSFS (2011:9), Stockholm: Socialstyrelsens.

SOSFS (2014) *Allmänna råd. Om våld i nära relationer* [*General Guidelines: About Violence in Close Relationships*], SOFS (2014:4), Stockholm: Socialstyrelsens.

Statskontoret (2014) *Sorgen finns det inga ord för. Om utredningar av vissa dödsfall* [*There Are No Words for Grief: Investigations of Certain Deaths*], Statskontoret (2014:19), Stockholm: Statskontoret.

Svensson, G. and Höjer, S. (2017) 'Placing Children in State Care in Sweden: Decision-Making Bodies, Laypersons and Legal Framework', in K. Burns, T. Pösö and M. Skivenes (eds) *Child Removals by the State: A Cross-Country Analysis of Decision-Making Systems*, New York: Oxford University Press, pp 65–88.

SWEA (2018) *Work Environment Report 2017*, Stockholm: Arbetsmiljöverket.

Swedish Government (2011a) *Vanvård i social barnavård. Slutbetänkande* [*The Swedish Inquiry on Child Abuse and Neglect in Institutions and Foster Homes: Final Report*] (SOU 2011:61), Stockholm: Fritzes.

Swedish Government (2011b) *Barnen som samhället svek – åtgärder med anledning av övergrepp och allvarliga försummelser i samhällsvården* [*The Inquiry on Redress for Past Abuse*] (SOU 2011:9), Stockholm: Fritzes.

UNCRC (United Nations Committee on the Rights of the Child) (2009) *Concluding Observations: Sweden 2009*, CRC/SWE/CO/ 4. Available from: www2.ohchr.org/english/bodies/crc/docs/co/ CRC-C-SWE-CO-4.pdf.

Wingfors, S.S. (2004) *Socionomyrkets professionalisering* [*The Professionalization of Social Work*], University of Gothenburg.

9

Errors and mistakes in child protection in Switzerland: a missed opportunity of reflection?

Brigitte Müller, Kay Biesel and Clarissa Schär

Introduction

For Switzerland, two lines of discourse can be roughly reconstructed in the field of errors and mistakes: a historically oriented discourse on abusive practices of child removals and placements and a contemporary oriented discourse on fatal cases in child protection in the context of a new organisation of authorities. What both lines have in common is that they have not (yet) led to an explicit debate on errors and mistakes in Switzerland.

The chapter begins with a short introduction to the Swiss child protection system and then summarises how coercive child removals practised until the mid-20th century have led to harm, injustice and suffering for many children and their families. It describes how the historical appraisal of this past practice fuelled a debate on abusive practices under the cover of child protection, which prompted a federal Act entitling survivors to reparation payments. The chapter further depicts which discourses and developments preceded the revision of the child and adult protection law in the Swiss Civil Code in 2013. The amended legislation aimed at professionalising child protection proceedings and included a pivotal shift from lay to professional decision-making bodies. The current state of this process that has led to criticism from politicians, the public and the media, particularly with regard to negative or even fatal outcomes of child protection cases, is analysed and discussed. Strategies for avoiding and dealing with errors and mistakes are described. Using this background, the need for an explicit discourse on errors and mistakes in child protection in Switzerland is outlined.

The child protection system in Switzerland today: a brief overview

Switzerland is a federal state consisting of 26 cantons, divided into 2,249 municipalities (Schnurr, 2017: 117). The cantons have their own parliaments, governments, courts and constitutions, and regulate the division of responsibilities between them and the municipalities (Bundeskanzlei, 2018: 13). Official languages are (Swiss-)German (63 per cent), French (23 per cent), Italian (8 per cent) and Romansh (0.5 per cent) (Bundeskanzlei, 2018: 8). Switzerland has 8.5 million inhabitants, 25 per cent of whom are foreign nationals (2.12 million) and 14.5 per cent (1.70 million) are children aged from zero to 19 (Bundesamt für Statistik, 2018: 7).

Child protection in Switzerland is described as a system with voluntary, public, civil law and criminal law sectors (Rosch and Hauri, 2016; Biesel and Urban-Stahl, 2018: 29–30). In the voluntary field, children and parents have access to multipurpose social services, child and youth welfare services, family centres, counselling services (maternal/paternal, parenting or victim counselling agencies), health promotion services, and medical and psychiatric treatment. In the public field, preschools (kindergartens) and schools have the task of cooperating with parents in the interest of the child. They may encourage and initiate support for children and their families (school social work, therapeutic and special educational support, speech therapy, school psychology). The staff of these institutions are legally required to inform the Child and Adult Authority (CAPA) if they suspect that a child is at risk. Under civil law, CAPAs are responsible for receiving and processing information on children at risk, for initiating further assessments and ordering child protection measures according to the Swiss Civil Code (SCC), if necessary against the will of the family. They are the only administrative bodies authorised to limit parents' rights, for example of custody. Lastly, the police and the judiciary are responsible for prosecuting crimes that threaten the well-being of children and for organising victim support under the criminal law.

Switzerland's child protection system is unique in international comparison. It is structured and organised differently in each canton. Two key institutions are relevant for child protection and children's welfare: social services or child and youth welfare services, and CAPAs. The CAPAs are court-like administrative bodies or courts led by either municipalities, cantons or inter-municipal alliances. Some 146 CAPAs cover regions with populations ranging from 16,000 to 396,000 (KOKES, 2017). Legislation allows the CAPAs to delegate the assessment of children at risk to social services or to child and youth welfare services.

Jud and Gartenhauser (2015: 342) describe the Swiss child protection system as family-oriented (compare Gilbert et al, 2011: 255). Schnurr (2017) by contrast argues that only CAPAs are institutionalised across the country and subject to federal legislation (SCC). In contrast, social services or child and youth welfare services differ considerably between the cantons with regard to types of services and accessibility. Less than half of the cantons have passed laws on access to services for children, young people and families, which illustrates the plurality of structures and systems. In the light of this, Schnurr states that the system in Switzerland is risk-oriented or child-protection oriented, with an emphasis on legal interventions (Schnurr, 2017: 118).

Child removals in Switzerland in the early and mid-20th century: coercive measures and the Reparation Initiative

'Protecting' children from disadvantaged families

From the 19th century up to the mid-20th century, children – mainly of poor families in rural areas – were 'thinged' or placed in children's homes in reaction to a still undeveloped welfare system. 'Thinging' was a practice in which the authorities placed children in foster families – often farmers – who received money for taking them. The children had to work for their subsistence, could not attend school regularly, and were often exposed to neglect and abuse, which for some even resulted in death (Hugger, 1998; Wohlwend and Honegger, 2004; Heller et al, 2005; Tabin et al, 2010). The exact number of children who were 'thinged' over the decades is unknown; some researchers estimate that in the early 20th century between 4 per cent and 10 per cent of all children were subject to this practice (Leuenberger et al, 2011). In residential care, children also often suffered harsh physical punishments and psychological and sexual abuse (Akermann et al, 2012; Expertenkommission Ingenbohl, 2013).

Other coercive measures practised in the 20th century concerned children of Yenish families, traditionally vagrant people in Switzerland (Leimgruber et al, 1998; Galle, 2016). A private foundation initiated the Relief Agency for the Children of the Country Roads in 1926 and, until 1973, removed about 600 children from their families. The stated goal of the Relief Agency was to end the vagrant lifestyle of the Yenish. Yenish people were negatively stereotyped as vagabonds who were stealing, begging and drinking. Against the background of contemporary eugenic, socio-racist ideas, they were perceived as genetically inferior and incapable of raising children to become settled and productive citizens (Ramsauer, 2000; Galle, 2016). Numerous Yenish children ended up in residential care, often in institutions for people with disabilities where many of them became victims of humiliation and abuse (Galle and Meier, 2009; Galle, 2016).

A common factor in these coercive measures taken to 'protect' children was the absence (or weakness) of the state's supervisory function, leaving children completely at the mercy of their carers (Leuenberger et al, 2011). The detrimental living conditions and victimisation of some of these children was a key factor for the historical appraisal of the early and mid-20th century practices of child removals and placements. These practices do not correspond to the criteria of errors or mistakes discussed in Chapter 2 of this book, by Biesel and Cottier, as the persons responsible for the removals were not child protection professionals deviating from legal or professional standards, but mostly laypersons. Nonetheless, the removals were clearly violations of the children's rights and integrity. The children were exposed to harmful and traumatic experiences in settings supposed to protect them and the state, if not approving it, tolerated it.

The Reparation Initiative

In the early 1990s, autobiographical reports of formerly placed children triggered a debate and historical appraisal of the coercive measures and child removals described previously (Leuenberger and Seglias, 2008; Nett and Spratt, 2012: 59). Later, a series of studies made clear that the 'well-being' of the children taken into custody was used to justify interventions such as those of the Relief Agency. However, in contrast to current practice, the concept was not rooted in knowledge about children's needs and rights but corresponded with prevailing moral conceptions about proper conduct and negative stereotypes of marginalised, poor or ethnic minority families (Leuenberger and Seglias, 2008). The practice of 'thinging' children or making them work for their keep served primarily as a cost-efficient way to manage poverty and to 'protect' society from those regarded as a potential threat to law and order (Spratt et al, 2015: 1516).

Taking into account the abusive character of coercive measures was the basis of the central claim of the Reparation Initiative: that the state was accountable for the suffering of the children who were removed from their families, and was thus obligated to pay reparations. The Reparation Initiative, submitted in December 2014, aimed at reappraising the history of the child removals in Switzerland up to the 1980s. The Swiss parliament and the Federal Council responded to the initiative by creating a federal Act entitling victims to receive payments from a terminable fund. In doing so, the state 'admitted' to having failed to protect children from harm, and publicly apologised to the victims for their suffering. In the years 2017 and 2018, approximately 8,000 persons applied for compensation and received payments. In addition to the apology and compensation, a comprehensive scientific review shed light on the conditions, dynamics and consequences of coercive measures directed at children in the 20th century. A crucial finding of these studies was that the children experienced the facts that their dignity was disregarded and the opportunity to participate and be heard in decision-making was denied as similarly traumatic to the abuse and neglect they suffered in foster families and care homes (Wohlwend and Honegger, 2004; Freisler-Mühlemann, 2011; Akermann et al, 2012).

The process that enabled victims of undue state interventions to speak out and experience justice and public discussion of past wrongs occurred in the two decades following Switzerland's ratification of the United Nations Convention on the Rights of the Child (UNCRC). In the same period, the Federal Council prepared the last of a series of revisions of the SCC, the revision of the 'custodian law'. Although from today's perspective the coercive measures practised in the early and mid-20th century clearly violate basic human rights and are incompatible with the UNCRC, the insights of the historical appraisal were only marginally linked to the revision of the law and the implementation of the UNCRC (Bundesrat, 2012). Debates such as what the experiences with past practice meant for the future structure and procedures in child protection or the threshold and conditions for state interventions in families were restricted to the academic community (Bütow et al, 2014).

Development of a professional child protection system

Raising awareness for child protection after the mid-20th century and the revision of the Swiss Civil Code

In Switzerland, the question how to protect children better from violence and neglect within the family became a public, political and professional concern only 30 years ago (Wiederkehr, 2013: 18). In the 1960s, child protection groups were operative in a few paediatric clinics, in 1975 the first child protection centre opened its gates and in 1982, the Swiss Child Protection League, dedicated to supporting families in need with the objective of preventing child maltreatment instead of merely prosecute it was founded (Wiederkehr, 2013: 18). These organisations saw a need to address child protection issues.

Paralleling these initiatives, child protection more and more became a political issue. The Swiss Civil Code of 1912 had defined the field as a lay-based system; a system in which the members of the Guardianship Authorities were elected political office holders in municipalities with a considerable scope to make decisions as they saw fit (Schnyder et al, 1995: 26–8; Affolter, 2013: 11). Moreover, the same (lay) person often assessed a child's situation and his or her well-being, decided on interventions, and executed and coordinated these interventions and measures (Affolter, 2013: 11). In small municipalities, the people who took decisions in child protection cases were personally acquainted with the families involved; a closeness that must be considered inadequate with regard to objective and neutral proceedings (Schnurr, 2012: 125–6). Moreover, the persons responsible for child protection as a rule did not have extensive professional knowledge and lacked in-depth judicial competence, which made them having to rely overly on external experts (Konferenz der kantonalen Vormundschaftsbehörden, 2008: 75; Schnurr, 2012).

In 1988, the Federal Department of Home Affairs mandated a group of experts to gather data about forms, prevalence and causes of child maltreatment and neglect, and to propose measures for the prevention and handling of physical and sexual abuse of children (Arbeitsgruppe Kindesmisshandlung, 1992; Bundesamt für Sozialversicherung, 2005: 12). Based on the report, the Swiss Federal Council (Bundesrat, 2006) initiated a decisive change in legislation in 1993. The revision was required because the 1912 law's conceptualisation and wording stemmed from the 19th century (Affolter, 2013: 10) and was thus outdated in many ways. As the same section of the SCC regulates child and adult protection, the reform affected and changed child protection substantially. The most pivotal change in legislation concerned the structure, organisation and procedures of child and adult protection under civil law: the guardianship authorities were completely restructured and transformed from lay boards to professionalised interdisciplinary authorities (CAPAs). The new organisational form aimed at reducing the number of authorities and persons in charge and at professionalising the child and adult protection system through appointing staff from different professional and disciplinary backgrounds (law, social work, accounting, psychology, medicine) (Cottier and Steck, 2012; Schnurr, 2012: 125–7). Child protection proceedings were to include – in accordance with the UNCRC – the right of the child to be heard 'in person' and to have a legal representative (Bundesrat, 2006; Cottier and Steck, 2012). The new law on child and adult protection and the new CAPA became operative in January 2013.

The law can be seen as a result of changing perspectives on the state's role in protecting children. Increased international awareness of children's needs and of the necessity to ensure adequate living conditions and protection from harm for every child had an impact on how the functionality of the Swiss child protection system was appraised. Another important impact was the ratification of the UNCRC in 1997 (Nett and Spratt, 2012: 31–3), which was a turning point for child protection both internationally and in Switzerland. Together, all these aspects led, in the sense of 'common imperatives' (Spratt et al, 2015: 1512), to a broader national discussion of child maltreatment and neglect and its prevention (Bundesamt für Sozialversicherung, 2005), and to the discussion of the legislative changes that might be necessary to develop a modern child protection system (compare Bundesrat, 2012). However, neither the general discussion nor the reform of the SCC have broached the topic of errors and mistakes in child protection, either with regard to the past or with regard to what sources of errors and mistakes the new system might generate and what measures could be taken to avoid, prevent or handle these.

Effects of the reorganisation and professionalisation of child protection

The short time that has passed since the new law on child and adult protection was implemented in 2013 precludes a concluding analysis of the advantages and disadvantages of the new regulations in comparison with the former system. For instance, although hearing the child's wishes, views and interests has been formally introduced to child protection proceedings, it remains unclear how this is put into practice (Hitz Quenon et al, 2014). To date there are few evaluations of the new system (Ecoplan and Hochschule für Soziale Arbeit Wallis, 2013; Rieder et al, 2016; Schwenkel et al, 2016; Bundesrat, 2017). Their findings – although preliminary – show that, as intended, the number of authorities and decision-making bodies reduced from over 1,400 to 146 (Rieder et al, 2016: 6). There is still a considerable heterogeneity in the organisation and form of the new CAPAs (Fassbind, 2013: 15) due to the federalist structures and the principle of subsidiarity that regulates the competencies between the federation, cantons and municipalities. The plurality of organisational forms makes it difficult to answer the question whether one specific model performs better or produces more favourable outcomes than another (Fassbind, 2013: 17; Rieder et al, 2016: 5). As the reform introduced a completely new administrative structure in the field, there were some initial challenges for the new CAPAs. They had to take over all the cases held by the former authorities, reorganise the dossiers and simultaneously start working in newly assembled, multi-professional teams. Moreover, the CAPAs had to establish procedures and build new forms of cooperation with other relevant stakeholders (Fassbind, 2013: 16). This led – in the beginning – to uncertainties and in some cases to delays in case handling and processing (Fassbind, 2013: 16).

Development of the political and public debate

The revision taking effect in January 2013 triggered considerable criticism from the media, which suggested the new system brought bureaucratisation and overly intrusive interventions in families by the authorities. This culminated in the great scandal of a child protection case in which a mother killed her two children, fearing they might be taken back to the children's home after a holiday stay at home in the village of Flaach in Zurich Canton (Direktion der Justiz und des Inneren, 2016). The 'Flaach case' was the starting point for a media campaign against the CAPAs creating a negative public attitude towards the authorities. Particularly criticised were supposedly poor and insensitive communications by CAPAs with families and other stakeholders, interventions perceived as disproportionate, the assumed cost overrun of the new system and the heterogeneity in structures and processes (Direktion der Justiz und des Inneren, 2016). On a political level, the critical appraisal condensed into several parliamentary motions that the Federal Council answered in a report in 2017 (Bundesrat, 2017). The report showed that since their formation in 2013 and despite the initial shortcomings, the CAPAs, together with the cantons, had already taken a multitude of measures to optimise their structures and proceedings (Bundesrat, 2017: 29). The report attested to the CAPAs' appropriate standard of work and negated the assumption that the number of statutory measures in child and adult protection had risen to a level where costs were significantly higher (Bundesrat, 2017: 29). The report further recommended the development of appropriate standards, for instance with regard to the assessment of children at risk. However, these regulations are not seen as requiring federal legislation (Bundesrat, 2017: 6). The Flaach and other cases treated as scandals by the media (see Rouiller, 2018) drew attention to deficiencies in Swiss child protection as outlined earlier. However, these cases are not analysed and compared systematically; consequently, it remains unclear whether their negative outcomes relate to the individual characteristics of the cases and the persons involved, to difficulties rooted in the respective cantons' specific structures and child protection proceedings, or to general flaws in the Swiss system.

Since 2017 and continuing at the time of writing, the public and political debate has taken two directions. On the one hand, the negative media coverage already mentioned has somewhat decreased, and a majority of political and administrative executive authorities acknowledge the advantages of the new system. On the other hand, there have been political initiatives to change basic paragraphs and standards in the new law. In 2017, the population of the canton Schwyz voted over the popular petition (*Volksinitiative*) 'No paternalism towards citizens and municipalities' that aimed to reallocate the competence to determine interventions in child and adult protection to the municipalities. Only a narrow majority of voters in the canton Schwyz (51.4 per cent) voted against this change in legislation. Another initiative, the 'CAPA initiative', launched in 2018 and at the time of this writing in the phase of collecting signatures from voters, aims at requiring CAPAs to appoint family members as legal guardians in any child or adult protection case, and to codify this in the Federal Constitution. If the initiative is signed by 100,000 voters, it will be summited to parliament by the end of 2019.

Apart from scepticism against state intervention in families that can be seen partly as a result of past practices, a reason for this articulated scepticism towards the newly created authorities is rooted in political tradition. The Swiss direct democracy understands 'the people' as the ultimate source of political power, sovereign (Nett and Spratt, 2012: 58–60), with civil rights at the core of participating in matters of public interest (Nett and Spratt, 2012: 58–60). Politicians in the Swiss parliament and office holders in executives of municipalities are voted into office while keeping 'regular', income-generating work. This long-standing tradition (called the militia system) may contribute to the reluctance of Swiss voters to delegate political power upwards, to courts or authorities. Moreover, a conservative-traditionalist view of the family means the protection of privacy is highly valued while state intervention in families is viewed critically.

Dealing with errors and mistakes in child protection in Switzerland

Strategies to avoid and handle errors and mistakes in child protection

Until now, neither the historical appraisal of the suffering of victims of welfare-related coercive measures nor the reform of the legislation that renewed the structures of the Swiss child protection system have triggered an open debate on errors and mistakes. Therefore, it is difficult to identify explicit strategies to avoid and manage errors and mistakes in child protection in Switzerland. Moreover, the question of what is seen as an 'error', a 'mistake' or 'critical incident' (Gehrlach et al, 2016) and who or what is responsible lacks any conclusive answer. For instance, the main purpose of one investigation of the Flaach case was to find out whether there were any legal violations by professionals of the CAPA involved. The investigation thus aimed at detecting errors made by the CAPA and their professionals. There was no intention to identify mistakes – actions or inactions based on misbeliefs, misconceptions or misunderstanding the situation – or to shed light on weaknesses or dysfunctions of the CAPA or other organisations in the system (see Chapter 2). The results of the investigation indicated that there was no clear correlation between the actions of the authority or the professionals and the children's killing (Kanton Zürich, 2016). No errors deviating from legal and/or professional standards, care or duties that violate the children's or the mother's personal rights were made in the case.

In sum, strategies for dealing with errors and mistakes in Switzerland have been limited to providing financial compensation and reviewing, scientifically, the coercive measures of the past, and analysing current critical or fatal child protection cases through investigations focusing on legal matters.

Such cases, however, and the respective reports are not common (Gehrlach et al, 2016) and there is no legal obligation to investigate child death or significant cases (Axford and Bullock, 2005: 34, 57). Again, it depends on the cantons whether a case is investigated further (Axford and Bullock, 2005: 84). The CAPAs' supervisory authorities in the cantons usually mandate official investigations in fatal cases. These, as in the Flaach case, examine whether members of CAPAs or other services have followed legal requirements, and to clarify questions of accountability. They usually include inspections of CAPAs and training for their members, but do not promote professional or organisational learning. The report recommendations instruct CAPAs and other services to adhere correctly to regulations, or to revise and refine their procedures. In light of the lack of systematic analysis of these cases, it comes as little surprise that they have, thus far, not triggered a more general discussion about errors and mistakes in child protection.

Other measures connected with the topic of errors and mistakes include evaluations of child protection practice, mostly commissioned by federal or cantonal administrations (Ecoplan and Hochschule für Soziale Arbeit Wallis, 2013; Rieder et al, 2016; Schwenkel et al, 2016; Bundesrat, 2017), but these do not refer to defined concepts of errors or mistakes explicitly. Their objective is to identify weaknesses in the current system in order to reform laws and regulations. Further, university research and development projects aim at increasing quality in child protection practice. In the last five years, a number of projects were initiated to develop and test assessment instruments and procedures. As in many other aspects of the Swiss child protection system, there are no guidelines or common standards on how to assess the situation and well-being of children at risk (Biesel and Schnurr, 2014). Two important frameworks for the improvement of assessment in child protection have been developed since 2013 in Swiss Schools of Social Work: the Bernese and Lucerne Assessment Instrument for Child Protection (Hauri et al, 2016) and the *Process Manual for Dialogical-Systemic Assessment of the Well-Being of the Child* (Biesel et al, 2017b). Of course, these tools are not patent solutions. They require qualified professionals and well-structured organisations, and are not designed to help professionals to avoid mistakes, but to support them in collecting, sorting and interpreting case information and reflecting on this information so as to consider and identify effective measures to protect children at risk.

New non-governmental organisations

Apart from the evaluations and development of new instruments and procedures, which are not linked directly to errors and mistakes, a number of non-governmental organisations in Switzerland are engaged in improving child protection. Examples are the foundation Child Protection Switzerland and the Child Rights Network. They advocate for greater consideration of children's rights, child-friendly justice and the prevention of domestic violence. A special organisation for child protection in Switzerland is the Conference for Child and Adult Protection (KOKES). The KOKES connects the cantonal supervisory authorities for child and adult protection by civil law. The reputation and legitimacy of the KOKES is considerable, but its work only focuses on child and adult protection matters relevant to civil law. New initiatives like the Contact Point for Child and Adult Protection (KESCHA) or the Association for Quality in Child Protection in Switzerland (IGQK) try to supplement the activities of the KOKES and the existing non-governmental organisations.

KESCHA is a non-governmental advisory centre founded in January 2017 to advise clients who feel they are inadequately involved in care order proceedings brought by CAPAs. However, KESCHA does not intervene in cases or contact the CAPAs directly. Its aim is to prevent escalation through offering telephone counselling and discussing the clients' perspective, rather than to identify and avoid errors and mistakes in child protection cases. A recent report (Jungo and Schöbi, 2018) highlights that KESCHA was contacted mostly by parents of children involved in child protection cases. The cases concerned conflicts over visiting rights, parental care, custody, or the child's place of residence, and, less frequently, placements and guardianship in general.

IGQK is an independent association, founded in 2016, whose members are either individuals from a variety of professional backgrounds, scientists of various disciplines, or organisations like CAPAs, social services or child and youth welfare services, or children's homes. IGQK has organised quality workshops on child protection themes and the first national 'Quality Dialogue in Child Protection' (Biesel and Hauri, 2018). An important result of the Quality Dialogue was the insight that in view of the different child protection systems in the Swiss cantons, it would be apt to establish a federal child protection or child and youth welfare law. A federal Act would allow child protection structures and services to be harmonised and generally binding quality standards to be developed. In addition, the Quality Dialogue made clear that practitioners lack the time to exchange ideas, take part in skill enhancement courses and to improve quality across the different fields of child protection and between different organisations and CAPAs in the cantons.

Conclusion

Child protection in Switzerland has undergone significant changes since 2013. Although empirical knowledge of the field is still limited, it is reasonable to assume that the newly established authorities and proceedings support more sound processes of assessment and decision making than the preceding system. The cantons are currently consolidating their implementation of the changes and adjustments described in this chapter, and the CAPAs continually try to improve their practice. The high degree of autonomy of the cantons that is typical in Switzerland allowed them to establish structures that fit local or regional needs and resources. However, it is also left to the cantons whether and how they address the potential sources of errors and mistakes in the several fields of child protection as an issue, and what measures to use where cases take a course detrimental to a child's well-being, or where structural problems such as case overload or lack of inter-organisational coordination accumulate. As at the time of writing, there has been no national public, political and professional debate on errors and mistakes in child protection in Switzerland. There are no comprehensive strategies to analyse, avoid and manage them, and thus far, the activities of the supervisory authorities have been almost entirely restricted to identifying breaches of legislation and regulations, not reviewing professional or quality standards. Moreover, there seems to be an implicit attitude in the field that the revision of the SCC aimed at professionalising the decision-making bodies and systemising procedures is sufficient both to improve the Swiss child protection system and to guarantee adequate standards in handling and processing cases.

There has been hardly any research on errors and mistakes in child protection in Switzerland (see Gehrlach et al, 2016). It is unclear whether, where and how errors and mistakes occur, what factors may contribute to them and how potential errors and mistakes could be avoided. In addition, there are many unknowns: what professionals think about errors and mistakes in child protection; what conceptualisations of errors and mistakes they work with; which approaches they use to prevent errors and mistakes; and what strategies they apply in dealing with incidents and outcomes of child protection cases they perceive as erroneous. Moreover, it is an open question how children and parents involved in child protection perceive and define as errors or mistakes. In the national research programme Welfare and Coercion (Swiss National Science Foundation, 2017), initiated in 2017, the mechanisms and effects of Swiss welfare policy and child protection practices are being analysed. The programme focuses mainly on coercive measures in the past; however, some of the research projects include the current practice of adult and child protection. It is as yet unclear how the study findings will influence future debates in the field. In addition, as experts, professionals, politicians, the media and the public focused on the structural changes and their effects, they temporarily lost sight of other important conceptual and methodical questions: what helps to protect children and youth at risk? What can be done, preventively, to support families in need before problems escalate? What is 'good quality' child protection and how can it be achieved in the current system? How can adequate communication between stakeholders be guaranteed? What does it take to involve children and parents better in child protection proceedings (Biesel et al, 2017a)?

Non-governmental organisations have taken up these matters and are presently advancing the discourse around quality in child protection, which – if only implicitly – includes the topic of errors and mistakes. In the near future, it will be necessary to move on to a more active, explicit and profound discussion about errors and mistakes in child protection in Switzerland, a discussion that goes beyond the question of accountability, produces knowledge that helps to understand families in which children are neglected or mistreated better, and creates opportunities to learn for practitioners and researchers alike.

References

Affolter, K. (2013) 'Die Totalrevision des Vormundschaftsrechts' ['The Complete Revision of the Custodian Law'], *SozialAktuell*, 45(1): 10–14.

Akermann, M., Furrer, M. and Jenzer, S. (2012) *Bericht Kinderheime im Kanton Luzern im Zeitraum von 1930–1970* [*Report on Children's Homes in the Canton Lucerne Between 1930 and 1970*], Lucerne: Gesundheits- und Sozialdepartement des Kantons Luzern.

Arbeitsgruppe Kindesmisshandlung (1992) *Kindesmisshandlungen in der Schweiz. Schlussbericht zuhanden des Vorsteher des Eidgenössischen Departements des Innern* [*Child Maltreatment in Switzerland: Final Report FAO Minister of Internal Affairs*], Bern: Schweizerische Eidgenossenschaft.

Axford, N. and Bullock, R. (2005) *Child Death and Significant Case Reviews: International Approaches – Report to the Scottish Executive*, Edinburgh: Information and Analytical Services Division, Scottish Executive Education Department.

Biesel, K. and Hauri, A. (2018) 'Kinderschutz im Dialog zwischen Anspruch und Wirklichkeit' ['Child Protection in Dialogue Between Claim and Reality'], *Zeitschrift für Kindes- und Erwachsenenschutz*, 73(6): 500–1.

Biesel, K. and Schnurr, S. (2014) 'Abklärungen im Kindesschutz: Chancen und Risiken in der Anwendung von Verfahren und Instrumenten zur Erfassung von Kindeswohlgefährdung' ['Assessment in Child Protection: Chances and Risks of Instruments and Tools to Assess Children at Risk'], *Zeitschrift für Kindes- und Erwachsenenschutz*, 69(1): 63–71.

Biesel, K. and Urban-Stahl, U. (2018) *Lehrbuch Kinderschutz* [*Textbook of Child Protection*], Weinheim: Beltz Juventa.

Biesel, K., Fellmann, L. and Schär, C. (2017a) 'Augen zu und durch?! Wie Klientinnen und Klienten Kindeswohlabklärungen erleben und was sie sich wünschen' ['Head Down and Charge?! How Clients Experience Assessments of Children at Risk and What They Wish For'], *Zeitschrift für Kindes- und Erwachsenenschutz*, 72(4): 291–303.

Biesel, K., Fellmann, L., Müller, B., Schär, C. and Schnurr, S. (2017b) *Prozessmanual. Dialogisch-systemische Kindeswohlabklärung* [*Process Manual for Dialogical-Systemic Assessment of the Well-Being of the Child*], Bern: Haupt.

Bundesamt für Sozialversicherung (2005) *Gewalt gegen Kinder: Konzept für eine umfassende Prävention* [*Violence Against Children: Concept for a Comprehensive Prevention*], Bern: Schweizerische Eidgenossenschaft.

Bundesamt für Statistik (2018) *Die Bevölkerung der Schweiz 2017* [*The Population of Switzerland 2017*], Neuchâtel: Schweizerische Eidgenossenschaft.

Bundeskanzlei (2018) *The Swiss Confederation: A Brief Guide*. Available from: www.bk.admin.ch/bk/en/home/dokumentation/the-swiss-confederation--a-brief-guide.html.

Bundesrat (2006) *Botschaft vom 28. Juni 2006 zur Änderung des Schweizerischen Zivilgesetzbuches (Erwachsenenschutz, Personenrecht und Kindesrecht)* [*Governmental Commentary on the Amendments in Swiss Civil Code (Adult Law, Personal Law, Children's Law) from 28 June 2006*], Bern: Schweizerische Eidgenossenschaft.

Bundesrat (2012) *Gewalt und Vernachlässigung in der Familie: notwendige Massnahmen im Bereich der Kinder- und Jugendhilfe und der staatlichen Sanktionierung* [*Violence and Neglect in Families: Necessary Measures in Child and Youth Welfare and in State Interventions*], Bern: Schweizerische Eidgenossenschaft.

Bundesrat (2017) *Erste Erfahrungen mit dem neuen Kindes- und Erwachsenenschutzrecht: Bericht des Bundesrates in Erfüllung der Postulate 14.3776, 14.3891, 14.4113 und 15.3614* [*Initial Experiences with the New Law in Child and Adult Protection: Report of the Federal Council Answering the Parliamentary Postulates 14.3776, 14.3891, 14.4113 und 15.3614*], Bern: Schweizerische Eidgenossenschaft.

Bütow, B., Pomey, M., Rutschmann, M., Schär, C. and Studer, T. (eds) (2014) *Sozialpädagogik zwischen Staat und Familie. Alte und neue Politiken des Eingreifens* [*Social Pedagogy Between State and Family: Old and New Policies of Intervention*], Wiesbaden: VS Verlag für Sozialwissenschaften.

Cottier, M. and Steck, D. (2012) Das Verfahren vor der Kindes- und Erwachsenenschutzbehörde, *La pratique du droit de la famille*, 13(4): 981–1000.

Direktion der Justiz und des Inneren (2016) *Aufsichtsrechtliche Würdigung der Handlungsweise der KESB Winterthur-Andelfingen im Fall Flaach* [*Supervisory/Regulatory Appraisal of the Actions of CAPA Winterthur-Andelfingen in the Flaach Case*], Zurich: Kanton Zürich, Direktion der Justiz und des Inneren als Aufsichtsbehörde im Kindes- und Erwachsenenschutz.

Ecoplan and Hochschule für Soziale Arbeit Wallis (2013) *Monitoring Umsetzung des Kindes- und Erwachsenenschutzgesetzes im Kanton Bern: Schlussbericht zur Übergangsphase* [*Monitoring of the Implementation of the Child and Adult Protection Law in the Canton Berne: Final Report on the Transition Phase*], Bern: Kantonales Jugendamt Bern.

Expertenkommission Ingenbohl (2013) *Ingenbohler Schwestern in Kinderheimen: Erziehungspraxis und institutionelle Bedingungen unter besonderer Berücksichtigung von Rathausen und Hohenrain* [*Ingenbohl Nuns in Children's Homes: Educational Practice and Institutional Conditions with Particular Regard to Rathausen und Hohenrain*], np: Gemeinschaft Ingenbohl.

Fassbind, P. (2013) 'Die Organisation der Kindes- und Erwachsenenschutzbehörden in der Schweiz' ['The Organisation of the Child and Adult Protection Authorities in Switzerland'], *SozialAktuell*, 45(1): 15–17.

Freisler-Mühlemann, D. (2011) *Verdingkinder – ein Leben auf der Suche nach Normalität* [*'Thinged' Children: Lives in Search of Normality*], Bern: hep.

Galle, S. (2016) *Kindswegnahmen: Das 'Hilfswerk für die Kinder der Landstrasse' der Stiftung Pro Juventute im Kontext der schweizerischen Jugendfürsorge* [*Child Removals: The Initiative 'Relief Agency for the Children of the Country Roads' of the Foundation 'Pro Juventute' in the Context of Swiss Child Welfare*], Zurich: Chronos.

Galle, S. and Meier, T. (2009) Von Menschen und Akten. Die Aktion «Kinder der Landstrasse» der Stiftung pro juventute [Of People and Files. The Mission «Children Of The Country Roads» of the Foundation pro juventute]. Zürich: Chronos.

Gehrlach, C., Hauri, A. and Iff, M. (2016) 'Fehler und kritische Zwischenfälle im zivilrechtlichen Kindesschutz: Wie Organisationen aus Einzelfällen lernen können!' ['Errors and Critical Incidents in Child Protection Under Civil Law: How Organisations Can Learn from Cases'], *Zeitschrift für Kindes- und Erwachsenenschutz*, 71(4): 297–311.

Gilbert, N., Parton, N. and Skivenes, M. (2011) 'Changing Patterns of Response and Emerging Orientations', in N. Gilbert, N. Parton and M. Skivenes (eds) *Child Protection Systems: International Trends and Orientations*, New York: Oxford University Press, pp 243–57.

Hauri, A., Jud, A., Lätsch, D. and Rosch, D. (2016) 'Anhang I: Das Berner und Luzerner Abklärungsinstrument zum Kindesschutz' ['Appendix I: Bernese and Lucerne Assessment Instrument for Child Protection'], in D. Rosch, C. Fountoulakis and C. Heck (eds) *Handbuch Kindes- und Erwachsenenschutz. Recht und Methodik für Fachleute* [*Handbook of Child and Adult Protection. Legislation and Methodology*], Bern: Haupt, pp 590–628.

Heller, G., Avvanzino, P. and Lacharme, C. (2005) *Enfance sacrifiée. Témoignages d'enfants placés entre 1930 et 1970* [*Sacrificed Childhood: Witnesses' Accounts of Children Placed Between 1930 and 1970*], Lausanne: Editions EESP.

Hitz Quenon, N., Paulus, E. and Luchetta Mytit, L. (2014) *Le droit de protection de l'enfant. Les premiers effets de la mise en oeuvre dans les cantons de Genève, Vaud et Zurich* [*Child Protection Law: First Effects of Implementation in the Cantons Geneva, Vaud and Zurich*], Bern: Swiss Centre of Expertise in Human Rights (SCHR).

Hugger, P. (1998) 'Das Verdingkind' ['The "Thinged" Child'], in P. Hugger (ed.) *Kind sein in der Schweiz* [*Being a Child in Switzerland*], Zurich: Offizin, 107–8.

Jud, A. and Gartenhauser, R. (2015) 'The Impact of Socio-economic Status and Caregiver Cooperation on School Professionals' Reports to Child Protection Services in Switzerland', *European Journal of Social Work*, 18(3): 340–53.

Jungo, A. and Schöbi, D. (2018) *Ein Jahr KESCHA. Kurzbericht* [*One Year KESCHA: Short Report*], Fribourg: University of Fribourg. Available from: http://docplayer.org/78754109-Ein-jahr-kescha-kurzbericht.html.

Kanton Zürich (2016) 'Erkenntnisse und Lehren aus dem Fall Flaach (Medienmitteilung und Dokumente)' ['Findings and Insights from the "Flaach Case" (Media Communication and Documents)']. Available from: www.zh.ch/internet/de/aktuell/news/medienmitteilungen/2016/erkenntnisse-und-lehren-aus-dem-fall-flaach.html.

KOKES (Konferenz für Kindes- und Erwachsenenschutz) (2017) 'KESB: Organisation in den Kantonen (Stand 01.01.2017)' ['CAPA: Organisation in the Cantons (Status 01.07.2017)']. Available from: www.kokes.ch/application/files/5214/9027/3916/KOKES_KESB_Organisation_Kantone_ZKE_1-2017.pdf.

Konferenz der kantonalen Vormundschaftsbehörden (2008) 'Kindes- und Erwachsenenschutzbehörde als Fachbehörde (Analyse und Modellvorschläge)' ['The Child and Adult Protection Authority as Specialist Authority (Examination, Models, Recommendations)'], *Zeitschrift für Vormundschaftswesen*, 63(2): 63–128.

Leimgruber, W., Meier, T. and Sablonier, R. (1998) *Das Hilfswerk für die Kinder der Landstrasse. Historische Studie aufgrund der Akten der Stiftung pro juventute im Schweizerischen Bundesarchiv* [*The 'Relief Agency for the Children of the Country Roads'. Historical Study Based on the Files of the Association of the Foundation 'Pro Juventute'*], Bern: Schweizerisches Bundesarchiv.

Leuenberger, M. and Seglias, L. (eds) (2008) *Versorgt und vergessen. Ehemalige Verdingkinder erzählen* [*Placed and Forgotten: Former 'Thinged' Children Tell Their Stories*], Zurich: Rotpunkt.

Leuenberger, M., Mani, L., Rudin, S. and Seglias, L. (2011) *'Die Behörde beschliesst' – zum Wohl des Kindes? Fremdplatzierte Kinder im Kanton Bern 1912–1987* [*'The Authority Decides' – For the Well-Being of the Child? Children Placed in Care in the Canton Berne 1912–1978*], Baden: hier+jetzt.

Nett, J. and Spratt, T. (eds) (2012) *An International Study Comparing Child Protection Systems from Five Countries (Australia, Finland, Germany, Sweden and the United Kingdom) that Provides Scientifically Founded Recommendations for Improving Child Protection in Switzerland*, Bern: Programme National pour la Protection de l'Enfant. Available from: https://www.bsv.admin.ch/dam/bsv/de/dokumente/kinder/studien/kindesschutzsysteme_international.pdf.download.pdf/studie_kindesschutzsystemeeininternationalervergleichguterpraxis.pdf.

Ramsauer, N. (2000) *'Verwahrlost': Kindswegnahmen und die Entstehung der Jugendfürsorge im schweizerischen Sozialstaat 1900–1945* [*'Neglected': Child Removals and the Development of Child and Youth Welfare in the Swiss Welfare State 1900–1945*], Zurich: Chronos.

Rieder, S., Bieri, O., Schwenkel, C., Hertig, V. and Amberg, H. (2016) *Evaluation Kindes- und Erwachsenenschutzrecht* [*Evaluation of the New Law of Child and Adult Protection*], Lucerne: Interface Politikstudien.

Rosch, D. and Hauri, A. (2016) 'Begriff und Arten des Kindesschutzes' ['Conceptualisation and Types of Child Protection'], in D. Rosch, C. Fountoulakis and C. Heck (eds) *Handbuch Kindes- und Erwachsenenschutz: Recht und Methodik für Fachleute* [*Handbook of Child and Adult Protection: Legislation and Methodology*], Bern: Haupt, pp 406–9.

Rouiller, C. (2018) *Rapport établi au terme de l'enquête administrative ordonnée par le Conseil d'Etat du Canton de Vaud après la découverte d'une grave affaire de maltraitance et d'abus sexuels* [*Report Regarding the Official Investigation Mandated by the State Council of the Canton Vaud After the Disclosure of a Case of Serious Maltreatment and Sexual Abuse of Children*]. Available from: www.vd.ch/fileadmin/user_upload/organisation/dfj/spj/Rapport_Claude_Rouiller.pdf.

Schnurr, S. (2017) 'Child Removal Proceedings in Switzerland', in K. Burns, T. Pösö and M. Skivenes (eds) *Child Welfare Removals by the State: A Cross-Country Analysis of Decision-Making Systems*, New York: University Press, pp 117–45.

Schnyder, B., Stettler, M. and Häfeli, C. (1995) *Zur Revision des Schweizerischen Vormundschaftsrechts: Bericht der vom Bundesamt für Justiz im Hinblick auf die Revision des Vormundschaftsrechts eingesetzten Expertengruppe vom Juli 1995* [*Revision of the Swiss Custodian Law: Report of the Expert Group Commissioned by the Federal Office of Justice*], Bern: Bundesamt für Justiz.

Schwenkel, C., Bieri, O. and Rieder, S. (2016) *Evaluation der Kindes- und Erwachsenenschutzbehörden im Kanton St. Gallen: Schlussbericht zuhanden des Amts für Soziales im Kanton St. Gallen* [*Evaluation of the Child and Adult Protection Authority in the Canton St. Gallen: Final Report FAO Department for Social Services*], Lucerne: Interface Politikstudien.

Spratt, T., Nett, J., Bromfield, L., Hietamäki, J., Kindler, H. and Ponnert, L. (2015) 'Child Protection in Europe: Development of an International Cross-Comparison Model to Inform National Policies and Practices', *British Journal of Social Work*, 45(5): 1508–25.

Swiss National Science Foundation (2017) *Welfare and Coercion: National Research Programme*. Available from: www.nrp76.ch/en.

Tabin, J.-P., Frauenfelder, A., Togni, C. and Keller, V. (2010) *Temps d'assistance: Le gouvernement des pauvres en Suisse romande depuis la fin du XIXe siècle* [*Time for Care: Poverty Policy in Western Switzerland After the 19th century*], Lausanne: Editions Antipodes.

Wiederkehr, K. (2013) 'Rück- und Ausblick auf den Kindesschutz in der Schweiz' ['Review and Outlook on Child Protection in Switzerland'], *SozialAktuell* 45(1): 18–19.

Wohlwend, L. and Honegger, A. (2004) *Gestohlene Seelen: Verdingkinder in der Schweiz* [*Stolen Souls: 'Thinged' Children in Switzerland*], Frauenfeld: Huber.

10

Discourses, approaches and strategies on errors and mistakes in child protection in Germany

Heinz Kindler, Christine Gerber and Susanna Lillig

Introduction

A detailed history of child protection scandals in Germany is yet to be written. But most early scandals in the German Empire (1871–1918) and the Weimar Republic (1918–33) seem to relate to cases of institutional neglect or institutional abuse (see, for example, Banach, 2007; Richter, 2011: 200). In addition, there was a lot of moral outrage regarding especially moral neglect in lower-class families (Dickinson, 1996). The idea that the state, as represented by state-funded child protection agencies, has the capacity and the obligation to detect maltreatment (however defined) in families in a reliable way and should be held liable for failing to do so, appears to have been absent. By contrast, in the last quarter of the last century the situation changed. Starting with cases in Osnabrück (Mörsberger and Restemeier, 1997) and Saarbrücken, both medium-sized towns in Germany, the failure of child and youth welfare authorities (*Jugendämter*) to protect children in their own or in foster families became the focus of media attention. This focus has continued ever since with a series of highly publicised child protection scandals referred to by the children's first names for example, Kevin (Brandhorst, 2015), Lea-Sophie and Jessica. Because maltreatment-related child deaths have actually become less prevalent over the whole period (UNICEF, 2003) and Germany has never had a strong culture of holding administration accountable, this phenomenon needs to be explained.

Several developments may have contributed. First, during a phase of social optimism between 1980 and 1990 there was a massive expansion of child and youth welfare in-home services for families in need (Siegner, 2009). This process signalled a changing conception of the role of the state in social matters in continental Europe. Beyond just providing financial benefits, the idea of a 'caring state' adopting a social investment strategy was formulated (van Kersbergen and Hemerijck, 2012). Such a state was far more present in the everyday life of vulnerable families and in their social networks, making the detection of maltreatment in families a much more realistic objective. Second, a liberal concept of the defence of children's personal rights against parents as well as the state took hold (Kessl, 2017). Compared with motifs such as compassion, state interest in healthy citizens or social justice, this made the fight against severe violations of children's rights an even more morally charged topic. Third, a wave of neoliberal thought led the public to turn a critical eye on poor families as well as on state agencies. From this perspective, both the poor and state agencies should be tightly controlled using methods developed in the private sector (such as key performance indicators, contract management and so on) (Bode and Turba, 2014). Within such a system, child maltreatment deaths became a kind of anomaly or disturbance that needed to be clarified. Finally, child and family social work in Germany has strong roots in hermeneutics, the tradition of understanding in continental philosophy (for an introduction see Hösle, 2018). Because of the very strong single case orientation within this tradition, plausible concepts of effect and effectiveness never emerged within social work research in Germany. Against the backdrop of general public scepticism regarding the usefulness of social work with maltreating parents as shown by media analysis (Brandhorst, 2015: 57–64), it was not possible to integrate cases of child maltreatment deaths into a more positive picture of largely effective child protection practice. As a result, criticism easily reached more fundamental levels.

Public debate may be one of the root causes why research on maltreatment-related child deaths has intensified in Germany since the turn of the millennium and it is definitely the main reason why it has been funded. For example, in 2008 a conference of the German chancellor and the prime ministers of all the German states (*Länder*) on child protection decided to start a programme of learning from problematic cases in child protection with the second and the third author of this chapter working in that programme. The main focus of research in Germany on fatal child maltreatment has never been on understanding the parents and families involved (for exceptions see Höynck et al, 2014; Kindler, 2017) but on analysing institutional dynamics and case worker behaviours in cases where the family has been in contact with child and family social services before the child was harmed. Researchers from medicine (Fegert et al, 2010), sociology (Büchner, 2014), psychology (Cinkl and Marthaler, 2009) and especially social work research (Biesel, 2011; Schrapper and Schnorr, 2012, for example) were drawn into the field. In addition, there have been some serious case reviews by public bodies (such as Bremische Bürgerschaft, 2007; Bürgerschaft der Freien und Hansestadt Hamburg, 2015) or multidisciplinary committees commissioned by public bodies (see, for example, Kindler et al, 2016) with the aim of learning how to prevent further cases. The resulting knowledge cannot be value free and several values are at stake. Most important, of course, is the humanitarian value of protecting children, as vulnerable members of society, from avoidable harm. Other values concerned include fairness to caseworkers, who may be confronted with unjustified criticism, and a duty of care for professionals working with parents at risk. This ethical dimension is important not only as a motivating factor for researchers and research participants but also because there are tensions with other societal approaches towards unsuccessful child protection cases (such as fact finding within criminal law procedures, punitive media coverage).

The German child protection system in a nutshell

Local child and youth welfare authorities (*Jugendämter*) and family courts are key institutions for child protection in Germany. For both institutions, child protection is only a fraction of their work and role. Social workers in more than 550 child and youth welfare authorities are responsible for the planning, funding, coordination and management of child and youth welfare services, including in-home parenting support, crisis intervention, foster and residential care. Due to the principle of subsidiarity, most services are provided by charities (*freie Träger*) but are funded by child and youth welfare authorities based on a service plan (*Hilfeplan*) that is developed together with the family. More than 630 family courts are responsible for divorce proceedings and all legal conflicts regarding children including child protection matters.

Parents have a strong legal position within the German child and youth welfare system. They have the right to receive child and youth welfare services if needed to ensure child welfare. Being at-risk for child maltreatment is not a prerequisite for services. In addition, parents have the right to choose between different services and service providers as long as caseworkers conclude that the service is necessary and promising. Parents and children have the right to participate in service planning and management. This is true even if there has been child maltreatment, providing parents are willing and able to work with the authority and service provider on re-establishing parenting capacity. The emphasis on partnership with, and participation of, parents is one of the reasons why the German child and youth welfare system has been called 'family service oriented' (Gilbert, 2012: 532). This does not mean that there are fewer out-of-home placements compared with other countries (see, for instance, Burns et al, 2017: 227) but that there is only a small number of involuntary placements. This is partly true, because parents can ask for a placement if they feel overwhelmed but have neither maltreated the child nor are at risk of doing so. However, even above the threshold for child protection intervention, a consensual solution is negotiated in most cases as a recent study has shown (Witte and Kindler, 2018). If a case goes to the family court, there are also some specifics (for a comparative analysis of legal regulations see Boele-Woelki et al, 2005). For example, there is no such thing as an irrevocable termination of parental rights in Germany. Parental rights may be removed temporarily but have to be returned if the situation improves in a significant way. But above all, in Germany, the court has quite an active role in reviewing the case and finding a solution (Burns et al, 2017: 227). It must carry out an examination, if it comes across a case where child protection measures might be needed. In most cases, there is an application by the child and youth welfare authority but the court is free to take up any other case. During the investigation, the court reviews available reports and hears the parents as well as children above the age of three years. It can order expert testimony, hear witnesses or visit the family's home. After clarifying the facts, a decision on involuntary state measures to protect children has to be made. Such measures can include removal of parental rights and the appointment of a legal guardian, as well as orders relating to the parents (such as to send the child to school each day) or other persons (to stay away from the child and the family home, for example).

Under German law, involuntary state interference with parental rights must take place if three criteria are met. First, there must be child endangerment (*Kindeswohlgefährdung*). A definition has been given by the Federal Court of Justice (*Bundesgerichtshof*) and the Federal Constitutional Court (*Bundesverfassungsgericht*). Both have defined it as a current danger that will most certainly cause significant harm to the child in the future. Therefore the decision whether there is child endangerment or not is a prognostic one. The concept of substantial harm includes to the physical, psychological, emotional, cognitive and social well-being of children. Second, (custodial) parents must be unable or unwilling to prevent actual danger even with support. Third, involuntary state intervention must be adequate and proportionate. The term 'adequate' means that the intervention has to show promise of the potential to prevent existing dangers. Considering the possible negative effects of state intervention (such as attachment disruption due to parent–child separation) it has to be likely that nevertheless the child will benefit overall. The term 'proportionate' means that there is an obligation to select the least intrusive measure that appears suitable to prevent the existing dangers.

Only the family court can interfere with parental rights, but just a small fraction of cases of possible child endangerment go to court. In most cases, notifications that a child might be endangered are addressed to the child and youth welfare authority. If the authority decides that the notification contains substantial grounds to suspect child endangerment, it must initiate a so-called 8a-procedure, named after the relevant paragraph in the Social Code No. 8. The aim of the procedure is to assess whether there is child endangerment and, if so, to identify the measures necessary to avert the dangers. During this procedure, caseworkers are required to involve parental figures and the child and to obtain an immediate impression of the child plus their personal environment. At least two professionals have to work together in making this assessment. If they conclude that child endangerment is present, there are several alternatives. If caseworkers and parents agree on a plan to avert existing dangers – the preferred option – no court procedure is necessary and some support measures (such as social-pedagogical in-home child and family services) are started. If an agreement is not possible but there is no emergency, an application is made to the family court. If there is an emergency, the child and youth welfare authority can make an emergency placement but where parents do not agree, there must be an immediate application to court. In 2017, there were 105.8 child protection investigations (8a-procedures) per 100,000 minors under the age of 18 years (Pothmann and Kaufhold, 2018). In 33.8 cases per 100,000 minors, child and youth welfare authorities decided that child endangerment was present and in 23.8 cases per 100,000 minors the family court had to intervene.

Professionals from other systems (including school, day care, health and police) are entitled to report cases of possible child endangerment to the child and youth welfare authorities and should do so, but only the police are required to report; mandatory reporting is the exception, not the rule, in Germany. Child and youth welfare authorities or courts can involve professionals from disciplines other than social work and law but how often they do so is unknown. Multi-professional case conferences rarely take place. In the German child protection system, caseworkers' professional skills and judgement are emphasised and, because of the philosophical roots of social work in Germany, this is positioned against evidence-based approaches in child protection. Although there have been commendable attempts to incorporate evidence-based approaches (see, for example, Sommerfeld and Hüttemann, 2007), there is hardly any empirical work guided by ideas from evidence-based practice (Ghanem et al, 2017), and no commitment towards evidence-based practice in child protection policy in Germany.

During recent years several more detailed descriptions of the child protection system in Germany have been published. Interested readers are referred to Wolff et al (2011), Haug and Höynck (2017) or Witte et al (2019).

Defining problematic case trajectories, errors and mistakes

In Germany, most of the literature avoids words like 'error' or 'mistake' because they are hard to define, value laden and might therefore generate resistance or fear in child protection caseworkers. Instead, expressions like 'problematic case trajectories' (Fegert et al, 2010) or 'failures in child protection' (Kindler, 2013) are more commonly used. Both expressions avoid value-laden attributions of responsibility. The phrase 'problematic case trajectory' is very open as problems may relate to case outcomes (perhaps the child was killed), special case characteristics or professional activities or inactivity and their contexts (perhaps no professional talked to child). For analytic reasons it is therefore often necessary to narrow down the category and most of the time it is reduced to problematic case outcomes, an expression quite similar to 'failures in child protection'. Both focus on avoidable, seriously negative case outcomes.

Some studies use the more embarrassing German term *Fehler*, which might be translated as mistake or as error (Biesel and Wolff, 2014; Biesel and Cottier, Chapter 2 in this book). Most often it is used in combination with the word 'learning' (as in 'learning from mistakes in child protection'), signalling a constructive intention. Biesel (2011) examines the concept in detail and introduces the German audience to international literature on errors and mistakes in social work and child protection. Although he is critical of the possibilities for defining standards in social work, deviations from standards, rules or norms are portrayed as one way to define errors. As described with reference to Reason (2008), the starting point of a second way to define mistakes is positive intentions that go wrong. Where there have been negative case outcomes, but alternative, more promising routes of action were available, it can be concluded that some kind of error or mistake must have happened. Most importantly, Biesel (2011) argues that, although errors or mistakes are made by professionals (such as caseworkers), it is useful to focus on the organisational context of such behaviours as this may offer effective ways to initiate organisational learning. This argument is echoed in large parts of the scientific literature in Germany (for example, in Gerber and Lillig, 2018). Reports by parliamentary inquiry committees, whose rules of procedure are designed following court procedures, have been more tempted to blame individuals, but have also considered system factors.

Both ways of defining errors and mistakes have some problems. Applying a definition with reference to rules, norms or standards may lead to meaningless or misleading results if rules, norms or standards themselves are not firmly based on evidence or if deviations had no substantial impact on the case outcome. In addition, this approach may reinforce some kind of mindless proceduralism that in itself can have negative side effects. Defining errors and mistakes in child protection as factors decisive for avoiding serious negative case outcomes despite good intentions introduces the difficulty of distinguishing avoidable from unavoidable negative case outcomes. Although some cases can clearly be assigned to one category or the other as highlighted by Munro (1996) there are many ambiguous situations. Deciding that a serious negative case outcome was avoidable and identifying critical contributing factors means engaging in counterfactual reasoning, because a control group of identical cases cannot be built. As thought experiments are ridden with epistemological problems (Illari and Russo, 2014) it is hard to draw firm conclusions from them and one is at best left with probabilities that a certain kind of action has contributed to a negative case outcome and another kind of action might have contributed to a better outcome.

Studies based on these two ways of defining errors may lead to results converging if deviations from standards, rules or norms can be pinpointed and if it seems likely that they have contributed substantially to a negative case outcome. Because other factors may also be identified as crucial for avoiding a serious, negative case outcome (such as a lack of knowledge, misunderstanding, over-reliance on rules), the second definition is more encompassing and parsimonious and should therefore be preferred in most scientific contexts. Quantitative empirical studies may be an exception because here errors defined as deviations from certain norms, standards and rules can be studied using larger samples. Information on the frequency and distribution of errors defined this way may be relevant for child protection reform if in-depth case studies (using the wider definition) highlight such deviations as important contributing factors to serious negative outcomes in some cases.

Empirical studies on errors as deviation from rules, norms and standards in child protection practice in Germany

In a recent comparative study, the Hestia study, central documents for child protection policies in Germany, the Netherlands and England as well as a total of 1,200 cases files on child protection investigations from child and youth welfare authorities at four sites per country were analysed. Relations between case practice and policy goals were studied (for example, Bouma et al, 2018). If an error is defined as clear deviation from rules or guidelines aimed to achieve a relevant policy goal, the results indicate the frequency of some errors in German child protection practice. Child participation is one such goal and there is a statutory regulation in Germany requiring the child and youth welfare authority to involve children and adolescents during child protection investigations (8a-procedures). Nevertheless in 37.4 per cent of the case files from Germany ($n = 419$) no contact between child protection caseworker and child was documented. An even greater number of children may have had no or only a limited opportunity to participate if a concept like meaningful participation (Bouma et al, 2018) is applied. Other studies from Germany (such as Münder, 2017, working with a sample of child protection court cases) have also found that the perspectives of a substantial minority of children were not recorded and therefore probably played no role in child protection decision-making. A lack of focus on the child and their perspectives has been identified in a number of case reviews as a contributory factor in insufficient protection and ineffective interventions (Schrapper and Schnorr, 2012; Gerber and Lillig, 2018). Consequently, these findings are relevant for the improvement of the German child protection system. Besides, it is an ethical imperative to offer children an opportunity to express their views in matters of central importance to their lives (Lonne et al, 2015).

For maltreated children, another policy goal in Germany and other countries is to protect them from further abuse. Several case reviews have concluded that missing or invalid risk assessments can make it more difficult for caseworkers to determine, if possible together with parents, appropriate protective measures (Schrapper and Schnorr, 2012; Gerber and Lillig, 2018). Knowledge of the risk factors that are present or absent in a family is a prerequisite for a valid risk assessment. Based on systematic reviews (Stith et al, 2009; White et al, 2015) a set of the most predictive risk factors was compiled in the Hestia study and case files were coded as to whether they contained any information on these factors (Witte and Kindler, 2018). For most risks, this was the case for only a minority of the German files. Information in case files from England was much more systematic. It was therefore concluded that an unsystematic way of gathering information may put many child protection investigations in Germany at risk from invalid and faulty assessments.

Outside the realm of research, some child and youth welfare authorities have drawn samples of child protection cases from their database and analysed compliance with rules and standards in them. Results, however, have rarely been published. A notable exception is a report by the audit office in Hamburg (Bürgerschaft der Freien und Hansestadt Hamburg, 2017). For this, a sample of service plans (*Hilfepläne*) from the child and youth welfare authority in a part of the city was analysed. It was criticised, that in less of 20 per cent of these child protection investigations (8a-procedures), was it recorded that two or more caseworkers worked together on the assessment as required by law. Moreover, in a majority of cases, assessment instruments were not completed, and case progress was not monitored sufficiently.

Overall, empirical data convey the impression that child protection practice in Germany is struggling to adhere to relevant norms and regulations. Given that these are seen as helpful for avoiding errors, this finding is troubling. However, it should be pointed out that there have been very few studies, especially no panel data, so it is unknown whether practice is improving.

Reviews of cases with serious negative outcomes

A detailed analysis of cases with serious negative outcomes (case reviews) constitutes a second method for learning about errors and mistakes in child protection practice in Germany. Case reviews are not mandatory nor is there an institution that draws together available reviews. Nevertheless, a growing number of case reviews has been undertaken. Compared with empirical studies case reviews cover a broader spectrum of factors from different levels (such as caseworker, team, authority, local child protection system) potentially associated with serious, negative outcomes. In addition, time-bound processes and interrelations between factors can be studied. Although the criteria for causal analysis are not satisfied, results from case reviews can be impressive and compelling. Methodological problems include the distinction between cases with avoidable and unavoidable negative case outcomes, identification of factors contributing to avoidable negative case outcomes and the generalisability of findings. Transfer into practice and identification of promising strategies to counter errors and mistakes have also been identified as challenges.

None of the case reviews from Germany has explicitly defined clear rules on how to identify avoidable, serious, negative outcomes and the factors that have contributed to such an outcome. Instead, group consensus was used as the criterion. In most of the reports, caseworkers and supervisors from the local child and youth welfare authority were asked to review the case trajectory and identify moments where alternative ways of assessing the situation and proceeding seemed possible and promising (Gerber and Lillig, 2018). Sometimes other members of the local child protection system, or parents and family members of children who were harmed have been included (Biesel and Wolff, 2014). Therefore, some kind of a collaborative or networking approach seems to be dominant in case reviews in Germany. However, researchers also took part in the review process so the results reflect views of researchers and local collaborators. Reliance on single experts, expert groups or commissions with elected officials is less common and limited to case reviews in the midst of political scandal (Bremische Bürgerschaft, 2007; Schrapper, 2013) but in one study both approaches were combined (Kindler et al, 2016).

In all published case reviews, the identification of factors that may have contributed to a negative outcome was based on some form of reconstruction of the case trajectory. Methods for this reconstruction differ; case files from the local child and youth welfare authority were often the starting point. Sometimes files from other institutions (such as charities providing child and youth welfare services) were also included. In most of the reviews interviews or testimonies served as a way to close gaps and enhance knowledge on the chronology. For example, information was obtained from parents, siblings, other family members, caseworkers, teachers and doctors. While some reviews tried to interview many informants, others were more restrictive. Criteria for determining the relevance of different informants for reviews have not yet been discussed. The resulting case chronology was analysed with regard to relevant phases and events, incoming information and turning points. Some methods had a focus on gaps and contradictions in the file (Gerber and Lillig, 2018), while others tried to synthesise the essence of the case (Schrapper and Schnorr, 2012). Case chronologies based on files and interviews were presented in different formats. For example, Gerber and Lillig (2018) distinguished three dimensions: developments and events in the family, service processes, and chronology of assessments relevant for child protection. Others focused on family history, organisational histories of the child and welfare authority and service providers, and the history of interactions between the family and institutions (Biesel and Wolff, 2014). Until now, effects of different ways of analysing and presenting the case history in case review outcomes have not been studied. Because service processes and organisational contexts are included in nearly all published reviews a 'systems approach' (Fish et al, 2008) emphasising the role of organisational factors can be seen as mainstream in Germany.

Results from case reviews

Two research groups have published reports on results from a series of their case reviews (Schrapper and Schnorr, 2012; Gerber and Lillig, 2018). Based on five case reviews, Gerber and Lillig (2018) identified 63 factors contributing to negative case outcomes. These were grouped into six higher-level categories: interactions between professionals and family; strategies to support families and protect children; processes of risk assessment; cooperation and communication in the child protection network; overall conditions for safeguarding; and dealing with parent's mental health issues. Most of the contributing factors identified by Gerber and Lillig (2018) have also been reported in studies on much larger samples of serious case reviews from England and beyond (see, for example, Brandon et al, 2010). For example: family members (such as stepfathers) not included in assessments and services; difficulties in relationship building with hard-to-reach parents; a lack of focus on children's voice and needs; information not shared or lost in collaborative practice; and delayed adaption of assessments to changing circumstances. Also, absence of supervision for caseworkers and overwhelmed professionals have been described in Germany and England as risks in child protection practice. There may, however, be particular issues for risks in child protection practice in Germany. For instance, the strong emphasis on gaining cooperation with parents has sometimes hindered professionals from confronting parents or insisting on medical examinations. In one case, court action was not taken because parents declared their willingness to cooperate although their behaviour did not match up. In addition, the role of service providers as contractors of the child and youth welfare authority sometimes has had the consequence that different views on a case were not discussed openly with caseworkers from the authority.

Schrapper and Schnorr (2012) based their description of ten 'patterns of risk' on a series of ten case reviews. Again, some factors contributing to negative case outcomes have also been identified in the international literature. For example, the problem of over-optimism in work with violent or hostile parents has already been highlighted by Dingwall et al (1983). But Schrapper and Schnorr (2012) also link their results to traditions in child and family social work in Germany. Several of their 'patterns of risk' emphasise the need for in-depth understanding of the case (*Fallverstehen*). Otherwise professionals remain in a reactive mode, cannot connect with parents and might get caught in ambivalent feelings. Most important, Schrapper and Schnorr (2012) underline that most 'patterns of risk' cannot be eliminated, but they can be recognised and controlled if caseworkers and supervisors engage in processes of case reflection.

Strategies to deal with errors and mistakes in Germany

The professional discourse in Germany on how to handle errors and mistakes in child protection was not initiated by critical awareness regarding quality in the disciplines involved or critical research on child protection outcomes but through child protection scandals in the media and criminal investigations against social workers. As a consequence, the first scientific publications on the topic had a somewhat defensive tone although the need for quality improvement in child protection was never denied (see, for example, Deutsches Institut für Jugendhilfe und Familienrecht, 2004). Some books tried to inform caseworkers about legal risks (criminal and civil) (Albrecht, 2004), while others summarised international discussions on errors and mistakes in child protection (Fegert et al, 2010).

Politicians were quick to respond to child protection scandals in the media, mostly with two strategies. One strategy was an increased level of regulation. For example, federal legislation in 2005 introduced detailed regulations on how to handle cases of possible child endangerment (8a-procedure) in the practice of child and youth welfare authorities. There were also federal laws clarifying court procedures in cases of child endangerment and giving health professionals and other professionals with duties of confidentiality permission to inform the child and youth welfare authority if they come across substantial grounds to suspect child endangerment (Lack, 2012). Mainly, however, the level of regulation was pushed forward in municipalities with lots of new instructions and forms. It is hard to decide whether increased regulation helped to avoid at least some errors and mistakes in child protection. Professional responses to changes in federal law were mostly positive (Mühlmann et al, 2015), but the increased level of regulation in municipalities also triggered criticism. For instance, caseworkers from child and welfare authorities in surveys complained about a rising proportion of their working time devoted to administrative tasks (Bürgerschaft der Freien und

Hansestadt Hamburg, 2018). A second political strategy consisted in expanding resources for child protection. For example, the number of full-time equivalent caseworkers in child and welfare authorities nearly doubled between the years 2006 and 2016 (Fendrich et al, 2018). To a lesser extent research projects on quality improvement in child protection were funded (Wolff et al, 2013) and official child protection statistics were improved. Finally, some municipalities tightened control of compliance with regulations in child protection. For example, in the city of Hamburg an inspectorate with competence for analysing child and youth welfare cases was founded (Biesel and Messmer, 2018).

Professional discourse and empirical research also produced some proposals. One strategy was to offer caseworkers better assessment instruments. Several studies examined the reliability, and the prognostic and incremental validity of screening and risk assessment tools (including Kindler et al, 2008). A second strategy was to invest in information materials, education and training. For example, the Federal Ministry for Family Affairs, Senior Citizens, Women and Youth financed a project that collected questions from caseworkers and produced a handbook with answers from experts in the field (Kindler et al, 2006). A third strategy was to focus on joint quality development within child protection networks. For instance, one project included workshops with network partners and parents (Wolff et al, 2013). Finally, attempts were made to enhance knowledge transfer with case reviews (such as including supervisors in the review process, producing easy to understand materials and creating an organisational climate that is open to constructive criticism). There are no empirical data for any of these strategies showing a reduction in rates of failure in child protection (for example, repeat maltreatments after an assessment, children reporting that they have not been heard). However, caseworkers evaluated all four strategies favourably.

Perspectives

There is an intensive discussion on errors and mistakes in child protection in Germany. This discussion is driven more and more by empirical studies and results from case reviews. However, the degree of systematisation in results from case reviews is low with hardly any work comparing results from different researchers or research groups. Moreover, strategies to deal with errors and mistakes are quite general with little discussion of strategies to address specific factors contributing to negative case outcomes. Finally, no studies have been able to document reduced rates of failures or problematic case outcomes in child protection in Germany. Therefore, much additional work remains to be done.

References

Albrecht, H.-J. (2004) 'Sozialarbeit und Strafrecht' ['Social Work and Penal Law'], in Deutsches Institut für Jugendhilfe und Familienrecht [German Institute for Youth Welfare and Family Law] (eds), *Verantwortlich handeln – Schutz und Hilfe bei Kindeswohlgefährdung. Saarbrücker Memorandum [Act Responsibly: Protection and Support with Child Endangerment – Memorandum of Saarbrücken]*, Bonn: Bundesanzeiger, pp 183–228.

Banach, S. (2007) *Der Ricklinger Fürsorgeprozess 1930 [The Court Process on the Ricklinger Residential Care Facility 1930]*, Opladen: Barbara Budrich.

Biesel, K. (2011) *Wenn Jugendämter scheitern: Zum Umgang mit Fehlern im Kinderschutz [If Child and Youth Welfare Authorities Fail: Dealing with Errors and Mistakes in Child Protection]*, Bielefeld: Transcript.

Biesel, K. and Messmer, H. (2018) *Konzeptentwicklung, wissenschaftliche Begleitung und Evaluation der Jugendhilfeinspektion in Hamburg [Concept Development, Scientific Monitoring and Evaluation of the Child and Youth Welfare Inspectorate in Hamburg]*, Basel: Fachhochschule Nordwestschweiz.

Biesel, K. and Wolff, R. (2014) *Aus Kinderschutzfehlern lernen. Eine dialogisch-systemische Rekonstruktion des Falles Lea-Sophie [Learning from Errors in Child Protection: A Dialogical-Systemic Reconstruction of the Lea-Sophie Case]*, Bielefeld: Transcript.

Bode, I. and Turba, H. (2014) *Organisierter Kinderschutz in Deutschland. Strukturdynamiken und Modernisierungsparadoxien [Organised Child Protection in Germany: Structural Dynamics and Paradoxes of Modernisation]*, Wiesbaden: Springer.

Boele-Woelki, K., Braat, B. and Curry-Sumner, I. (2005) *European Family Law in Action, Vol. 3: Parental Responsibilities*, Antwerp: Intersentia.

Bouma, H., López, M.L., Knorth, E.J. and Grietens, H. (2018) 'Meaningful Participation for Children in the Dutch Child Protection System: A Critical Analysis of Relevant Provisions in Policy Documents', *Child Abuse & Neglect*, 79: 279–92.

Brandhorst, F. (2015) *Kinderschutz und Öffentlichkeit: Der 'Fall Kevin' als Sensation und Politikum [Child Protection and the Public: The Case of Kevin as Sensation and Political Issue]*, Wiesbaden: Springer.

Brandon, M., Bailey, S. and Belderson, P. (2010) *Building on the Learning from Serious Case Reviews: A Two-Year Analysis of Child Protection Database Notifications 2007–2009*, Research Brief DFE-RB040, London: Department for Education.

Bremische Bürgerschaft (2007) *Bericht des Untersuchungsausschusses zur Aufklärung von mutmaßlichen Vernachlässigungen der Amtsvormundschaft und Kindeswohlsicherung durch das Amt für Soziale Dienste* [*Report of the Inquiry Commission on Possible Neglect of Obligations by Official Guardian and Child Welfare Protection by the Office for Social Services*], Drucksache 16/1381.

Büchner, S. (2014) 'Der Fall Kevin – Warum wird geholfen, wenn Hilfe nicht mehr hilft?' ['The Case of Kevin: Help When Help Does Not Help Anymore'], in J. Bergmann, M. Hahn, A. Langhof and G. Wagner (eds) *Scheitern – Organisations- und wirtschaftssoziologische Analysen* [*Failure: Analysis by Sociology of Organisations and Economy*], Wiesbaden: Springer, pp 131–58.

Bürgerschaft der Freien und Hansestadt Hamburg (2015) *Bericht des Parlamentarischen Untersuchungsausschusses 'Aufklärung der Vernachlässigung der Kindeswohlsicherung im Fall Yagmur durch staatliche Stellen und Erarbeitung von Empfehlungen zur Verbesserung des Kinderschutzes in Hamburg'* [*Report of the Parliamentary Inquiry Commission 'Elucidation of Neglect of Child Welfare Protection in the Case of Yagmur by State Offices and Suggestions for Improving Child Protection in Hamburg'*], Drucksache 20/14100.

Bürgerschaft der Freien und Hansestadt Hamburg (2017) *Jahresbericht 2017 des Rechnungshofs der Freien und Hansestadt Hamburg* [*Annual Report 2017 of the Audit Office in Hamburg*], Drucksache 21/8000.

Bürgerschaft der Freien und Hansestadt Hamburg (2018) *Bericht der Enquete-Kommission 'Kinderschutz und Kinderrechte weiter stärken'* [*Report of the Enquete Commission 'Further Strengthening of Child Protection and Children's Rights'*], Drucksache 21/16000.

Burns, K., Pösö, T. and Skivenes, M. (eds) (2017) *Child Welfare Removals by the State: A Cross-country Analysis of Decision-Making Systems*, New York: Oxford University Press.

Cinkl, S and Marthaler, T. (2009) *Machbarkeitsstudie für eine unabhängige Kommission zur Untersuchung von gravierenden Kinderschutzfällen* [*Feasibility Study Regarding an Independent Commission for Serious Case Reviews in Child Protection*], Potsdam: Brandenburger Ministerium für Bildung, Jugend und Sport.

Deutsches Institut für Jugendhilfe und Familienrecht (2004) *Verantwortlich handeln – Schutz und Hilfe bei Kindeswohlgefährdung* [*Act Responsibly: Protection and Support with Child Endangerment*], Bonn: Bundesanzeiger.

Dickinson, E.R. (1996) *The Politics of German Child Welfare from the Empire to the Federal Republic*, Cambridge, MA: Harvard University Press.

Dingwall, R., Eekelaar, J. and Murray, T. (1983) *The Protection of Children: State Intervention and Family Life*, Oxford: Blackwell.

Fegert, J.M., Ziegenhain, U. and Fangerau, H. (2010) *Problematische Kinderschutzverläufe: Mediale Skandalisierung, fachliche Fehleranalyse und Strategien zur Verbesserung des Kinderschutzes* [*Problematic Case Trajectories in Child Protection: Media Scandals, Analysis of Errors and Mistakes and Strategies for Improving Child Protection*], Weinheim: Beltz Juventa.

Fendrich, S., Pothmann, J. and Tabel, A. (2018) *Monitor Hilfen zur Erziehung 2018* [*Monitor Socio-educational Support Measures for Parents and Children 2018*], Dortmund: Forschungsverbund DJI/TU Dortmund.

Fish, S., Munro, E. and Bairstow, S. (2008) *Learning Together to Safeguard Children: Developing a Multi-agency Systems Approach for Case Reviews*, SCIE Report 19, London: Social Care Institute for Excellence.

Gerber, C. and Lillig, S. (2018) *Gemeinsam Lernen aus Kinderschutzverläufen* [*Joint Learning from Child Protection Case Trajectories*], Cologne: Nationales Zentrum Frühe Hilfen.

Ghanem, C., Lawson, T.R., Pankofer, S., Maragkos, M. and Kollar, I. (2017) 'The Diffusion of Evidence-Based Practice: Reviewing the Evidence-Based Practice Networks in the United States and German-Speaking Countries', *Journal of Evidence-Informed Social Work*, 14(2): 86–118.

Gilbert, N. (2012) 'A Comparative Study of Child Welfare Systems: Abstract Orientations and Concrete Results', *Children and Youth Services Review*, 34(3): 532–6.

Haug, M. and Höynck, T. (2017) 'Removing Children from Their Families Due to Child Protection in Germany', in K. Burns, T. Pösö and M. Skivenes (eds) *Child Welfare Removals by the State: A Cross-Country Analysis of Decision-Making Systems*, New York: Oxford University Press, pp 89–115.

Hösle, V. (2018) *A Short History of German Philosophy*, trans. S. Rendall, Princeton, NJ: Princeton University Press.

Höynck, T., Behnsen, M. and Zähringer, U. (2014) *Tötungsdelikte an Kindern unter 6 Jahren in Deutschland* [*Homicide of Children Under Age 6 in Germany*], Wiesbaden: Springer.

Illari, P. and Russo, F. (2014) *Causality: Philosophical Theory Meets Scientific Practice*, Oxford: Oxford University Press.

Kessl, F. (2017) 'Kinderrechte als emanzipatorische Menschenrechte?' ['Children's Rights as Emancipatory Human Rights?]', *Berliner Debatte Initial*, 28: 46–8.

Kindler, H. (2013) *Qualitätsindikatoren für den Kinderschutz in Deutschland* [*Quality Indicators for Child Protection in Germany*], Cologne: Nationales Zentrum Frühe Hilfen.

Kindler, H. (2017) 'What Explains Dangerous Parenting and How Can It Be Changed?', *Journal of Family Research*, 11: 195–214.

Kindler, H., Gerber, C. and Lillig, S. (2016) *Wissenschaftliche Analyse zum Kinderschutzhandeln des Allgemeinen Sozialen Dienstes im Landkreis Breisgau-Hochschwarzwald im Todesfall des Kindes A.* [*Scientific Analysis of Child Protection Procedures in the County of Freiburg-Hochschwarzwald in the Death Case of the Child A*], Munich: Deutsches Jugendinstitut.

Kindler, H., Lillig, S., Blüml, H., Meysen, T. and Werner, A. (2006) *Handbuch Kindeswohlgefährdung nach § 1666 BGB und Allgemeiner Sozialer Dienst (ASD)* [*Handbook of Child Endangerment According to Section 1666 BGB and General Social Service*], Munich: Deutsches Jugendinstitut.

Kindler, H., Lukasczyk, P. and Reich, W. (2008) 'Validierung und Evaluation eines Diagnoseinstrumentes zur Gefährdungseinschätzung bei Verdacht auf Kindeswohlgefährdung' ['Validation and Evaluation of a Diagnostic Tool for Cases of Suspected Child Endangerment'], *Zeitschrift für Kindschaftsrecht und Jugendhilfe*, 12: 500–5.

Lack, K. (2012) *Möglichkeiten und Grenzen der Gesetzgebung zur Effektivierung des Kinderschutzes* [*Possibilities and Limits of Lawmaking for Improving Child Protection*], Bielefeld: Gieseking.

Lonne, B., Harries, M., Featherstone, B. and Gray, M. (2015) *Working Ethically in Child Protection*, New York: Routledge.

Mörsberger, T. and Restemeier, J. (eds) (1997) *Helfen mit Risiko. Zur Pflichtenstellung des Jugendamtes bei Kindesvernachlässigung* [*Helping with Risk: Obligations for Child and Youth Welfare Authorities in Cases of Child Neglect*], Neuwied: Luchterhand.

Mühlmann, T., Pothmann, J. and Kopp, K. (2015) *Wissenschaftliche Grundlagen für die Evaluation des Bundeskinderschutzgesetzes* [*Scientific Basis for the Evaluation of the Federal Child Protection Law*], Dortmund: AKJHS.

Münder, J. (ed.) (2017) *Kindeswohl zwischen Jugendhilfe und Justiz* [*Child Welfare Between Child and Youth Welfare Services and Family Court*], Weinheim: Beltz Juventa.

Munro, E. (1996) 'Avoidable and Unavoidable Mistakes in Child Protection Work', *The British Journal of Social Work*, 26(6): 793–808.

Pothmann, J. and Kaufhold, G. (2018) 'Mehr "8a-Verfahren", aber keine Zunahme der Kindeswohlgefährdungen' ['More "8a-Procedures", but Not More Cases with Child Endangerment'], *Kom-Dat*, 2/2018: 5–8.

Reason, J. (2008) *The Human Contribution: Unsafe Acts, Accidents and Heroic Recoveries*, Farnham: Ashgate.

Richter, J. (2011) *'Gute Kinder schlechter Eltern': Familienleben, Jugendfürsorge und Sorgerechtsentzug in Hamburg, 1884–1914* [*Good Children of Bad Parents: Family Life, Child and Youth Welfare Services and Removal of Custody in Hamburg, 1884–1914*], Wiesbaden: VS Verlag.

Schrapper, C. (2013) 'Betreuung des Kindes Anna. Rekonstruktion und Analyse der fachlichen Arbeitsweisen und organisatorischen Bedingungen des Jugendamts der Stadt Königswinter im Fall "Anna"' ['Caring for the Child Anna: Reconstruction and Analysis of Case Handling and Contexts in the Child and Youth Welfare Authority in Königswinter in the Case of Anna'], *Das Jugendamt*, 86(1): 2–16.

Schrapper, C. and Schnorr, V. (2012) *Risiko erkannt – Gefahr gebannt. Risikoanalyse als Qualitätsentwicklung im Kinderschutz* [*Risk Detected – Danger Banned: Risk Analysis as a Means for Quality Development in Child Protection*], Mainz: MIFKJF.

Siegner, G. (2009) 'Öffentliche Sorge für Jugendliche – Kritik der öffentlichen Jugendfürsorge' ['Public Care for Adolescents: Criticism of Public Child and Youth Welfare'], in W. Helsper, C. Hillbrandt and T. Schwarz (eds) *Schule und Bildung im Wandel* [*Change in School and Education*], Wiesbaden: VS Verlag, pp 93–126.

Sommerfeld, P. and Hüttemann, M. (2007) *Evidenzbasierte Soziale Arbeit. Nutzung von Forschung in der Praxis* [*Evidence-Based Social Work: Utilisation of Research in Practice*], Baltmannsweiler: Schneider Verlag Hohengehren.

Stith, S.M., Liu, L.T., Davies, L.C., Boykin, E.L., Alder, M.C., Harris, J.M., Som, A., McPherson, M. and Dees, J. (2009) 'Risk Factors in Child Maltreatment: A Meta-analytic Review of the Literature', *Aggression and Violent Behavior*, 14(1): 13–29.

UNICEF (2003) *A League Table of Child Maltreatment Deaths in Rich Nations*, Florence: UNICEF Innocenti Research Centre.

Van Kersbergen, K. and Hemerijck, A. (2012) 'Two Decades of Change in Europe: The Emergence of the Social Investment State', *Journal of Social Policy*, 41(3): 475–92.

White, O.G., Hindley, N. and Jones, D.P. (2015) 'Risk Factors for Child Maltreatment Recurrence: An Updated Systematic Review', *Medicine, Science and the Law*, 55(4): 259–77.

Witte, S. and Kindler, H. (2018) 'Decisions at the End of Child Protection Investigations: Varying Thresholds for Interventions and Their Relation to Policy', lecture given at the NORFACE Welfare State Futures Programme Final Conference, Florence. www.dji.de/ HESTIA.

Witte, S., Miehlbradt, L.S., van Santen, E. and Kindler, H. (2019) 'Preventing Child Endangerment: Child Protection in Germany', in L. Merkel-Holguin, J.D. Fluke and R.D. Krugman (eds) *National Systems of Child Protection: Understanding the International Variability and Context for Developing Policy and Practice*, Cham: Springer, pp 93–114.

Wolff, R., Biesel, K. and Heinitz, S. (2011) 'Child Protection in an Age of Uncertainty: Germany's Response', in N. Gilbert, N. Parton and M. Skivenes (eds) *Child Protection Systems: International Trends and Orientations*, New York: Oxford University Press, pp 183–203.

Wolff, R., Flick, U., Ackermann, T., Biesel, K., Brandhorst, F., Heinitz, S., Patschke, M. and Röhnsch, G. (2013) *Aus Fehlern lernen– Qualitätsmanagement im Kinderschutz* [*Learning from Mistakes: Quality Management in Child Protection*], Opladen: Barbara Budrich.

11

Dysfunctions in French child protection

Hélène Join-Lambert and Gilles Séraphin

Introduction

The child protection system in France has experienced successive dysfunctions since the 1990s, translated into poor quality protection and even children's deaths. These have led to large-scale administrative and legislative reforms. Most of the time, the element that triggers the reforms has been media coverage of the dysfunction: a particular event (often a death) moves public opinion and the authorities have to provide a response almost immediately. Occasionally, the media focus on situations of distress and suffering, often alerted by the results of research that have made them visible and understandable. Whatever the situations, users' defence associations have also played a key role in this function of alerting public opinion and proposing reforms.

Following a presentation of the child protection system in France, we will analyse the way in which the term dysfunction (*disfonctionnement*) seems most suitable to understand the situation in the country, as the terms error (*erreur*) and failure (*faute*), used less frequently, do not account for the cases found. Our analysis will focus on major dysfunctions that have moved public opinion (cases that have led to deaths), or that have been gradually revealed by researchers and users' associations (lack of participation by parents, difficulties in making the transition to adulthood due to lack of support) and led to reforms or proposals for reform. Our study considers situations classified as dysfunctions in the child protection system from the 1980s onwards, a period in which children's rights have become a priority for French society.

The child protection system in France

In France, child protection is a public policy based on a substantial body of legislation, established originally by legislation in 1889 and largely reformed by Acts in 2007 and 2016. This system of child protection, including all prevention and protection measures, is now heavily decentralised by the state to the 101 departments (*départements*, administrative and political divisions) that make up the territory of France. It is therefore managed and funded by departments via their child welfare service (Aide sociale à l'enfance) (Gabriel et al, 2013; Bolter and Séraphin, 2018).

The child protection system is based on the principle of subsidiarity between an administrative authority and a judicial authority. The administrative authority is held by the President of the Department Council. The judicial authority, embodied by the public prosecutor and the juvenile court judge, deals with both criminal and civil cases. The President of the Departmental Council is also responsible for carrying out legal measures and for continuity in monitoring children's personal trajectories within child protection.

In matters within the scope of criminal proceedings, the magistrate rules whether it is an offence (*délit*, such as theft, or crime, as in murder or rape) and passes a sentence that reflects the guilt of a perpetrator. The decentralised services of the state are responsible for executing decisions made by the criminal courts.

Civil proceedings, which make up the child protection legal system, enable the judge to make a ruling on an endangered child; civil protection measures can be imposed independently of any penal measure against a perpetrator. It is neither necessary nor useful to identify a perpetrator or establish an offence to protect an endangered child legally (Séraphin, 2017).

Any citizen who witnesses a situation of violence or simply has doubts about it is obliged to notify the above authorities, by phoning the free, confidential 24/7 emergency number *Allo Enfance en danger*/119, which offers the possibility of discussing the issue with professional listeners and run by Service national d'accueil téléphonique de l'enfance en danger (SNATED: National Agency for Phone Calls Regarding Children in Danger). They can also contact the Centre for Collecting Information of Concern (CRIP: Centre de recueil de l'information préoccupante) in each Department or, in certain circumstances, report directly to the prosecution service.

Professionals can also issue concerns (*information préoccupante* – IP), and in certain circumstances even report cases to the legal authorities. As regards issuing IPs, Departments' statistics show that it is mainly social and education professionals who do this and, to a lesser extent, healthcare practitioners.

This information is evaluated either by CRIP or by the prosecution service and then by the juvenile court judge, with the help of a dedicated service if required. After the evaluation at the administrative level, the Department services consider the possibility of assistance outside the field of child protection (such as financial assistance) or child protection assistance with the agreement of the family. If evaluation is not possible, the agreement with the family is withheld or withdrawn, and if assistance fails to remove the risk or the danger is serious and immediate, the judicial authority takes over. In this case, the family's formal agreement is not required, although informal agreement should still be sought with a view to obtaining cooperation.

The administrative services (with the agreement of the family) and the legal measures (seeking the approval of the family) are performed at home, out of home (mainly in an institution or foster care, involving a placement with an unpaid relative or a professional foster family) or a combination of these. The number and diversity of child protection services has increased since 2000. Apart from fostering by unpaid relatives, support in the home or in a placement is carried out by trained professionals with a diploma recognised and governed by the Labour Code.

Services and measures are implemented directly by the Department or by associations authorised and monitored by the Department or, in the case of legal measures, authorised and controlled by the state child protection services.

Generally, child protection in France covers 300,000 minors (around 2 per cent of minors living in the country) and 20,000 young people between 18 and 20 years of age (including unaccompanied minors);[1] 80 per cent of the measures are court ordered. Over 50 per cent of measures relate to placement, 58 per cent of them in foster families.[2]

A key feature of the French system is that in most situations where children are placed, the parents retain parental authority. Parental authority is withdrawn only in cases of serious breach of responsibilities or prolonged abandonment (when the child is already placed). In 2016, this was the case for 1,067 children, with 139 withdrawals of parental authority and 928 legal declarations of abandonment (ONED/ONPE, 2016: 12). In the same year, 143,440 children were placed. Therefore, when children are placed, most parents have legal rights as users of child protection services.

The understanding of *erreur* (error) and *faute* (failure) as *dysfonctionnement* (dysfunction)

Rather than errors, politicians, researchers, practitioners and users' associations refer to *dysfonctionnement* (dysfunctions) which relate to different issues within child protection. In general, the terms 'error' and 'failure' are mostly reserved for situations of death, serious physical violence and sexual abuse. Furthermore, in French the term *faute* (failure) has a moral and legal dimension that is automatically linked to the notion of guilt. The term *erreur* (error) is often used so as not to make a condemnation a priori, although the notion of guilt is always hanging in the air. Therefore, for types of error committed without individual liability being brought into play, the preferred term is 'dysfunction'.

Indeed, since 2000 some highly publicised court cases have shown that, in most dramatic situations, no observed individual or legal mistakes have been committed and there are no (or very few) major individual errors of judgement in cases that serve as benchmarks. However, there have been chronic dysfunctions identified in the evaluation and decision-making chain. In several cases, it is not worth changing the law, but it is essential to create the right conditions for correct evaluations, transmission of information and quick decision-making.

In this chapter we will highlight several kinds of dysfunctions that have been identified in practice and research, and addressed by changes in public policies or law. The terms 'error', 'failure' or 'dysfunction' are used in different contexts by different stakeholders.

Dysfunctions in the past

Looking back in time, most of the public debate around errors, failures or dysfunctions in child protection occurred in the 1990s and after. Researchers and organisations defending users' rights were active in the 1970s, whereas the notion of child maltreatment itself only became central to child protection in the 1980s (Gabel, 2000: 29). Two types of association work to defend users and press for reforms: those that mainly focus on defending the rights of families and parents, such as ATD Quart Monde, set up in 1957 to defend all poor families; and others that defend children who have suffered maltreatment, such as La Voix de l'enfant, created in 1981. Dysfunctions related to children's rights, such as institutional abuse or failed protection in cases of sexual abuse and death, only appeared as public scandals after the turn of the century. The fact that parents' rights were initially more of a concern than children's rights probably illustrates the slow evolution of the status of children and their rights in France.

Interventions not respecting parents' rights

Back in the 1970s, child protection services were criticised for exercising social control, hidden behind the function of child protection, and depicted as 'family police' (Donzelot, 1977). Certain associations have denounced abusive removals of children on the basis only of the precarious conditions in which families lived, without evidence of maltreatment. In the 1990s, government inspectors picked up on the argument of these non-governmental organisations to recommend that parents' rights be respected more in decision-making and protection processes (Naves et al, 2000). In certain situations, parents who could, in principle, benefit from legal assistance and whose children are placed following a court order, manage to get an error recognised, and their children returned. However, the number of such returns, which could result from changed family circumstances, is unknown.

Since 2015, France has been shaken by a series of debates about children with autism being put under protection and placed. Parents and associations for their defence now generally accuse judicial and Department services of placing children on the basis that they are at risk of maltreatment, while the main problem is a lack of healthcare and social solutions adapted to these children's condition. In contrast, experts point out that children with autism can also – and sometimes more than others – be victims of maltreatment, including neglect, and should therefore benefit from protection. In summary, it is estimated that the evaluation phase is decisive: only an adapted evaluation based on expertise that takes into account autistic disorders can go beyond the passionate and sterile debate about the well-being of the children concerned (Défenseur des droits, 2015).

Research on parents' rights

Since the early 2000s, some studies have focused on the parent–practitioner relationship within child protection services (Fablet, 2008; Boddy et al, 2014; Boutanquoi et al, 2014; Tillard et al, 2015) and, more specifically, on the perspectives of parents of placed children (Mackiewicz, 2002; Euillet and Zaouche-Gaudron, 2008; Sécher, 2009; Touahria, 2011).

In the more general context of the contractualisation of social assistance, the 2002 Act[3] introduced a contract in the form of an individual document for care, and the 2007 Act[4] did so in the form of a 'personal plan' for the child. The contract can lead one to believe that each party has a margin for manoeuvre, at least to be able to accept or reject its terms (Erbès-Seguin, 1999). However, researchers remind us that within social work, relations between practitioners and users are marked by the power of the former and the dependence of the latter. In their relations with practitioners from the socio-educational sector, parents often feel that they are on the receiving end of decisions about the measures applied to them, rather than contributing to those decisions (Join-Lambert, 2016).

The question that emerges from recent research is the exercise of parents' rights within the framework of child protection. Indeed, since most of the parents maintain their rights throughout the duration of the placement, professionals and institutions have a legal duty to encourage parental links with their children and, therefore, to enhance processes of joint upbringing. Successive legislation has strengthened practices and institutions in this regard.

Institutional maltreatment

Only a few cases of institutional child abuse have become public over the years in France. The most famous one occurred in 1998 when the head of a home called Cheval pour tous (Horse for All) was convicted of sexual abuse and maltreatment of seven young people between 1992 and 1998. Several young people had made allegations before their right was eventually recognised (Tomasovitch, 2002). It is striking that the number of trials for institutional abuse is very low, although cases of sexual abuse within child protection institutions, committed either by adults or by fellow protected children have been documented (Boitout, 2015; CEDIF, 2018). It seems that this is due not only to children's fear that their testimonies are not taken seriously and cases will be dismissed, but also to practitioners' fear of being sacked for revealing details of abuse (Daadouch, 2017).

Research on this issue is scarce. Researchers addressing institutional abuse tend to investigate abuse and neglect as the consequence of institutional dysfunction rather than individual mistakes (Durning, 1985).

Misuse of children's testimonies in cases of sexual abuse

In 2004 and 2005, two highly publicised trials brought situations of serious sexual abuse inflicted on children within the family to public attention. In 2004, the Outreau trial concerned paedophilia where 12 children were recognised as victims. The trial followed revelations made by four children towards the end of 2000. These children had already been placed following rulings by juvenile court judges, in 1995 for one and in early 2000 for the other three. The parents' visiting and custody rights were immediately suspended after these disclosures (Garapon and Salas, 2006; Joxe, 2010). The dysfunction highlighted in this trial related to the status of the children's testimonies. Indeed, these testimonies alone initially led to charges against 17 adults in 2004. Cases against 13 of these were later overturned on appeal. The events recounted could not be proven and may possibly never have happened. The credibility of the children's testimonies was thus seriously undermined, which led the inquiry committee to propose measures aimed at taking into account the child's age and his/her development in a better way (Ministère de la Justice, 2005).

During this process, the terms 'error' and 'failure' – even 'shipwreck' – regarding the judiciary were extensively used in the press, particularly in relation to the young examining magistrate, who committed no legal mistake that could have influenced the outcome. However, associations defending families, and even child victims, researchers and several magistrates identified chronic dysfunctions (Garapon and Salas, 2006).

In 2005, a second paedophilia case was heard in Angers. It involved 66 adults charged with rape, prostitution and sexual abuse against 45 children between 1999 and 2002. The first revelations, made in 2001, came from adults. The Department social services were criticised on this occasion for not having identified the maltreatment and not protecting the children. Many of the adults accused had been monitored by these services, as they depended on them financially; some had already been sentenced and even jailed for the rape of minors. Moreover, most of the children had already been supported and protected by child protection prevention services for other reasons (Johannès, 2005).

These two cases highlighted the difficulties involved in considering and analysing children's statements, and more generally in prosecuting child sexual abuse. In the Outreau trial, testimonies accused – either wrongly or without decisive elements that could lead to prosecution – adults presumed innocent, while in the Angers case, the child victims said very little, and even covered up for their guilty parents.

Research available on taking children's statements into account

The status of the child's word in child protection has been the subject of only a few research studies. In her doctoral thesis, Pierrine Robin studied the consideration of the child's point of view during the evaluation of his/her situation, within a French–German perspective. As she reminds us, it was after the Outreau trial that a working group made recommendations aimed at improving the collection of child victim testimonies (Robin, 2013: 87). Her empirical study showed that, despite the inclusion of a formal participation tool in the 2007 law, children are not closely involved in the process of evaluating their situation prior to being taken into care, and there is a wide variety of professional practice. In general, children say that they feel that their statements have less value than those of adults, practitioners or parents (Robin, 2013).

In her research into the collection of testimonies of small children under the protection of child welfare, Elsa Zotian observes that 'practitioners in the field initially stand out for the extreme attention they pay to the way in which young children express themselves' (Zotian, 2017: 145). In the absence of words, the slightest behaviours are interpreted from a psychological perspective, sometimes even a psychoanalytical one, with major consequences that, on occasion can even lead to breakdown in parenting arrangements. Here, the child's expression seems to be both overvalued and over-interpreted.

Despite the call for research launched by the National Observatory for Children in Danger, ONED, in 2015[5], to which Robin and Zotian responded, the question of the conditions for listening to the child before, during and after protection decisions has not been much researched in France. This means it remains rather random, depending on the sensitivities of practitioners and teams.

Dysfunctions in fatal cases

More recently, another case ('Marina') attracted public attention. It concerned a girl who died in 2009, aged eight, following physical and psychological maltreatment, probably suffered since birth. The services in many schools she attended had pointed out her situation. Doctors also alerted the prosecution service when she was admitted to hospital for one month due to physical marks, which had been diagnosed. However, neither the child protection services nor the judicial police detected maltreatment during their inquiries (Dupont, 2014); Marina always defended (and even protected) her parents during these inquiries.

As in the Outreau case, the terms 'error' and 'failure' were extensively used in the press, particularly with regard to the Department's child protection services. Despite everything, nobody was held criminally responsible. In contrast, associations for the defence of child victims, researchers and other experts revealed chronic dysfunctions. As a result, the Children's Ombudsman, who reports to the Human Rights Defender, ordered a detailed report on the matter. This confirmed, based on detailed arguments, not only a few dysfunctions but a chain of dysfunctions throughout the system (Défenseur des droits, 2014).

The reform of the Child Ombudsman institution in France enabled this comprehensive study. Indeed, by becoming Deputy Defender of

Human Rights in 2011, the Child Ombudsman now has the power to collect any information considered necessary on matters brought to their attention, without any restriction related to their secret or confidential nature. The Ombudsman may even proceed with on-the-spot checks at the administrative or private premises of the people suspected. Based on these powers, the Child Ombudsman and Deputy Defender of Human Rights 2011–14, Marie Derain, asked a specialist in child welfare, Alain Grevot, to analyse all the events and the chain of decisions that preceded Marina's death. The report presented in 2014 (Défenseur des droits, 2014) is a very detailed explanation of all the dysfunctions that characterised the little girl's case, starting with reports by primary school teachers that were not properly taken into account, and continuing with the non-consideration of hospital stays lasting several weeks because of marks all over her body. The general principle of the study was not to determine errors, even legally condemnable failures, but to understand how a chain of dysfunctions could have led to this tragedy. The key phrase was 'Learn from mistakes so it does not happen again'.

Dysfunctions in the support of young adults

Another dysfunction has been increasingly mentioned, particularly in professional circles: children's and young people's trajectories within child protection, and shortly after leaving the system. This does not get much coverage in the media. It appeared briefly after the attacks on *Charlie Hebdo* magazine in 2015, when it emerged that two of the criminals had spent six years in a home and then had a wayward record after they left at 18 years of age (Duparc, 2015; *Le Parisien*, 2015). When there are questions of chaotic trajectories or situations of extreme precariousness for care-leavers, the expression used is 'dysfunction', and never 'error' or 'failure'.

Research on the subject

Experts on this topic conclude that this is a case of a dual dysfunction. On the one hand, among children placed, an entire category is identified as having chaotic trajectories involving several placements, disruption, returning to their families and movement from one placement to another (Potin, 2012). These trajectories lead to considerable instability in the lives of these young people, and when they reach adulthood (Firdion, 2006). The dysfunction is identified as stemming from placement breakdown, which has a big impact on forming a child's or young person's personality. These youngsters experience accumulated disruption in terms of family and socio-educational care, and also in education and healthcare. In adolescence, they reach a stage where no institution is able to provide them with what they need (Barreyre et al, 2008).

Another dysfunction has also been identified in terms of support at the end of care: adolescents who are not ready for autonomy, either in terms of decision making or in their everyday life (Join-Lambert Milova, 2006), and are unable to enter the labour market and become economically independent (Frechon and Marquet, 2016). The ONPE also points out the lack of information for young people leaving the child protection system about the support they can apply for (ONED/ONPE, 2015). Furthermore, the context of public sector budget cuts makes it more difficult to extend support beyond the age of 18. The *aide jeune majeur* (young adult support) envisaged to support young people leaving placement (18–21 years of age) is not mandatory for local authorities. The ways of implementing this vary widely and often only a small number of young adults can benefit.

Improvement strategies and measures taken to recognise and avoid errors, failures and dysfunctions

Measures taken to better recognise parents' rights

In the French child protection system, the agreement (administrative protection) or adhesion/participation (legal protection) of families is generally sought during the decision-making process and the implementation of measures. Furthermore, parental rights have been reinforced through the Acts of 2002 and 2007. An 'individual care document' must be made between the parents and the institution for each child placed (Act 2002-2 of 2 January 2002 overhauling social and medical-social action). Since the Act 2007-293 of 5 March 2007 reforming child protection, once a protection measure is declared the Department draws up a 'plan for the child' with the minor and the parents. This document is signed by the service and the parents, and includes an analysis of the situation, the plans for the child and the action to be taken.

The Act 2007-293 incorporated innovative mechanisms that respond to a range of needs, often somewhere between 'home help' and 'placement' (Breugnot, 2011). Several types of mechanisms have been implemented since 2007. 'Placement at home' is undertaken in the child's own home with the parents. It includes visits by professionals several times a week and emergency, contingency arrangements for stays elsewhere in the event of a family crisis. 'Sequential placement' envisages alternating, predefined periods during which the child will either be with the parents or in a placement. 'Day reception' aims at caring for the child during out-of-school periods (evenings, Wednesdays, weekends), or even in school time when the child does not attend school. The idea here is to prevent situations of danger where the risk is identified within the family. The child sleeps at the parents' home every night, and no placement is envisaged (Join-Lambert, 2012). These innovations aim at obtaining better information on the skills and resources of the parents, to involve them more and more in the protection of their child. The accent is on joint working, meaning that the parents are in charge of the child's upbringing wherever this is possible and secure. A second aim –for the public authorities – is to make savings in comparison with traditional placement systems.

Strategies implemented to avoid errors in sexual abuse trials

The Outreau (2004) and Angers (2005) trials helped to determine the extent of the phenomenon of intrafamily sexual abuse, and above all to take the specific nature of children's statements into account, within both the police and the social and child protection services (Neyrand and Mekboul, 2014). The 2007 Act aimed at strengthening the prevention system by collecting and cross-checking all testimonies more systematically (Chemin, 2006).

In general, this is about listening to anyone who expresses a doubt about a situation or has witnessed someone at risk. Since 1989, the endangered children call centre (119/SNATED) has been available to listen to anyone with concerns. Calls are received by specially trained personnel. An IP can be transmitted immediately to the Departments concerned, and an emergency intervention may be set in motion, if required. Communications are made continuously, and the number of calls received and IPs issued is considerable. In 2015,[6] of 304,176 calls, 33,010 (+7.8 per cent since 2009) were dealt with by professionals because they were related to potential dangers. Some 56 per cent of the calls processed, mainly from a close relative, resulted in advice, prevention and guidance, and 44 per cent of calls were transferred to the appropriate departments in the form of an IP.

The IP is, in effect, the cornerstone of the alert and identification system. Since Act 2007-293, all Departments have a CRIP that centralises the information received about a child and expedites a specific evaluation, according to the current procedures. Depending on the child's ability for self-expression, their testimony is also taken during the evaluation process.

In more serious situations of criminal offences, the legislator and the government have made reforms. The main ones arise from the implementation (by decrees and circulars) of Act 98-468 of 17 June 1998 'on the prevention and repression of sexual offences and the protection of minors', which notably imposes an obligation to film any testimony involving a minor (Mallevaey, 2012). The most significant developments have taken place in professional and institutional practice. The police and *gendarmerie* services receive specific training particularly on the use of the National Institute of Child Health and Human Development protocol to ensure that testimonies from minors are taken in appropriate conditions (Cyr, 2014). The voluntary sector has also shown considerable interest. The association La Voix de l'enfant supports the creation of multidisciplinary office and reception units in hospitals for child victims of maltreatment and/or sexual violence, aimed at collecting statements from child victims under the best possible conditions, particularly in a safe environment specially designed for the purpose (ONED/ONPE, 2014). The creation of these units (around 60 in the country at present) intends to bring together consideration of the child's suffering in medical, psychological and social terms with the need to carry out inquiries and/or start legal proceedings to establish the truth. The child is thus seen in hospital by health practitioners, forensic doctors and psychologists. A child who needs a medical examination is referred to paediatrics and is then questioned by one or more members of the judicial police or the *gendarmerie*. This session is recorded with equipment approved by the judiciary. A one-way window allows medical personnel to follow the session and intervene if necessary, to allow the child to take a break and, as required, to make the testimony more accurate. Once recorded, the child will not have to give testimony again.

Strategies for improvement to avoid fatal cases

Marina's case led to several, far-reaching, changes. Above all, the analysis of dysfunctions confirmed that the main guidelines indicated in Act 2007-293 pointed in the right direction. Indeed, in 2008, the last year of the young girl's life, the obligations arising from this Act had not all been applied in the Department where she lived. There is every reason to believe that the new mechanisms would probably have corrected this chain of dysfunction. In particular, the case has created awareness around the urgency of setting up collection units for IPs and interservice and inter-institution protocols for sharing and analysing information on dangerous situations experienced by children. It has also enabled us to understand that the mere alignment of institutions with the law, as essential as it is, is not sufficient. It is also necessary to create the right context for good decision-making. Therefore, Departments have jointly prepared some shared evaluation standards and have trained all their personnel so they can respond adequately to their obligation to assess situations of danger. This process is yet to be formalised in terms of judicial investigations, expedited directly by the prosecutor or the juvenile court judge.

Furthermore, following the signature of the interservice and inter-institution protocols, Departments receive and deal with ever more IPs. The procedure works well, for example with the National Education Service. In contrast, great difficulties persist in the healthcare sector, especially with private family doctors. Although they are in contact with children, very few report cases with concerns. In 2014, the High Authority on Healthcare (Haute autorité de la santé), together with the French Medical Board, issued a recommendation to encourage doctors to be more vigilant and draft reports on worrying signs. The recommendation included practical annexes (legal references, forms, procedures, contacts and so on).[7] Moreover, the latest Act on child protection (2016-297 of 14 March 2016) requires each Department to appoint a referring doctor (article 7) for the child protection service. From now on, the Department's 'child protection referring doctor' is responsible for organising standard working procedures and coordination between the Department's services and the unit for the collection, the treatment and evaluation of information that is of concern, on one hand, and private and hospital doctors, as well as school medical doctors, on the other(Code d'action sociale et des familles [Code of Social Action and Families] L. 221–2).

As knowledge emerged about the story of Marina and some other children who died from parental violence subsequently, it was seen that a large proportion of these children were originally born secretly[8] and only formally recognised by their parents at the end of the two-month period after the birth allowed (Bolter et al, 2018). The Act 2016-297 of 14 March 2016 requires that these parents are systematically offered support within the child protection framework.

More generally, following the publication of the Children's Ombudsman's report, it appeared possible to 'learn from one's errors'. On 1 March 2017, the Minister of Families and Women's Rights launched the first inter-ministerial plan to mobilise and fight against violence perpetrated on children: 'Given the improvement of our understanding of violence, [these measures] aim to analyse the functioning of institutions that have not been able to prevent violent child deaths. It is, therefore, a case of learning from our errors by systematically feeding information back.'[9] She also commissioned a report from the ministerial inspectorates (IGAS: Inspection générale des Affaire sociales [General Inspectorate of Social Affairs]; IGJ: Inspection générale de la Justice [General Inspectorate of Justice]; and IGAE: Inspection générale de l'administration, de l'éducation nationale et de la recherche [[General Inspectorate of Administration, Education and Research]). The report issued a range of recommendations to improve identification, evaluation and prevention of danger, for example: medical follow-up of children at school and through a digital health book, sharing information on school drop-out, investigation of situation with high risk factors, reinforcement of parenting support and information on contraception, better collaboration and sharing of information in child protection organisations, training measures for professionals contributing to child protection (IGAS, IGJ, IGAE, 2018). Likewise, in order to create a system for the analysis of errors within this inter-ministry plan, the ONPE has been requested to develop with its partners, especially the Departments, a feedback method for sharing 'dramatic experiences' (measure 5). This was published in 2019 and gives guidelines for learning from dramatic events in child protection through "understanding together what happened and what contributed to making the drama happen" (ONED/ONPE, 2019) This approach shows that people are gradually gaining awareness: an error can be a source of knowledge; analysing procedures that have led to errors and dysfunctions will mean that they can be avoided in future, at least partly.

Improvement strategies regarding rights of young adults leaving care

The notion of 'trajectory' entered the legislative structure for child protection with the 2016 Act, but the effects are not yet visible. On the government's initiative, the Economic, Social and Environmental Council (CESE: Conseil économique, social et environnemental) issued an opinion (13 June 2018) on the measures to be taken to improve the trajectories of minors in care and the support given to young adults when they leave care. This opinion refers to an 'economic and social mess and educational nonsense' (Dulin, 2018:7).

In France, people who benefit from a public policy have long been identified according to 'statutory' characteristics (age, gender, disability, income threshold and so on). As a result, it is difficult to create complementary public policies that support *personal* trajectories (Séraphin, 2014; Séraphin and Bolter, 2017). This is particularly the case for securing the autonomy of minors who were subjects of child protection. The Act 2016-297 of 14 March 2016 on child protection introduced some provisions to make this process of autonomy more effective. At 17 years of age, placed children should have an interview with an official of the Department Council to discuss their life plans and the means for achieving them. Furthermore, any minor who comes of age during a school, university or vocational training year have support to complete the year. However, a young person placed as a minor does not have rights to specific or even partial support during the early years of adult life. The CESE's opinion proposes solutions that allow:

- better coordination of the different stakeholders and existing measures for young people in these two circumstances;
- safeguarding trajectories by adapting the working of institutions to the specific needs of young people; and
- providing better support for young people placed before and after 18 years of age, particularly with finances and accommodation.

Conclusion

This overview of the dysfunctions in the French child protection system highlights the importance and complexity of the system. It has been built on institutions whose spheres of activity evolve (justice, welfare, healthcare) and on professions that defend their own skills and codes of conduct (social professionals, psychologists, lawyers, doctors and so on). However, it also reflects a series of specific and evolving rules and values: for example, the importance of parents, even where they have been identified as 'failed'; the rejection of paedophilia; attaching importance to what children say. Cooperation among the different sectors and the coexistence of different standards give rise to misunderstandings and flaws in the system.

The research studies partly explain these dysfunctions, and also highlight the potential for new practices to improve prevention and the protection of children and young people. In addition to the measures to improve child protection referred to in this chapter, the law also obliges stakeholders at all levels with responsibilities in the sector to follow a specialised 240-hour training course on the different options in the field. Despite all precautions, children continue to lack protection from their parents and to suffer. However, the attention paid to children, their experiences and their views have continuously increased in France and elsewhere in Europe. This has been accompanied by greater sensitivity to tragedies. It is this increased awareness that leads to better identification of the system's weaknesses and, on the whole, to improving standards, laws and practices to strengthen protection and consider everyone's rights.

Notes

[1] The structure of the French population on 1 January 2018 is the following: Total: 65,018,096 people; 0–19 years old: 15,687,985; 20–59: 32,491,805; 60–4: 3,959,701; 65 and above: 12,878,605. Source: Insee.

[2] For the figures for 2014, see www.onpe.gouv.fr/chiffres-cles-en-protection-lenfance.

[3] Loi n° 2002-2 du 2 janvier 2002 rénovant l'action sociale et médico-sociale [Act 2002-2 of 2 January 2002 overhauling social and medical-social action].

[4] Loi n° 2007-293 du 5 mars 2007 réformant la protection de l'enfance [Act 2007-293 of 5 March 2007 reforming child protection].

[5] The name changed in 2016 to the National Observatory for Child Protection (ONPE).

[6] See www.onpe.gouv.fr/chiffres-cles-en-protection-lenfance.

[7] See www.has-sante.fr/portail/jcms/c_1775839/fr/maltraitance-des-children-y-penser-pour-reperer-savoir-reagir-pour-proteger.

[8] In France, a woman can give birth in a maternity ward without having her or the father's identity registered in the civil registry. Such children, without any established filiation, are wards of the state and adoptable.

[9] See www.egalite-femmes-hommes.gouv.fr/wp-content/uploads/2017/02/PlanVIOLENCES_-ENFANTS_2017-2019.pdf.

References

Barreyre, J., Fiacre, E.P., Joseph, V., Makdessi, Y. Cizeau, A., Vasseur, M. and Ecoffet, M.-C. (2008) *Une souffrance maltraitée. Parcours et situations de vie de jeunes dits 'incasables'* [*A Maltreated Suffering: Trajectories and Life Situations of Young People Classified as 'Unmarriable'*], Paris: Cedias.

Boddy, J., Statham, J., Danielsen, I., Geurts, E., Join-Lambert, H. and Euillet, S. (2014) 'Beyond Contact? Policy Approaches to Work with Families of Looked After Children in Four European Countries', *Children & Society*, 28(2): 152–61.

Boitout, J. (2015) '"La cabane de l'amour": Ou le traumatisme des équipes éducatives quand le passage à l'acte sexuel vient s'inscrire dans les failles des fonctionnements institutionnels' ['The Love Hut': Or the Trauma of Educator Teams When Sexual Intercourse Takes Place as a Result of the Failures of Institutional Functioning], in C. Savinaud and A. Harrault (eds) *Les Violences sexuelles d'adolescents* [*Adolescents' Sexual Abuse*], Toulouse: Eres, pp 175–83.

Bolter, F. and Séraphin, G. (2018) 'Child Protection in France', in L. Merkel-Holguin, J.D. Fluke and R.D. Krugman (eds) *National Systems of Child Protection: Understanding the International Variability and Context for Developing Policy and Practice*, Basel: Springer, pp 75–92.

Bolter, F., Keravel, E., Momic, M. and Séraphin, G. (2018) 'Protéger les enfants, protéger les parturientes: le double impératif de l'accouchement sous le secret en France' ['Protect Children, Protect Women Giving Birth: The Dual Imperative of Giving Birth in Secret in France'], *Chronique Revue de l'association internationale des magistrats de la jeunesse et de la famille* [*Chronicle Magazine of the International Association of Youth and Family Magistrates*], 12(1): 61–6.

Boutanquoi, M., Ansel, D. and Bournel-Bosson, M. (2014) *Les entretiens parents/professionnels en protection de l'enfance construire la confiance, Rapport pour l'ONED/ONPE* [*Interviews Between Parents and Child Protection Practitioners: Building Trust – Report for ONED/ONPE*], Besançon: Laboratoire de psychologie, Université de Franche-Comté.

Breugnot, P. (2011) *Les innovations socio-éducatives: Dispositifs et pratiques innovants dans le champ de la protection de l'enfance* [*Socio-educational Innovations: Innovative Mechanisms and Practices in the Field of Child Protection*], Rennes: Presses de l'EHESP.

CEDIF (Comité Élargi de Défense de l'Individu et des Familles [Enlarged Committee for the Defence of Individuals and Families]) (2018) *Une nouvelle affaire de viols en foyer* [*A New Case of Rapes in a Foster Institution*]. Available from: https://comitecedif.wordpress.com/2018/10/10/une-nouvelle-affaire-de-viols-en-foyer/.

Chemin, A. (2006) '"Il y a trop de lacunes dans la prise en charge des enfants"' ['"There Are Too Many Gaps in Child Care"'], *Le Monde*, 16 March. Available from: www.lemonde.fr/societe/article/2006/03/16/lacunes-dans-la-prise-en-charge-des-enfants_751401_3224.html.

Cyr, M. (2014) *Recueillir la parole de l'enfant témoin ou victime: De la théorie à la pratique* [*Listening to a Child Who Has Been a Witness or a Victim: From Theory to Practice*], Paris: Dunod, coll.Enfances.

Daadouch, C. (2017) 'Maltraitance au sein des établissements sociaux et médico-sociaux et levée du secret: derniers développements' ['Maltreatment Within Social and Medical-Social Establishments and Lifting Secrecy: Latest Developments]', *Journal du droit des jeunes*, 366/7: 39–44.

Défenseur des droits [Defender of Human Rights] (2014) *Compte rendu de la mission confiée par le Défenseur des droits et son adjointe, la Défenseure des enfants, à M. Alain Grevot, délégué thématique, sur l'histoire de Marina* [*Report on the Mission Requested by the Ombudsman on Rights and His Assistant, the Defender of Children in M. Alain Grevot, Thematic Delegate, on the Story of Marina*], Paris: La Documentation Française. Available from: https://juridique.defenseurdesdroits.fr/index.php?lvl=notice_display&id=12514.

Défenseur des droits [Defender of Human Rights] (2015) *Handicap et protection de l'enfance: des droits pour des enfants invisibles* [*Disability and Child Protection: Rights for Invisible Children*] Paris: Le défenseur des droits.

Donzelot, J. (1977) *La police des familles* [*The Family Police*], Paris: Editions de Minuit.

Dulin, A. (2018) *Prévenir les ruptures dans les parcours en protection de l'enfance. Avis du Conseil économique, social et environnemental* [*Prevent Disruptions in the Trajectory in Child Protection: Opinion of the Economic, Social and Environmental Council*], Paris: Journal officiel de la République française.

Duparc, A. (2015) *La jeunesse ébranlée des frères Saïd et Chérif Kouachi en Corrèze* [*The Harrowing Youth of the Kouachi Brothers (Saïd and Chérif) in Corrèze*]. Available from: www.mediapart.fr/journal/france/130115/la-jeunesse-ebranlee-des-freres-said-et-cherif-kouachi-en-correze?onglet=full.

Dupont, G. (2014) 'Mort de Marina: l'enquête énumère de multiples dysfonctionnements' ['The Death of Marina: The Inquiry Lists Multiple Dysfunctions'], *Le Monde*, 30 June. Available from: www.lemonde.fr/societe/article/2014/06/30/les-multiples-dysfonctionnements-avant-la-mort-de-marina-8-ans_4447622_3224.html.

Durning, P. (1985) 'Education et suppléance familiale en internat: Etude psychosociologique du climat socio-émotionnel et de ses incidences sur les enfants accueillis en établissements de rééducation et de thérapie, 1980/1985' ['Education and Family Susbstitution in Child Care Institutions: A Psycho-sociological Study of the Socio-emotional Climate and Its Effects on Children Staying in Re-education and Therapy Establishments, 1980/1985]', *Les cahiers du CTNERHI: Handicap et inadaptation*, n° 140.

Erbès-Seguin, S. (ed.) (1999) *Le contrat. Usages et abus d'une notion* [*The Contract: Use and Abuse of a Notion*], Paris: Desclée de Brouwer.

Euillet, S. and Zaouche-Gaudron, C. (2008) 'Des parents en quête de parentalité: le cas des parents dont l'enfant est accueilli à l'Aide sociale à l'Enfance [Parents in search of parenting: the case of parents whose child is under the care of Child Welfare Services]', *Sociétés et jeunesses en difficulté, revue pluridisciplinaire de recherche* [*Societies and Young People in Distress*], 5(Spring). Available from: https://journals.openedition.org/sejed/2703.

Fablet, D. (2008) 'L'émergence de la notion de parentalité en milieu(x) professionnel(s)' ['The Emergence of the Notion of Parenting in Professional Circles'], *Sociétés et jeunesses en difficulté, revue pluridisciplinaire de recherche* [*Societies and Young People in Distress*], 5(Spring). Available from: https://journals.openedition.org/sejed/3532.

Firdion, J.M. (2006) 'Influence des évènements de jeunesse et héritage social au sein de la population des utilisateurs des services d'aide aux sans-domicile' ['Influence of Events of Youth and Social Legacy Within the Population of Users of Assistance Services for Homeless People'], *Economie et statistique* [*Economy and Statistics*], 391(1): 85–114.

Frechon, I. and Marquet, L. (2016) 'Comment les jeunes placés à l'âge de 17 ans préparent-ils leur avenir?' ['How Do Young People Placed at the Age of 17 Prepare Their Future?'], Documents de travail INED 227 [INED Working Document 227]. Available from: www.ined.fr/fichier/s_rubrique/25515/document_travail_2016_227_sortie.de.placement_autonomie.des.jeunes.place.s.fr.pdf.

Gabel, M. (2000) 'La maltraitance faite aux enfants' ['Maltreatment of Children'], *Actualité et dossier en santé publique* [*Public Health Current Issues*], 31: 26–34.

Gabriel, T., Keller, S., Bolter, F., Martin-Blachais, M.P. and Séraphin, G. (2013) 'Out of Home Care in France and Switzerland', *Psychosocial Intervention*, 22(3): 214–25.

Garapon, A. and Salas, D. (2006) *Les Nouvelles Sorcières de Salem. Leçons d'Outreau* [*The New Salem Witches: Lessons from Outreau*], Paris: Seuil.

IGAS, IGJ, IGAE (2018) Mission sur les morts violentes d'enfants au sein des familles, *Évaluation du fonctionnement des services sociaux, médicaux, éducatifs et judiciaires concourant à la protection de l'enfance*. Available from www.justice.gouv.fr/art_pix/2018-044%20Rapport_Morts_violentes_enfants.pdf

Johannès, F. (2005) 'Au procès d'Angers, un avocat de la défense dénonce les erreurs des travailleurs sociaux et des magistrats' ['In the Trial in Angers, a Defence Lawyer Denounces Errors Made by Social Workers and Magistrates'], *Le Monde*, 5 July. Available from: www.lemonde.fr/societe/article/2005/07/05/au-proces-d-angers-un-avocat-de-la-defense-denonce-les-erreurs-des-travailleurs-sociaux-et-des-magistrats_669520_3224.html.

Join-Lambert Milova, H. (2006) 'Autonomie et participation d'adolescents placés en foyer (France, Allemagne, Russie)' ['Autonomy and Participation of Adolescents Placed in Care (France, Germany, Russia) '], *Sociétés et jeunesses en difficulté, revue pluridisciplinaire de recherche* [*Societies and Young People in Distress*], 2(Autumn). Available from: https://journals.openedition.org/sejed/188.

Join-Lambert, H. (2012) *Les accueils de jour en protection de l'enfance. Une nouvelle place pour les parents?* [*Day Care in Child Protection: A New Role for Parents?*], Paris: L'Harmattan.

Join-Lambert, H. (2016) 'Parental Involvement and Multi-Agency Support Services for High-Need Families in France', *Social Policy and Society*, 2(15): 317–29.

Joxe, P. (2010) 'L'affaire d'Outreau et les enfants' ['The Outreau Case and Children'], *Après-demain*, 3(15): 12–15.

Le Parisien (2015) 'Ici, on a vu grandir les frères Kouachi' ['The Kouachi Brothers Were Seen Growing Up Here'], *Le Parisien*, 28 January. Available from: www.leparisien.fr/week-end/ici-on-a-vu-grandir-les-freres-kouachi-28-01-2015-4486299.php.

Mackiewicz, M.P. (2002) 'Early Residential Foster Care: Parental Experiences Concerning Their Co-operation with Professional Workers', in E.J. Knorth, P.M. Van Den Bergh and F. Verheij (eds) *Professionalization and Participation in Child and Youth Care: Challenging Understandings in Theory and Practice*, Burlington, VT: Ashgate, pp 201–11.

Mallevaey, B. (2012) 'La parole de l'enfant en justice' ['The Child's Word in the Field of Justice'], *Recherches familiales* [*Family Research*],1(9): 117–29. Available from: www.cairn.info/revue-recherches-familiales-2012-1-page-117.htm17-129.

Ministère de la Justice [Ministry of Justice] (2005) *Rapport du groupe de travail chargé de tirer les enseignements du traitement judiciaire de l'affaire dite 'd'Outreau'* [*Report of the Working Group Responsible for Learning the Lessons from the Judicial Treatment of the 'Outreau' Case*], Paris: La Documentation française.

Naves, P., Cathala, B. and Deparis, J.-M. (2000) *Accueils provisoires et placements d'enfants et d'adolescents: des décisions qui mettent à l'épreuve le système français de protection de l'enfance et de la famille* [*Provisional Care and Placements of Children and Adolescents: Decisions that Test the French Child and Family Protection System*], Paris: Ministère de l'Emploi et de la Solidarité et du Ministère de la Justice.

Neyrand, G. and Mekboul, S. (2014) *Corps sexué de l'enfant et normes sociales. La normativité corporelle en société néolibérale* [*Sexual Body of a Child and Social Norms: Standard Body Rules in a Neoliberal Society*], Toulouse: Eres.

ONED/ONPE (2014) *Considérer la parole de l'enfant victime. Étude des Unités d'accueil médico-judiciaires* [*Considering the Child Victim's Word: Study on Medico-Judicial Units*], Paris: La Documentation française.

ONED/ONPE (2015) *L'accompagnement vers l'autonomie des 'jeunes majeurs'* [*Support for the Autonomy of 'Young Adults'*], Paris: La Documentation française.

ONED/ONPE (2016) *La situation des pupilles de l'Etat. Enquête au 31 décembre 2014* [*The Situation of Wards of the State: Survey of 31 December 2014*], Paris: La Documentation française.

ONED/ONPE (2019). *Le retour sur événement dramatique en protection de l'enfance : sens et repères méthodologiques* [*Feedback on dramatic events in Chuild Protection : sense and methodoligcal guidelines*]. Available from: www.onpe.gouv.fr/system/files/publication/livret_red_complet_web_0.pdf

Potin, E. (2012) *Enfants placés, déplacés, replacés: parcours en protection de l'enfance* [*Placed, Displaced, Re-placed Children: Trajectory in Child Protection*], Toulouse: Eres.

Robin, P. (2013) 'L'évaluation de la maltraitance: Comment prendre en compte la perspective de l'enfant' ['The Evaluation of Maltreatment: How to Take the Child's Perspective into Account'], doctoral thesis, Rennes: Presses Universitaires de Rennes.

Sécher, R. (2009) *Reconnaissance sociale et dignité des parents d'enfants placés en protection de l'enfance* [*Social recognition and dignity of the parents of children placed in child protection*], Université de Nantes: Thèse en Sciences de l'éducation.

Séraphin, G. (2014) 'Protéger un enfant en accompagnant la construction de son parcours de vie. Les récents rapports "Enfance/Famille" en perspective' ['Protect a Child by Helping with the Construction of His/Her Life Path: Recent Reports *"Childhood/Family"* in Perspective'], *Journal des droits de jeunes* [*Youth Law Journal*], 338/9: 47–63.

Séraphin, G. (2017) 'Les mesures de protection. Enfant maltraité, en danger... de quoi parle-t-on ?' [Protection measures. Maltreated child, child in danger... What are we talking about?], in H. Romano (ed.) *Accompagner en justice l'enfant victime de maltraitance ou d'accident* [*Accompanying the Child Victim of Abuse or Accident*], Paris: Dunod, pp 45–56.

Séraphin, G. and Bolter, F. (2017) 'Making Better Sense of Children's Trajectories in Child Protection in France', *Children and Youth Services Review*, 73: 145–8.

Tillard, B., Vallerie, B. and Rurka, A. (2015) 'Intervention éducative contrainte. Relations entre familles et professionnels intervenant à domicile' ['Constrained educational intervention. Relations between families and practitioners at home'], *Enfances, familles, générations* [*Childhood, Families, Generations*], 24. Available from: https://efg.revues.org/1011.

Tomasovitch, G. (2002) 'Douze ans de réclusion pour François Supéri [Twelve years in jail for François Supéri]', *Le Parisien*, 15 March. Available from: www.leparisien.fr/faits-divers/douze-ans-de-reclusion-pour-francois-superi-15-03-2002-2002896777.php.

Touahria, A. (2011) 'La force des liens dématérialisés. Associations de parents d'enfants placés, technologies de l'information et mobilisations [The power of dematerialised links. Parents' associations of placed children, IT technologies and mobilisation]', in M.C. Bureau and I. Sainsaulieu (eds) *Reconfigurations de l'Etat social en pratique: les interactions entre institutionnels, professionnels et citoyens dans le champ de l'intervention sociale* [*Reconfigurations of the Social State in Practice: Interactions Between Institutional, Professional and Citizens in the Field of Social Intervention*], Lille: Presses Universitaires du Septentrion, pp 265–80.

Zotian, E. (2017) *Les professionnels face aux modes d'expression des jeunes enfants confiés à l'Aide sociale à l'enfance* [*Professionals Faced with the Modes of Expression of Young Children Entrusted to Child Welfare Services*], Paris: Rapport final pour l'Observatoire national de l'enfance en danger.

12

Errors and mistakes in child protection: an unspoken issue in Italy?

Teresa Bertotti

Introduction

In Italy there has been no explicit debate about errors and mistakes in child protection, nor is there a system for reviewing fatal and serious cases, as there is in many of the countries cited in this book. Generally speaking, the debate tends to address failures of the system or emerging problems in society, rather than specific professional misconduct. Discussion and doubts about failures and uncertainties seem to develop only within individual child protection teams. Apparently, the problem in Italy is non-existent; or more precisely we may say that it is unspoken. In order to discover this characteristic of the Italian perspective, this chapter will first outline the context of the population, the welfare system, the organisation of the Italian child protection system and provide a brief overview of its development, with a focus on child removals. On this basis, the second section illustrates how errors and mistakes are acknowledged in child protection in Italy. The third section focuses on the effects that publicly apportioning blame might have on child protection, and serves as a bridge to the description of the responsibilities and main strategies adopted to tackle and prevent errors. Some considerations of the unspoken character of the Italian approach to errors will conclude the chapter. Because of the lack of specific studies, this chapter is mainly based on the author's years of experience in the field, as both a professional and an academic, and on analysis of existing materials, with the abiding hope that further research will be carried out.

The context

According to Istat (2018), in 2017, the Italian population numbered 60,500,000 persons, of whom 10,008,033 were children under 18

(16.6 per cent of the overall population). Italy is an ageing country, with 21.7 per cent of the population aged over 65 and a steadily declining birth rate since 2008. Families are becoming smaller and 'long', decreasing in breadth, growing older and more unstable. Single parents are on the increase (totalling 15.8 per cent in 2016, compared to 5.5 per cent in 1983), and so is the rate of separations and divorces (+63 per cent from 1996 to 2015) involving almost 65,000 children. The economic crisis has had a strong impact on levels of family poverty; 10 per cent of households and 14.3 per cent of children were living in absolute poverty in 2013, with an evident impact on educational performance (UNICEF, 2014).

Italy is classed as having a Southern Europe and Mediterranean welfare system (Ferrera, 1996) characterised by the strong role for families in the provision of care. Although the family has the main responsibility for protecting individuals from socio-economic risks, the level of allowances for families is low and unequal; Italy has been classified as a country with one of the lowest degrees of defamiliasation (Naldini and Saraceno, 2008; Cho, 2014). The Italian welfare system is also characterised by a preference for cash transfers, and a great and continuing disparity between the north and south of the country (Ascoli and Pavolini, 2015). The bases for its universal welfare system were laid in the 1980s, with the establishment of the National Health Service depending on the regional authorities, and a network of fundamental services that still constitute the backbone of the present welfare system. During the 1990s, the health system underwent a radical transformation, with the separation of social provision and the introduction of managerial and neoliberal principles (Maino and Neri, 2011). The social welfare system was regulated at the national level later in 2000 (Law 328/2000) as an integrated system of social services based on the principle of devolution and subsidiarity, with the establishment of basic levels of assistance guaranteed cross-nationally. The welfare system is managed at the local level by the 20 Italian regions for the health system and by the municipalities for social welfare; there being more than 8,000 of them, small municipalities group together in 'territorial areas' for the management of social services.

Although policies for child welfare have existed since the establishment of Italy as a nation and after the Second World War, the real boost to child welfare came in the 1990s, with the implementation of the United Nations Convention on the Rights of the Child (UNCRC) and the approval of the landmark Bill (no. 285/1997) significantly called 'Promotion of the Rights and Opportunities in Childhood and Adolescence'. This law marked a change, fostering a global approach to child well-being focused on children's rights and the modernisation of services, and establishing a set of institutional bodies devoted to implementing the UNCRC and promoting best interventions.

The Italian system of the child protection today

The Italian child protection system is based on a complex relationship between the welfare system and the judicial authorities whose regulation stems from a patchwork of norms from different sources that operate at different levels. Briefly, the legal framework operates at the national level, with some fundamental norms dating back to the 1930s, (during the fascist regime) while the welfare system operates at the regional level. Since the 1970s legislative powers on education, social welfare and health have been decentralised to the 20 Italian regions.

The reference point for child welfare intervention is the municipality, the *Comune*, as the point of the public administration closest to the general public, subject to democratic control through elections (Bifulco, 2017). According to Social Reform No. 328/2000, municipalities are responsible for the 'promotion of children's rights' and the 'promotion and support of family responsibilities', which includes 'the protection of children in distress, at risk, or in danger' (art. 16, 22). Within this frame, they have also the duty of implementing court orders. Hence, there are two scenarios in which children in need are supported. The first, and most common, is on a voluntary basis, following the request from the parents. The second, less frequent, scenario is compulsory, following orders of the Juvenile Court. In both situations, services offered by the municipality are linked with the community and may range among social support and counselling, pedagogical support, combining housing and education resources, income, and employment support. In order to implement court orders, social services cooperate with services in the health system, which provides therapeutic support for adults and children, and with non-profit organisations, which provide residential care homes and home educational support services. Social workers and psychologists are the main professionals involved in a child protection team, with social workers usually employed by municipalities and psychologists by health agencies.

The legal framework provides that only the Juvenile Court is entitled to intervene in the private life of the family for the protection of children. The threshold for intervention is broadly defined: whenever parental behaviour leads to 'serious injuries' or is 'detrimental' to the child, according to the Civil Code (art. 330, 333) or when a child is in a 'state of moral or material abandonment', according to the laws on Adoption and Foster Care (no. 184/1983, and no. 149/2001). In these cases, the Court can impose obligations on parents, assign the child to the care of the local authority, order out-of-home placement of the child, and can remove the parents' parental powers. The law also states that a child can be adopted, replacing his/her birth parents with adoptive parents whenever the support given fails, in the long run, to resolve the problems of the family.

The Italian system imposes an obligation to report to the Court on all public officials or those carrying out public functions who have knowledge of any situation of 'abandonment or detriment' to children (art. 9 of Law no. 149/2001) or of certain crimes regarding children.

Referrals are made to the Juvenile Prosecution Office, for protection measures involving the Court, if needed. The Court makes its decisions through a council chamber composed of two magistrates and two lay judges; this is done after hearings involving the parents and children aged 12 or over, and including psychological and social assessments from local services. Following these investigations, the Court establishes the protection measures deemed necessary and the level of limitation of parental responsibilities. The implementation of court orders is a matter for the local authorities, through their child protection services. Crossnationally, there is a wide variation in the responsibilities and powers attributed to local authorities by the Courts, hence leading to a high degree of discretion and heterogeneity on how local services manage relations with the family.

As this complex interplay between local services and the Juvenile Court develops, the responsibility of each system is overlapping, muddled and unclear, causing much dispute and tension. The lack of a comprehensive law, such as a Children Act intended to clarify several issues raised, mainly related to the relation between administrative and judicial powers, has been repeatedly criticised, without any significant results until now (UNCRC, 2017).

The development of the child protection system

The present Italian child protection system originated in the 1980s and developed through various stages over the years, including modifying its laws, the organisation of services and professional cultures, oscillating between child protection and family-oriented approaches (Gilbert et al, 2011; Fargion, 2014). As in other Western countries, it started with the 'discovery' of child maltreatment and the acknowledgement that risks for children might also arise from within the family, and not only from the outside (Spratt et al, 2015). For Italian society, this was a shocking discovery because of the ideal of family and maternal bonding which is inherent to Italian culture. The new awareness was initiated by AIPAI (the Italian Association for the Prevention of Abuse to Children), the establishment of the first national child helpline, and the opening of a few pioneer centres for the protection and treatment of abused children and their families. The main ones were in Milan, the CBM, Centro per il Bambino Maltrattato e la cura della crisi familiare [Centre for Maltreated Children and Treatment of Family Crises] and in Rome, attached to the Bambin Gesù Paediatric Hospital. This stage was marked by a child protection approach, acknowledging the existence of child maltreatment, addressing the need to detect abuse and to protect children. Nonetheless, according to Bertotti and Campanini (2013) it was moderated by a family-oriented approach witnessed by the definition of child maltreatment as a 'family problem' and a call to link child protection with the 'treatment of family relationships'. In this approach, professionals, especially psychologists, were challenged to learn how to work with families who have not asked for help, deploying the mandatory context created by the court orders to induce positive changes in family relationships, starting from the judicial request to evaluate parental capacities (Cirillo and Di Blasio, 1989). Through this approach 'a third way between neglecting abused children and mere sentencing of the abusing parent' would have be possible (Cirillo and Di Blasio, 1989: 2).

This approach informed the following development of public specialised teams that were created within the framework of the health system, throughout the country in the 1990s. The creation of a national network of professionals and services (CISMAI, Coordinamento Italiano Servizi contro Maltrattamento e Abuso all'Infanzia [National Network of Services Against Child Maltreatment]), operating on the basis of the principles embraced by International Society for Prevention Child Abuse and Neglect (ISPCAN) supported the development of new competences among professionals. The focus of the system moved towards a child protection approach and decisive improvements to Italian legislation on prosecutions of child abuse were made.

Later, in the second decade of the 2000s, a more family-oriented approach emerged. It was linked to the impact of the economic crisis that, on one hand, increased the level of poverty of families and, on the other, cut financial resources for services, as well as the introduction of neoliberal policies in the health sector. Many specialised teams were dismantled, and new local 'child and family services' were created by the municipalities. The focus on protection was replaced by a call for 'shared responsibilities', for the 'involvement of the community' and a stronger commitment to supporting families. This encouraged the call for a 'new paradigm' based on an ecological and relational perspective, and for a greater involvement on the part of families (Serbati and Milani, 2013). The topic of child abuse disappeared from public debate, substituted by the need to reduce out-of-home placements and deinstitutionalisation and a new discourse on the importance of family bonds.

Child removals in Italy

From the end of the Second World War throughout the 1970s, child placement in large institutions was a widespread policy. Through the action of national bodies, such as ONMI (Opera Nazionale Maternità Infanzia [National Body for Maternity and Childhood]) and ENAOLI (Ente Nazionale Assistenza Orfani del Lavoro Italiani [National Orphan Aid Institution]), hundreds of children from poor and large families, orphans with disabilities or born outside marriage, were housed in big institutions, managed by religious or secular bodies. At that time, placements were mainly voluntary, following the parents' request because of their inability to take care of children, the lack of local services and the family legislation prohibiting the recognition of children born out of wedlock. It was calculated that during the 1970s, around 200,000 children (from an overall population of around 53,000,000) were accommodated. Some of these institutions were reported for maltreating and abusing children, making them live in harmful hygienic conditions, without minimum care for their needs. Guidetti Serra and Santanera described, in their 1973 published book, that around 18 judicial proceedings against institutions for abuse resulted in convictions; testifying how children were exploited by the owner for the income provided by the state for their upkeep. The trials also demonstrated the tangle of complicity, connivance and corruption that allowed these institutions to continue to operate for years, despite reports from supervisory bodies like ONMI. Moreover, despite the convictions, no reparation was made to the victims, neither at that time nor more recently.

The issue has recently re-emerged with regards to a residential institution in Tuscany, called Il Forteto, where children were maltreated and sexually abused. Although the managers were convicted in 1985, the institution remained open until 2015, and Bertani and colleagues (2017) argue that this was possible because of ideological bias, lack of control, and scepticism concerning the victims' allegations remained as it was in the 1970s. These scandals contributed to the inclusion of childcare structures in the movement for 'deinstitutionalisation', that spread in the 1970s fostered by Franco Basaglia, against 'total institutions' and psychiatric asylums.

In the 1980s, in connection with the decentralisation and the development of local services, new forms of alternative care, such as foster care and small residential units, spread through Italy. Also, thanks to the impetus imparted by the new law on adoption and foster care (no. 184/1983), the number of children placed progressively declined to 45,000 at the end of the 1980s. It is interesting to note that these changes were often supported by juvenile judges collaborating with social services, who depicted themselves as on the same side for the protection of children (De Carolis et al, 1979). In 2001, a new call for deinstitutionalisation was made, establishing a five-year plan for the closure of all large institutions for children and giving a child the right to live within a family or foster care, as the preferred form of alternative care. In the following years, the number of children placed decreased to almost 30,000, almost equally divided between family-based foster care and residential care, reaching a placement rate of 2.9/ 1,000 children, which is one of the lowest in Europe (Belotti, 2009; Del Valle et al, 2013).

Understanding errors and mistakes in child protection in Italy

Dealing with unclear rules

The debate on errors and mistakes in Italian child protection can be reconstructed retrospectively by considering the main issues of discussion that accompanied the principal changes described in the preceding section. In fact, many of the developments were accompanied by debates at different levels among practitioners, such as at conferences, in parliament or in political forums. Two specialised journals were also an important arena for discussion: *Minori e Giustizia* [*Minors and Justice*], a historical journal supported by the national association of juvenile judges, and *Maltrattamento e Abuso all'Infanzia* [*Maltreatment and Abuse Against Children*], a specialised academic journal originally linked to CISMAI. As noted earlier, the Italian child protection system is characterised by a patchwork of norms providing an unclear picture of roles and responsibilities, mainly in the relations between local social services and the judicial authorities.

The initial debate focused on misunderstandings and errors in the interpretation of norms. Reciprocal allegations of omissions of the necessary protection tasks between the judiciary and the social services' sector were made. Discussions also accompanied the efforts to clarify the aspects of the process. Unclear aspects ranged from professionals' obligation to refer to the judicial authorities to the role of social services in the implementation of court orders. For practitioners, the obligation to refer represented a highly sensitive issue because of the radical change that moving from a voluntary to a mandatory context creates in the relation to the family. Many tensions in the relationship between professionals and family are situated at this stage. And this tension increases when referrals also have to be made to the adult criminal court. To overcome this problem, many organisations have created two different types of services, mandatory and voluntary, already mentioned. Child protection services have also been criticised for inappropriate assessments of the risk for the child, both in the direction of neglecting as well as of emphasising the need for protection. Also, the management of care orders has been criticised because of the extent of limitation of parental responsibilities and the regulation of visits to children.

Many of these tensions qualify the relations between social services and families, as demonstrated by a recent study on aggression against social workers, where 64.2 per cent of such incidents are related to child protection matters (Sicora et al, 2018).

At first, in line with the initial conception that juvenile judges were 'partners' of child protection services and played a role as 'reconcilers' toward the family (Moro, 2002), many doubts were resolved through direct contact between judges and practitioners. Afterwards, with the increase in referrals in the late 1990s, the belief began to spread that social services had too much power, more power than the Juvenile Court. The idea that the rights of parents and families were not sufficiently safeguarded became equally widespread. In 2001, the amendment of the Constitution introducing greater guarantees for the defence in all court hearings brought elements of adversarial proceedings also in the civil Juvenile Court hearings, including a greater role for parents' lawyers and the possibility to name the lawyer for the child. The juvenile judges changed their position from being a partner to being a third party making their judgment in the confrontation between contrasting positions. Consequently, child protection services had to rethink their position: no longer allied with the judges but just one of the parties.

The impact of the 'discovery' of child sexual abuse

The 'discovery' that children could be also sexually abused marked a turning point in this process. Until 1996, child abuse was considered only as incest and classed as a crime against morality; however, with the first cases beginning in the 1990s, Italy acknowledged the backwardness of its system regarding both the norms and professional competences; professionals were not acquainted with the complex traits of secrecy and difficulties to detect this kind of abuse; judges and investigators were unprepared to involve children in judicial procedures. These shortcomings on both sides lead to false-positive as well as real-negative cases. The effort to improve developed through harsh confrontations on the battlefield of the criminal courts with reciprocal accusations, realising that clinical needs of children could not be easily matched with the needs of judicial proceedings (Malacrea, 2011).

Nevertheless, professional competences and the law improved, increasing the number of referrals and conviction of abusers. However, the recognition of this kind of abuse provoked a backlash at the turn of the millennium. Professionals and specialised teams were accused of exaggerating facts, influencing the children, and were heavily criticised for overzealous protection. This happened in a case that occupied the media headlines in 1998. It concerned a group of children involved in satanic ritual abuse in a small rural area in northern Italy. Fourteen adults were investigated following allegations of abusing and prostituting their children, the production of child pornography in satanic rituals, and 15 children were placed in out-of-home care. The parish priest, who was indicated as the mastermind of the ritual abuses, died of a heart attack before the end of the trial. Professionals involved in forensic assessments were heavily attacked, accused of manipulating the children. The trial proved the truth of the allegations and convicted half of the accused; the other half were acquitted for lack of evidence. Despite this result, this case increased practitioners' concerns in dealing with such cases. A parliamentary inquiry was also launched by one of the abuser's lawyers, denouncing the excess of power of child protection services. The case contributed to the reform of judicial hearings mentioned previously. More generally, since then public discourse on child maltreatment began to decline.

Effects of blaming in the public debate on child protection

During the 1990s, when Italy begun to realise the existence of child maltreatment and abuse, the media were very active in covering the issue of child protection. They did so in two ways: considering specific cases, in the various stages of the judicial hearings, or conducting wider debates, addressing shortcomings of the system. With the advent of a more family-oriented approach in the first decade of the 2000s, the media debate appears less polarised. Moreover, thanks to codes of conduct established with journalists, there is a greater respect for confidentiality and the anonymity of children.

In Italy, there seem to be no studies providing evidence of public blame shaping professional decision-making and practices. Information can be indirectly obtained from Allegri's studies on the media image of social workers, showing that social workers are mentioned in the press mainly in relation to child protection matters (Allegri, 2011).

Stories of service malpractice are more often covered by the local than the national press; these stories usually stem either from parents, complaining that they are victims of unjust decisions, or from judicial proceedings. For instance, in 2012, the forceful removal of a ten-year-old child from school, following a court order, was filmed by his aunt and reported in the newspapers. The behaviour of the social workers and the police was heavily criticised in national and local media.

The impact of public blaming on services is always stressful; however, it is managed differently internally and externally. In terms of the external, practitioners do not have a direct contact with the press. Publicly, it is the managers who take the stand with the aim of safeguarding the institution and the professionals. If they are employed by a public administration, practitioners are not even allowed to participate in public debates and, as social workers, they also have deontological obligation to client confidentiality. On the one hand this helps to protect the individuals involved but it also feeds the notion that errors exist, due to the silence of practitioners.

Public administrations may also have political concerns due to the need to maintain consent and defend unpopular positions; this is especially relevant in small communities and when children who are to be protected are linked to eminent families from the community. As Malacrea (2001) commented, this was evident in the case of the satanic abuse, mentioned earlier, where public blaming on the media was expressly used to put pressure on the court.

Internally, the impact of public blaming is dealt with in different ways. Usually, the distress is handled within the professional team, where practitioners may feel a sense of support to work out what happened. However, real errors are rarely handled within the team; they are more likely to be discussed either in individual conversations between the manager and the practitioner, or during team supervision, which in Italy is always external. Due to restrictions imposed by austerity measures, this opportunity is becoming rarer (Bertotti, 2016). In cases where the organisation is not sufficiently sensitive and professionals are involved in judicial proceedings, individuals are left to deal with the judicial consequences and the painful feelings of failure and guilt on their own.

Because of the general character of condemnation in the debate and because they are involved in court hearings, the prevailing attitude among practitioners and managers is defensive and reserved. This climate rarely leaves room for open debate on errors and seldom constitutes a source of learning.

Dealing with errors and strategies to handle and avoid errors

Different levels of responsibilities and strategies to avoid errors should be viewed from a systemic perspective considering macro, meso and micro levels (Munro, 2005).

At the micro level, errors are explicitly considered only when they fall within the legal framework: this occurs following a complaint from a person alleging that she or he has been victim of misconduct by practitioners; complainants may seek compensation in the civil domain or may make an accusation of crime. In the former case, the first to be interrogated is the public administration, on which the primary responsibility falls. If the administration has been found liable, it may claim internally against the practitioner. While the public administrations, through the managers, have a responsibility to act according to the law, professional practitioners are required to act 'scientifically and consciously', according to their technical and professional autonomy, as quoted in Law n. 84/1993, art. 1, recognizing the social work profession. When the allegation relates to a criminal offence the responsibility is personal and the practitioner is subjected to the legal process. In these cases, organisations are not obliged to provide legal support for their employee: in some cases they do so, in others they do not. Rather, they may consider having been harmed themselves by the behaviour of the employee. For this reason, professional associations started to suggest their members to activate special forms of insurance.

Finally, social workers or psychologists, as registered professions, are also called on to respond to their professional organisations, which have the duty to investigate and the power to impose penalties in case of professional misconduct. In Italy, every person is entitled to complain to the disciplinary board of a profession, requesting the investigation of alleged unprofessional conduct. This seems to happen quite frequently as shown by recent research among 12 social workers' disciplinary councils that found that 38 per cent of the complaints involved child protection matters (Soregotti, 2019).

Beyond the legal framework, it is not easy to find strategies clearly aimed at preventing errors or at providing indications for handling them. However, scattered and almost concealed in the many articulations of the system, strategies can be detected indirectly; they could also be drawn from analysing the public debate and claims about the most pressing needs. As a consequence of the economic crisis, the actual debate is more focused on the ways to combat the persistent child and family poverty rather the need to protect children and related errors. It could be speculated that intervention in private family life is something that the state cannot afford nowadays. Already burdened by many endeavours, families are more and more irreplaceable as the cornerstone of the welfare system and need to be protected and supported, without any further intrusion. Politically, the position of children and their maltreatment is no longer an urgent problem thus driving to a potential lower level of protection (Belotti, 2013). However, somehow embedded in the system, changes introduced in previous periods to deal with child maltreatment have partly remained. For instance, providing abused children with specific psychosocial support for care and during judicial hearings is a minimum level of assistance that should be guaranteed throughout the country.

At the macro level, control, monitoring and specific guidelines seem to be the main strategies to prevent errors. Out-of-home placements have been monitored since 1983, by the law on adoption and fostering that established a regular system of monitoring placements. Every six months, all residential units are obliged to inform the Juvenile Court and the local authorities about the children placed and must report on the frequency of their contact with parents; the court is obliged then to start the procedure for adoption, if it is found that a child is abandoned. Residential units are also subject to a system of accreditation and control, administered at the local level. However, this is not mandatory for all local authorities and, in 2014, the National Ombudsman for Children (AGIA: Autorità Garante Infanzia e Adolescenza) issued national quality standards in order to reduce the cross-national disparities.

At the national level, several bodies have the role of monitoring and orienting policies and practices. The main one is the National

Observatory on Childhood and Adolescence (NOCA), which is composed of representatives from government, local authorities and civil society. It has the duty of drawing up the three-year national plan for childhood and the Italian report on the implementation of the UNCRC, responding to recommendations made by the United Nations Committee on the Rights of the Child. Also, coordinated by Save the Children Italy, more than 150 associations write the UNCRC non-governmental report, addressing the main shortcomings of the system. Attached to NOCA, the National Documentation Centre carries out research and monitoring activities of existing laws and needs related to children's rights. The Childhood Parliamentary Commission is the legislative body entitled to discuss new laws but also to deal with parliamentary inquiries that may results from alleged misbehaviour. In 2011, the National Ombudsmen for Children was also established, with the task of monitoring children's rights, collecting complaints on their violations and producing guidelines to address major shortcomings in the system.

The meso levels of service organisation and professional practice are the most important for preventing and handling errors in daily practice.

Guidelines and protocols are commonly used also at this level to clarify uncertainties in relations between child protection services and the judiciary, to organise inter-agency cooperation, and to support internal working. In the absence of national law, several juvenile courts provided directions for social services regarding the vaguer steps in the judicial process, resulting in very different regulations across the country. Moreover, when the health system withdrew from the direct management of specialised child protection teams, inter-institutional agreements became necessary. These now provide the framework for organising inter-agency cooperation and the various forms of multi-professional teams existing in Italy; they are also responsible for defining institutional responsibilities, financial loads and professional recommendations. The multitude of local regulations indicates the high degree of fragmentation and heterogeneity in the country, as demonstrated in a study carried out by Bollini in 2009, who found that more than 40 documents were produced by different bodies between 1998 and 2008.

Collective decision-making is another strategy widely adopted at the micro level of decisions in single cases. Collective decisions are quoted as 'best practice' both in in multi-agency work, as well as at the level of a single service. Sharing different views and team discussion are considered very important by practitioners for obtaining a better understanding and minimising possible errors. However, some research has shown that team discussion is influenced by factors far removed from the features of the case, such as professional status or access to resources, and are hampered also by the risk of bureaucratisation (Motta, 2013; Bertotti, 2016).

A number of agencies have also developed procedures and assessment tools aimed at supporting good practice and avoiding errors, specifically for the investigation of the risks for a child and the assessment of parental capabilities. At the local level, examples are the project on social evaluation of parental care carried out in Bologna and the guidelines on assessment produced in Naples (Comune di Napoli, 2013; Cheli et al, 2015). At the national level, the RISC project on the appropriateness of risk assessments, promoted by the Zancan Foundation, and the PIPPI project on prevention of placement promoted by the University of Padua, are examples (RISC, 2011; LabRIEF, 2015). Also, professional associations have issued guidelines for good practice: CISMAI is very active as are the national boards of social workers and of psychologists.

Finally, at the level of the single service, *the professional team* is an important place where complex decisions are made, and difficulties could be discussed. It is mainly up to service managers to foster a climate for exchange so that discussion becomes a learning opportunity. Teams may also have external supervision, dealing with the emotional impacts and the overall management of a case (Allegri, 1997). In connection with the introduction of the adversarial judicial proceedings, many services hired a legal advisor, who has the task of advising both the administration and practitioners about their duties and obligations.

Concluding remarks: the unspoken issue

From the preceding discussion, it might seem that the issue of errors is almost non-existent in Italy, as it is rarely addressed explicitly. However, it seems very present, implicitly, in the pervading feeling of caution and mistrust between all sectors within the system. In the absence of further studies, it may be speculated that this is linked to the structure of the Italian child protection system, based on a muddled collaboration between the justice and the welfare systems that are characterised by very different logics and regulations. In the absence of a law that coherently remedies the overlaps and contradictions, errors seem related to misunderstanding and potentially diverse lines of accountability.

The possibility of committing errors remains unspoken. It is seldomly mentioned, either in the multitude of guidelines or in the various organisational settings. Informal discussions with practitioners and experts in various fields carried out in the preparation of this chapter triggered surprise and reluctance to recognise the issue. Proposals for more detailed research also provoked some resistance and even outright refusal. Recognising explicitly the possibility of making mistakes could risk damaging further the already fragile image of child protection services and might increase the existing criticism and mistrust of professionals. In other words, it seems that professionals, or the overall system, cannot acknowledge the possibility of errors, thus indicating the preponderance of a no-failure culture (Sicora, 2017).

This culture is fostered by a system where errors are only recognised explicitly when they fall within the legal framework, by way of civil or criminal complaints or referrals to disciplinary boards. Unavoidably, since these work with a binary code of guilt/innocence, they induce defensive attitudes. In addition, when revealed to the media this 'sport' of blaming is often magnified, and professionals are left to deal with the painful feelings of failure and suffer in silence. According to Malacrea (2001), it might also reflect a collective reluctance to recognise the existence of aberrant behaviours by adults against children.

Nevertheless, day-to-day practice highlights many scenarios that produce an awareness of making errors, such as multidisciplinary teams, collective decisions, supervision and legal advisors; however, none of these deals openly with the possibility of acknowledging errors and learning from them. The idea exists in theory, but is left implicit, almost hidden and unexpressed, as something of which to be ashamed.

This is also evident at the macro level, in how the Italian child protection system approaches improvement. Legislation, guidelines and other regulations are issued with the intent of addressing shortcomings and shortages. However, very rarely do they take their cue from an explicit and shared analysis of the errors and shortcomings that they are intended to address. Thus, the new measures may appear to be driven by ideology, such as 'defending' the family or the child, rather than by an analysis of facts. It seems that the prevailing attitude in Italy is to respond more promptly to top-down indications coming from an external source because it possesses moral or institutional authority, rather than because it is the result of reflective and rational practice (Fronte quoted in Sicora, 2017:48-49).

A positive counter-tendency is reflected in the initial steps of research focusing on various aspects of child protection. This is only a beginning: there is still a lack of studies investigating the effectiveness of arrangements adopted to address failings. The hope is that a more realistic and rational culture may develop, where it will be possible to consider the different points of view, including that of parents, children, experts and institutions, specifically in regard to errors and mistakes in child protection. This may allow a culture characterised by blame and moralistic judgement to be overthrown and lead to the development of a 'generative approach, where it is possible to combine different views [and build up] a different attitude toward failure' (Sicora, 2017: 49). However, it should also be recognised that responses to abuse are often influenced by the emotional impact that can pervade the public and political spheres, in connection with the issue of abuse of children as the story of the development of the Italian system demonstrates.

References

Allegri, E. (1997) *Supervisione e lavoro sociale* [*Social Work and Supervision*], Rome: Carocci.

Allegri, E. (2011) '(S)parlano di noi: Il sistema di tutela minorile su stampa e televisione' ['They Talk About Us: Child Protection System on the Media'], *Lavoro Sociale*, 11(2): 243–54.

Ascoli, U. and Pavolini, E. (2015) *The Italian Welfare State in a European Perspective: A Comparative Analysis*, Bristol: Policy Press.

Belotti, V. (2009) 'Introduzione' ['Introduction'], in V. Belotti (ed.) *Accogliere bambini, biografie, storie e famiglie Quaderno n. 48* [*Out-of-Home Children, Biographies, Stories and Families: Exercise Book No. 48*], Firenze: Centro Nazionale Documentazione e Analisi per l'infanzia e l'adolescenzam, Istituto degli Innocenti, pp v–xxiv.

Belotti, V. (2013) 'Bambine, bambini e politiche in tempi di recessione' ['Children and Policies in the Recession'], in M. Guerra (ed.) *Dalla parte del futuro. Risignificare parole e pratiche nei luoghi dell'infanzia* [*On the Future's Side: To Rename Words and Practices in Places of Childhood*], Parma: Edizioni Junior, pp 43–50.

Bertani, M., Borraccetti, V., Curci, P. and Secchi, C. (2017) *Aberrazioni Comunitarie: A partire dalla tragedia del Forteto* [*Community Aberration: From the tragedy of The Forteto*], Florence: Antigone.

Bertotti, T. (2016) 'Resources Reduction and Welfare Changes: Tensions Between Social Workers and Organizations – The Italian Case in Child Protection Services', *European Journal of Social Work*, 19(6): 963–76.

Bertotti, T. and Campanini, A. (2013) 'Italy', in P. Welbourne and J. Dixon (eds) *Child Protection and Child Welfare: A Global Appraisal of Cultures, Policy and Practice*, London: Jessica Kingsley, pp 97–119.

Bifulco, L. (2017) *Social Policies and Public Action*, Abingdon: Routledge.

Bollini, A. (2009) 'Procedure e protezione: l'utilizzo di linee guida e protocolli sull'abuso all'infanzia in Italia' ['Protection and Procedures: Using Guidelines on Child Abuse in Italy'], *Maltrattamento e abuso all'infanzia*, 11(3): 139–50.

Cheli, M., Mantovani, F. and Mori, T. (eds) (2015) *La valutazione sociale delle cure parentali. Manuale per l'operatore* [*Social Assessment of Parental Care: A Handbook*], Milan: Franco Angeli.

Cho, E.Y.-N. (2014) 'Defamilization Typology Re-examined: Re-measuring the Economic Independence of Women in Welfare States', *Journal of European Social Policy*, 24(5): 442–54.

Cirillo, S. and Di Blasio, P. (1989) *La famiglia maltrattante: Diagnosi e terapia* [*Families that Abuse: Diagnosis and Therapy*], Milan: Raffaello Cortina.

Comune di Napoli (2013) *Spunti metodologici sulla funzione di tutela dell'infanzia nei servizi sociali del comune di Napoli* [*Methodological Suggestion for Child Protection in Social Services of the Municipality of Naples*], Naples: Comune die Napoli e Cooperativa Sociale L'Orsa Maggiore. Available from: www.comune.napoli.it › files › D.3984b9ab18f1cca10c6a.

De Carolis, G., Moro, A.C., Petrella, G. and Sgritta, G.B. (1979) *Riforma delle leggi sull'adozione e l'affidamento* [*Reform of Laws on Adoption and Foster Care*], Padua: Fondazione Zancan.

Del Valle, J.F., Canali, C., Bravo, A. and Vecchiato, T. (2013) 'Child Protection in Italy and Spain: Influence of the Family Supported Society', *Psychosocial Intervention*, 22(3): 227–37.

Fargion, S. (2014) 'Synergies and Tensions in Child Protection and Parent Support: Policy Lines and Practitioners' Cultures', *Child & Family Social Work*, 19(1): 24–33.

Ferrera, M. (1996) 'The "Southern Model" of Welfare in Social Europe', *Journal of European Social Policy*, 6(1): 17–37.

Gilbert, N., Parton, N. and Skivenes, M. (2011) 'Changing Patterns of Response and Emerging Orientations', in N. Gilbert, N. Parton and M. Skivenes (eds) *Child Protection Systems: International Trends and Orientations*, New York: Oxford University Press, pp 243–57.

Guidetti Serra, B. and Santanera, F. (eds) (1973) *Il paese dei celestini: Istituti di assistenza sotto processo* [*The Country of Celestines: Care Institutes Under Trial*], Turin: Einaudi.

Istat (Istituto Nazionale di Statistica) (2018) *Annual report 2018 - The state of the Nation*, https://www.istat.it/en/archivio/217955 accessed Oct 2019.

LabRIEF (Laboratorio di Ricerca e Intervento in Educazione Familiare) (2015) *Programma d'Intervento Per la Prevenzione dell'Istitituzionalizzazione: Quaderni della ricerca sociale*, 24, 34 [*Intervention Programme for the Prevention of Institutionalisation*, Papers of Social Research, 24, 34], Padua/Rome: Labrief/Ministero del Lavoro e delle Politiche Sociali.

Maino, F. and Neri, S. (2011) 'Explaining Welfare Reforms in Italy Between Economy and Politics: External Constraints and Endogenous Dynamics', *Social Policy & Administration*, 45(4): 445–64.

Malacrea, M. (2001) 'Quando l'abuso sui bambini va in cronaca' ['When Child Abuse Is On the Media'], *Prospettive Sociali e Sanitarie*, 31(18): 19–20.

Malacrea, M. (2011) 'Esperienze sfavorevoli infantili e percorsi giudiziari' ['Adverse Childhood Experience and Court Hearing'], in D. Bianchi (ed.) *Ascoltare il minore. Interventi di protezione e tutela di bambini e adolescenti* [*Listening to Children: Protection and Protection Interventions for Children and Adolescents*], Rome: Carocci, pp 65–97.

Moro, A.C. (2002) *Manuale di diritto minorile* [*Handbook of Juvenile Law*], Bologna: Zanichelli.

Motta, M. (2013) 'Le relazioni tra servizi e operatori: alcuni snodi rilevanti' ['Services and Professional Relations: Some Relevant Issues'], in R. Albano and M. Dellavalle (eds) *Organizzare il servizio sociale* [*Organising Social Work*], Milan: Franco Angeli, pp 185–219.

Munro, E. (2005) 'Improving Practice: Child Protection as a System Problem', *Children and Youth Services Review*, 27: 375–91.

Naldini, M. and Saraceno, C. (2008) 'Social and Family Policies in Italy: Not Totally Frozen but Far from Structural Reforms', *Social Policy & Administration*, 42(7): 748–73.

RISC (Rischio per l'infanzia e soluzioni per contrastarlo [Risk for Childhood and Solution to Contrast]) (2011) *Rapporto finale di ricerca. Quaderni della ricerca sociale, 12* [*Final Research Report*, Papers of Social Research, 12], Rome/Padua: Ministero del Lavoro e delle Politiche Sociali/Fondazione Emanuela Zancan onlus.

Serbati, S. and Milani, P. (2013) *La tutela dei bambini. Teorie e strumenti di intervento con le famiglie vulnerabili* [*The Protection of Children: Intervention Theories and Tools with Vulnerable Families*], Rome: Carocci.

Sicora, A. (2017) *Reflective Practice and Learning from Mistakes in Social Work*, Bristol: Policy Press.

Sicora, A., Nothdurfter, U., Rosina, B. and Sanfelici, M. (2018) 'Service User Violence Against Social Workers in Italy: Prevalence and Characteristics of the Phenomenon', presentation at 8th European Conference for Social Work Research, Edinburgh, UK, April 2018, https ://www.eswra.org/documents/ECSWR2018.pdf.

Soregotti, C (2019) Le violazioni disciplinari degli assistenti sociali. Studio esplorativo nazionale sul procedimento di segnalazione ed elaborazione.[Social workers' disciplinary violations. An exploratory study of disciplinary procedure for alleged violations committed by social workers] Phd Thesis, University of Milano - Bicocca, https://boa.unimib.it/handle/10281/241131?mode=full.556.

Spratt, T., Nett, J., Bromfield, L., Hietamäki, J., Kindler, H. and Ponnert, L. (2015) 'Child Protection in Europe: Development of an International Cross-Comparison Model to Inform National Policies and Practices', *British Journal of Social Work*, 45(5): 1508–25.

UNCRC (2017) *Combined Fifth and Sixth Periodic Reports Submitted by Italy Under Article 44 of the Convention, Due in 2017 CRC/C/ITA/5-6*. Available from: http://docstore.ohchr.org/SelfServices/FilesHandler.ashx?enc=6QkG1d%2fPPRiCAqhKb7yhsunkTiY%2fvDoWjbtx8Nu6M%2by%2fL7IzI23dbypRkrAsz0TA%2btK55sjDCZ4diMpGKwDYsvGTLFYGhOZSiIcIPGKE9r%2f0j%2f9iiNAQT%2bBxosV9hEwm.

UNICEF Office of Research (2014) *Children of the Recession: The Impact of the Economic Crisis – Innocenti Report Card 12*, Florence: UNICEF Office of Research.

13

Preventing and responding to errors in US child protection

Jill Duerr Berrick and Jaclyn Chambers

Introduction

The US, in comparison to many other Western industrialised countries, hosts a welfare state that is highly residual in nature. The safety net is comparatively thin and individuals and families are considered an important defence against market, health or other unanticipated hardships (Hacker and Pierson, 2017). Family support policies in the US are relatively weak, though it should be noted that there is considerable diversity in family and child policy within and across the 50 states and territories (Meyers et al, 2001). The US does not provide federal paid family leave, it does not provide child allowances, childcare services are typically arranged through private pay (though some subsidised services are provided to low-income families), and healthcare is not universally provided. Federal policy and the funding that follows provide limited support for family strengthening services. Within this context, the child protection system is designed to serve children who have been or who are at risk of being harmed by their parents or other caregivers. With few prevention services available, child maltreatment, once discovered, may be serious and may require an intrusive state response. An inappropriate state response – whether unnecessarily intruding on the privacy of the family, or inaccurately assessing the need for protective measures offered to the child – can be consequential. These inaccurate judgements are typically referred to as 'errors'. This chapter reviews the primary approaches utilised in the US to prevent errors from happening, and also discusses strategies in place to assess errors after they occur.

An overview of child protection in the US

Children represent 23 per cent of the total US population of 327 million residents (US Census, 2017). The child protection system designed to serve these children is highly decentralised. The federal government provides an overarching framework and some funding, but there is a high degree of variability in the delivery of child welfare services across the 50 states and territories. In about a dozen states, the administration of services is further decentralised to the county level where variability in policies and practices is notable. Drawing on the framework provided by Gilbert et al (2011), the US is typically referred to as a *child protection* system, characterised by a notion that maltreatment is the result of challenged parenting resulting in substantial risk or harm to the child and warranting a government response to determine evidence of harm and to discern an appropriate state response. As such, eligibility for the child protection system turns on a narrow conceptualisation of child safety, rather than the broader notion of child well-being. Contacts with families are usually conducted by child welfare professionals working in public or private non-profit agencies; intrusive interventions into family life must be affirmed by a juvenile court judge.

Signals of risk are communicated to child welfare agencies by means of a child maltreatment referral to a child abuse hotline. Child-serving professionals are typically mandated by the government to file child abuse referrals if they suspect child maltreatment; other community members who are not mandated to report may also lodge their concerns. These signals of risk are assessed by child welfare staff to determine whether child welfare intervention is warranted. Nationwide, somewhat less than half of referrals (approximately 40 per cent) are screened out by child welfare agencies. In 2016, of the remaining 60 per cent of referrals that were screened in (approximately 4.2 million children), about 17 per cent (9.1 per 1,000 children) were *substantiated*, meaning that the referral was verified as maltreatment following a child welfare investigation; these children were thus eligible to receive child welfare services. An additional 14 per cent of referrals received an *alternative response*, meaning that their family information was forwarded to a community-based agency to offer voluntary, family-based support services. In the US, referrals for young children are especially likely to be substantiated; as such, most children served by child welfare are under the age of six (US DHHS, 2018).

Available data suggest that of all children who had substantiated referrals, about one fifth were removed from their homes (usually involuntarily) and placed in foster care. Almost one third of children with substantiated referrals (29.4 per cent) were subject to services imposed following court proceedings (US DHHS, 2018).

How are errors and mistakes characterised in the US?

In the US context, conversations about errors and mistakes in child welfare have several dimensions, and they can occur at many points along a continuum from eligibility determination to voluntary or involuntary services that may be more or less intrusive. In our conceptual map for this chapter, we use Reason's (1990) classification of *rule or knowledge-based mistakes* and *slips and lapses*, though for our purposes we use language that may be more germane to child welfare: *errors of decision making* and *errors of practice*.

Errors of decision making

According to Gelles (2017), the core task of child welfare professionals is decision making. In some countries, child welfare staff provide direct services to families, but in the US most services that families receive are provided by staff who are employed in non-profit agencies contracting with the public agency. Child protection professionals who work in public child welfare agencies therefore play the role of *decision maker* determining eligibility for services, making recommendations to the courts, and referring children and families to community-based agencies. Gelles refers to each of the major decision points as *gates* in the system (see Table 13.1).

Errors in decision making can occur at any of Gelles's gates. We draw the reader's attention to Gates #1 (screening), #3 (substantiation) and #5 (removal), as these may be especially important to our discussion regarding errors in child welfare. In these, one of two types of error might occur. First, a child who is not in danger, has not been harmed or is not at risk of harm is nevertheless perceived as unsafe and is drawn into the child welfare system to receive involuntary services. These are referred to as *false positive* errors. The second type of error, or *false negative*, occurs when a child who is in danger, has been harmed or is at risk of harm, is passed over and is not engaged with child protection services.

The consequences of errors in decision making are serious. False positive errors are especially consequential for family justice. For example, an error in decision making that results in the involuntary separation of a child and parent is an extreme violation of the family and the family's right to privacy and integrity (Guggenheim, 2005).

Table 13.1: Summary of major decision points as gates in the child protection system

Gate #1	Should the child welfare referral be screened in or screened out?
Gate #2	Among screened-in cases, is an investigation warranted? (In most jurisdictions, the decision is affirmative.)
Gate #3	Is the referral valid/substantiated, invalid/unsubstantiated, or unknown? (A substantiated referral typically results in a case being opened for services.)
Gate #4	Should services to the parent be denied due to an aggravated circumstance?
Gate #5	Is the child safe, or is the risk of harm high while remaining with the parent? If yes, should alternative care be offered for the child?
Gate #6	If out-of-home placement is required, which placement setting should be recommended to the court?
Gate #7	Should reunification be recommended to the court?
Gate #8	If reunification is not possible, is there an alternative, legally binding and lasting home setting that can be recommended?
Gate #9	Are the child's circumstances sufficiently safe and stable that the case can be closed?

Some families may have the legal resources to argue against the state and prevail, but ample evidence suggests that the child welfare system is disproportionately involved in the lives of low-income families in the US (Jonson-Reid et al, 2009). As such, the likelihood that these families will have the resources or adequate legal counsel to overcome the power of the state (even with state-sponsored legal assistance) is uncertain.

False positive errors have more far-reaching effects still. An injustice against a single family is grave. Yet when violations such as erroneous family break-up occur or are perceived to occur disproportionately within a single neighbourhood or community, the damage reverberates (Roberts, 2008). These concerns are especially pronounced in the US where the data show that some racial or ethnic groups are disproportionately affected by child welfare involvement. According to several data sources, African American and Native American / Alaska Native children are especially likely to have contact with and be served by child protection agencies compared with White children. African American children are twice as likely and Native American / Alaska Native children three times more likely to be reported for maltreatment compared with White children (Magruder and Shaw, 2008). Moreover, over half of all African American children in the US will be investigated following a child maltreatment referral before their 18th birthday. This is in contrast to about 37 per cent of all children in the country (Kim et al, 2017). African American children also find their child welfare investigation substantiated (verified) at twice the rate of White children (Putnam-Hornstein et al, 2013). And in any given year, African American and Native American / Alaska Native children are about twice as likely as White children to be placed into out-of-home care (Putnam-Hornstein et al, 2013). A study by Wildeman and Emanuel (2014) shows that the prevalence of foster care throughout childhood has stark racial/ethnic implications. Their research suggests that about 5 per cent of all US children will spend some time in foster care before their 18th birthday. For African American and Native American / Alaska Native children, the rates are about two and three times higher respectively.

The weight of the evidence suggests that these disproportionalities can largely be explained by disproportionate need, often reflecting the structural barriers that traditionally marginalised groups have in accessing resources such as safe housing, gainful employment, adequate healthcare and other services (Drake et al, 2009, 2011; Kim and Drake, 2018). Nevertheless, when rules or knowledge-based mistakes occur affecting families and communities that are already heavily burdened by extensive child welfare involvement, the errors may be experienced as especially consequential. False positive errors, felt privately by individual families and collectively when a number of families in a given community share their experiences with one another, are not usually made public through the mainstream media (though, of course, there are notable exceptions – see, for example: Clifford and Silver-Greenberg, 2017; Therolf, 2017; Janney, 2018). Some social media outlets publicise unjust child removals (for example, parentalrights. org), but these are usually considered fringe stories, and they may be perceived as suspect. Perhaps because the large share of families touched by the child welfare system are poor, their social capital may not give them access to the mainstream media outlets that might otherwise investigate and tell their story.

False negative errors in decision making are, of course, equally consequential and are – we would argue – more likely to be made public. In Gates #1, #3 or #5, false negative errors may occur because a decision was made *not* to screen in a referral, *not* to open a case, or *not* to place a child in out-of-home care, in spite of real danger to the child. We should clarify that errors of decision making typically occur because the information available to the social worker or perceived to be available to the social worker at that time suggested the selection of one decision over another (such as screen in/out; substantiate / not substantiate; remove / remain home).

A decision that results in a child being ineligible for service, when a service might have mitigated against serious harm is often made public through the mainstream media. For example, headlines from various news outlets suggest the gravity of these errors: 'Child Welfare Officials Previously Investigated Tampa Mom Accused of Drowning Girl in River' (WFLA Staff, 2018) and 'Lawsuit Faults County for Placing Infant Who Later Died with "Overwhelmed" Foster Parents' (Moran, 2018).[1]

In these and other news stories, child welfare professionals are characterised as having selected a decision path for the child that resulted in catastrophe. Of course, when children are harmed or killed, and the child welfare agency is implicated, the tragedy is felt profoundly by the child's family and community, and by professionals in the child welfare agency. But in making the case public through the mainstream media, the errors also have the effect of shaking the community's confidence in the agency and in its mission of child protection.

Errors of practice

In contrast to *errors of decision making* are *errors of practice*. We indicated previously that the core task for child welfare professionals is decision making. We also note that most services provided to families that could result in changed family circumstances are typically provided by professionals who work in community-based, non-profit agencies. But child welfare professionals also engage in practice with children and families. For example, they are typically required to regularly visit and speak with children who are living in out-of-home care; they may be required to supervise visits between a birth parent and child, conduct a background check on a caregiver, or provide referrals to a parent to access services. Errors of practice may happen with some frequency and – we would argue – occur largely outside public view. For example, a staff member who is required to visit a child monthly might miss a visit now and again. The staff member, in this instance, has made an error of practice the results of which might be perfectly benign, or might result in harm to the child. Where no injury occurs, the mistake happens outside public view. But serious errors of practice often come to the attention of the public.

Although Reason's classifications of slips and lapses (our errors of practice) combine both errors of omission and commission, we believe these are distinct classifications rooted in distinct intentions or contexts. We define errors of omission as mistakes that arise when a child welfare professional acts or fails to act, typically due to circumstances beyond his/her control. This could be because of lack of information, time or resources, for example. Errors of commission, on the other hand, occur as a result of a child welfare professional's intentional action or inaction. Because child welfare case files are kept confidential it is often difficult to discern whether an error of practice occurred due to omission or commission. What is reported in the mainstream media simply assigns responsibility regardless of intentionality: 'Jurors Blame L.A. Social Workers for Repeated Sexual Abuse of El Monte Girl and Award Her $45 Million' (Winton, 2018); 'County Failed Repeatedly to Stop Sexual Abuse of Foster Children, Lawsuit Alleges' (Cook, 2018); and 'Report Says DHHS Failures Preceded Abuse Deaths of 2 Girls, but Lack of Details Frustrates Lawmakers' (Lawlor, 2018).

Irrespective of whether the error is due to decision making or practice, there is anecdotal evidence that grave errors – particularly those resulting in serious harm or death at the hands of a parent – tilt child welfare agencies toward conservative decision making and result in higher rates of child removal – gates #3 and #5 (minimising false negatives, but possibly exaggerating false positives). Philip Browning, the director of Los Angeles' County's child welfare agency from 2012 to 2017 – arguably the largest child welfare agency in the country – indicated that the large increases in foster care under his watch were a result of a child death.

> I think that numbers went up frankly because of this tragic situation we had in the Antelope Valley [the 2013 death of eight-year-old Gabriel Fernandez], … I think what happened was that the public and I were shocked at what happened to that young child, and I think the public started calling in, and maybe they wouldn't have in the past. We got thousands more phone calls, which resulted in thousands more investigations that resulted in more children being detained.
>
> (Heimpel, 2018)

Because errors of decision making and errors of practice have consequences for children, families, communities and agencies, efforts to reduce mistakes in child welfare are imperative. In the US, significant federal and state funds are available to improve the overall quality of the workforce in child welfare (see, for example, the National Child Welfare Workforce Initiative at www.ncwwi.org) and thereby reduce *errors of practice*. The goals of these efforts are to ensure an ample supply of professionally trained staff, to reduce turnover so that agencies can spend their limited resources on supporting existing staff rather than training new staff, and ensuring that high quality services are provided to children and families. As the workforce improves over time, the expectation is that errors of practice (of omission and commission) will diminish.

***

Errors of decision making are, in part, responsive to workforce conditions. It is presumed, for example, that staff will make more thoughtful and perceptive decisions if they have sufficient time to consider all of the information available in selecting a decision path. But unlike reducing errors of practice – where government agencies and their staff have taken the lead in addressing the issue – researchers in the US have largely focused attention on errors of decision making. In fact, researchers have expended considerable time and effort since the 1990s attempting to identify scientific strategies that will reduce false positive and false negative errors. In particular, a body of evidence has emerged focused on decisions that occur at Gates #1 (screening), #3 (substantiation) and #5 (removal), in part because of substantial concern relating to the family justice consequences of false positives, and influenced heavily by ongoing concerns about racial/ethnic disparities in the outcomes of these decisions.

Research to address errors in decision making

It has been well documented that decision-making errors can be rife in the child welfare system (Munro, 1999; DePanfilis and Girvin, 2005). Child welfare professionals are tasked with gathering complex and sometimes contradictory information to decide when and how to intervene with families. Individual preferences and biases can strongly influence these decisions (Arad-Davidzon and Benbenishty, 2008). Additionally, practitioners often disagree about crucial decisions, despite relying on the same case characteristics and decision-making tools to determine outcomes (Bartelink et al, 2014). Even when using a decision-making tool, reasons for workers' decisions are still largely absent from case records (de Kwaadsteniet et al, 2013). Thus while studies on child welfare decision-making are plentiful, much remains to be understood about the mechanisms that drive decisions and how to improve decision making – thereby reducing false-positive and false-negative errors – from an empirical perspective (Bartelink et al, 2015). Nevertheless, researchers have developed tools to aid the decision-making process and standardise decisions across and between staff, with the goal of creating more equitable decisions between individual families, and between racial and ethnic groups.

Structured decision-making models have proliferated in the US as an alternative to clinical intuition when determining a family's risk level. These decision-making models have typically fallen into two categories: consensus-based assessments and actuarial assessments (Baird and Wagner, 2000; D'Andrade et al, 2008; Crea, 2010). Consensus-based assessments utilise underlying theories and expert opinion about child maltreatment to structure the information that a caseworker collects about a family. Staff then typically utilise this information to make a clinical determination regarding the most appropriate child welfare response. Examples of consensus-based instruments include the Washington Risk Assessment Matrix, California Family Assessment Factor Analysis, Child Emergency Response Assessment Protocol, and Utah Risk Assessment Scales (D'Andrade et al, 2008).

Actuarial risk assessments are structured to collect and analyse data points that are empirically related to risk of future maltreatment. Actuarial assessments may include factors that are not theoretically related to maltreatment; each factor on an actuarial assessment is given a weight based on its statistical probability of predicting future maltreatment (Cuccaro-Alamin et al, 2017). These assessments are typically completed by an individual worker and result in a risk score (of high risk to low risk) that is used to support the professional's decision about the preferred course of action. Some prominent actuarial models are the National Council on Crime and Delinquency's Structured Decision Making, the ACTION for Child Protection and National Resource Center for Child Protective Services model, and the Signs of Safety model (Cuccaro-Alamin et al, 2017). Most child welfare agencies in the United States utilise at least one form of structured risk assessment, with some using a combination of multiple approaches. A recent study by Casey Family Programs indicates that – alone or in combination with other tools – 23 states use Structured Decision Making, 11 states use Signs of Safety, 17 states use the ACTION model, and 10 states use other tools (SACHS, 2012).

The purported benefits of structured decision-making tools are the increased likelihood that decisions will more accurately reflect actual risk than clinical judgement alone, thus reducing the likelihood of false positives. Tools such as these are also designed to minimise staff members' unobserved or unacknowledged biases in decision making, thereby reducing racial disparities in outcomes that might otherwise arise. Further, utilisation of these tools among many professionals increases the likelihood of uniform decision making between different staff who might interact with the same family, thus increasing reliability and reducing the likelihood that the state will be perceived as capricious in its actions.

More recently, researchers have extended the structured decision-making framework to include predictive risk modelling (PRM). PRM 'is a statistical method of identifying characteristics that risk-stratify individuals in a population based on the likelihood each individual will experience a specific outcome or event' (Cuccaro-Alamin et al, 2017: 293). Similar to actuarial models, PRM results in a risk score that guides how much intervention is warranted with a particular family. Also, like actuarial models, the risk score should be combined with professional judgement in decision making. PRM differs from traditional actuarial models in the amount and type of information it uses to predict maltreatment risk, as well as the processes used to generate the risk score. Specifically, data mining and sophisticated analytic techniques are utilised to predict risk, using as many data points as possible. Child welfare agencies are beginning to utilise PRM to classify families' risk and reduce the number of decision-making errors made by child welfare professionals.

While the implementation of structured decision-making models has been the primary intervention to reduce child welfare decision-making errors, there have been other approaches to improve decision-making and reduce errors. As noted earlier, child welfare errors that lead to racial disparities have been a primary concern in the child welfare field since at least the 1980s. With the idea that racial disparities are due at least in part to worker bias in decision making, many child welfare agencies have instituted cultural competency training designed to reduce worker bias, reduce decision-making errors, and ultimately address racial disparities. Cultural competency training aims to help child welfare professionals 'respond respectfully and effectively to people of all cultures, classes, races, ethnic backgrounds, sexual orientations, and faiths or religions in a manner that recognises, affirms and values the worth of individuals, families, tribes, and communities, and protects and preserves the dignity of each' (CWLA, 2001 2). As a nation with a deeply problematic history concerning race, this model has become a key element of core training in child welfare agencies in the United States.

Effectiveness of these strategies in reducing errors

Structured decision-making models are believed to reduce errors because they decrease worker bias, help streamline what information staff collect and how they synthesise that information, and utilise statistical methods to determine a risk level. As structured decision-making gained momentum and popularity among researchers and policy makers in the 1990s, there were sceptics among those providing direct services within the child welfare field. Namely, some child welfare professionals expressed concern that important clinical and discretionary skills, which allow staff to understand the nuances and unique needs of each family and respond accordingly, would be replaced by rote assessment tools that could not adequately make these crucial decisions (Goddard et al, 1999; Gillingham, 2011). While there is some contradictory evidence (for instance, Baumann et al, 2005), the vast majority of the literature has found that actuarial and consensus-based instruments perform better in predicting maltreatment risk than clinical judgement alone (DePanfilis and Girvin, 2005; Ægisdóttir et al, 2006; Johnson, 2011). Furthermore, actuarial assessments are more effective in determining risk than consensus-based assessments (Baird and Wagner, 2000; D'Andrade et al, 2008). Thus, structured decision-making models do appear to help reduce errors and mistakes within child welfare practice. However, structured decision-making assessments are only one tool in a child welfare professional's toolbox, and clinical skills are still crucial in how staff assess and interact with families.

Perhaps the most controversial strategy to reduce errors in child welfare has been PRM. While the literature base is still nascent, early assessments of predictive analytics indicate that it does aid in decision making, resulting in fewer false positives and false negatives (Vaithianathan et al, 2013; Cuccaro-Alamin et al, 2017; Hurley, 2018). However, there is an impassioned academic and public debate surrounding the merits and possible collateral consequences of using PRM to guide decision making in child welfare. Specifically, scholars and other stakeholders have indicated concerns about consent and privacy related to families' data, operational challenges related to specificity and sensitivity, and the potential privatisation and opaqueness of PRM techniques (Keddell, 2015; Cuccaro-Alamin et al, 2017). Perhaps the most controversial criticism of PRM involves the debate about whether PRM exacerbates the racial and socio-economic disparities that are entrenched in the child welfare system. Some argue that if PRM uses data that are already biased, because they are based on flawed human decision-making that is inherently and often systematically biased, then PRM may end up unintentionally replicating and extending racial and socio-economic disparities (Eubanks, 2018). Advocates for PRM emphasise that PRM does not explicitly focus on race or socio-economic status as predictors of risk, that it may actually reduce bias in decision making as it is meant to remove human bias from risk assessment decisions and that transparency in the PRM process is key to help all parties understand how various factors are being weighed in the resulting risk decisions (*Los Angeles Daily News*, 2017; Hurley, 2018). Further evaluation of PRM and its impact on families should help to shed light on the potential benefits and drawbacks of this approach for child welfare decision-making.

Unlike structured decision-making and PRM, cultural competency training has generally been a welcome shift within child welfare practice. However, there is limited evidence for the effectiveness of cultural competency training on reducing decision-making errors. After engaging in cultural competency training, child welfare staff have shown improved skills working with diverse families and increased cultural awareness (De Jesús et al, 2016). It is possible that these improvements in skills and attitudes may reduce decision-making errors. Yet, there is little to no literature that directly examines the impact of cultural competency training on decision-making errors related to worker bias. Considering the prevalence of cultural competency efforts among child welfare agencies in the United States and its aims to reduce worker bias, research in this area is needed.

Assessing errors after they occur

When very serious mistakes are made, whether due to errors of practice or errors of decision making, a resulting child death typically initiates a child fatality review in the US. The first Child Fatality Review Teams (CFRT) were established in Los Angeles in the 1970s to examine all child deaths regardless of the connection to a child welfare service (Durfee and Tilton-Durfee, 1995); since that time, CFRTs have been established in most states and many counties (Douglas and McCarthy, 2011). Following federal legislation in 1996, Citizen Review Panels were established in most states to examine child fatalities specifically as they relate to child welfare–related cases (Palusci et al, 2010). These multidisciplinary teams examine the facts of the case and attempt to determine the circumstances surrounding the death in order to develop policies and procedures to prevent future similar incidents.

To our knowledge, there is no research showing an association between CFRTs and a reduction in child welfare errors. Some evidence indicates that CFRTs reveal the cause of death as related to non-compliance with established policies, procedures or practices within the agency (Douglas and Cunningham, 2008) – what we have referred to as errors of practice. Other evidence suggests that child deaths may not necessarily be related to the child welfare agency or child welfare professionals, but to other ancillary agencies in the community (Palusci et al, 2010). In both instances, these data may help individual communities assess their web of child protection, but will typically offer little information relevant to adjacent communities. In general, CFRTs can reveal limitations in policy or procedures at the agency level, but because these are backwards-looking reviews focused on individual outlier cases, their capacity to generate knowledge that can be generalisable for prevention purposes that are forward-facing will always be limited.

Is a wrong decision always an error?

Research evidence is rapidly accumulating in the US to develop decision-assistance tools designed to reduce the likelihood that errors in decision making (either false positives or false negatives) will be made by child welfare professionals. But these are not a guarantee that the correct decision will always be made. The individual families who come to the attention of child welfare and their wide range of rapidly changing circumstances are too varied to be captured entirely by data analytics. Once the uncertainty has been narrowed as far as science will allow, will some children and families still get hurt? And if so, will that outcome presuppose that an error in decision making was implicated?

After a recent child death in Los Angeles County, a public investigation ensued, not unlike the process that typically follows a high-profile incident in any other jurisdiction in the country (Gainsborough, 2010). Addressing the County Board of Supervisors (the legislative body that oversees the child welfare agency) the newly hired director of child welfare services made the following sober remarks: 'We have no known interventions that can be 100 percent effective, 100 percent of the time. We try our best, sometimes we make mistakes, but we have people that go out every single day and risk their own lives to try and save these children' (City News Service, 2018).

His comments speak to the uncertainty that surrounds the field of child welfare; a field with a limited number of interventions that have a sound evidence base (see: California Evidence-Based Clearinghouse for Child Welfare, 2019); and a field of enormous complexity in terms of the families and the difficulties of their lives. But his comments also speak to the passion and professionalism that many staff bring to this work, and it is in that context that we suggest another perspective on the question of errors in decision making.

Child welfare professionals make decisions every day that are based on fundamental principles that undergird the field. These principles centre on honouring notions of safety, family, permanency, culture, family privacy, home, kinship and client voice (see Berrick, 2018). In some cases, it is clear that one of these principles should prevail and should therefore serve as a guide to subsequent decisions. But a close examination of average cases suggests that at least one of the principles that is fundamental to practice typically competes with at least one other principle – that the principles serve as contradictory guides to decision making. As such, when a case presents as ambiguous or especially complex, data from risk assessment tools may not say enough about how to proceed. In these instances, child welfare professionals often return to the principles of the profession as a supplementary decision-making guide. Without the benefit of a window into the future, cases may have bad outcomes, even if the decisions leading to these outcomes were made using data (where available) and even if the child welfare professional enacted good practice. Are these errors? We argue that although they may result in bad outcomes, if there were neither errors in decision making nor errors in practice, these poor outcomes do not necessarily reflect mistakes.

Looking to the future, agency leaders can set an organisational context to support professional standards that minimise errors of practice (by omission and commission). And evidence-based decision-making tools, as well as cultural competency training, can aid child welfare professionals in reducing the likelihood of errors of decision making (false positives and false negatives). After the fact, Child Fatality Review Teams can closely assess the unique circumstances that resulted in tragedy. In the US, robust efforts are under way to address the potential for errors both from a forwards-looking and backwards-looking perspective. As these efforts continue, we believe families' interactions with the state will be more fair, uniform, responsive and transparent. But profoundly weighty choices are always at stake in child welfare, and neither leadership nor science may be able to definitively chart a course for all families that guarantees the right choice in all circumstances.

Note

[1] Because most child welfare files are highly confidential in the US, we cannot determine whether the cases described in these headlines are due to errors of decision making, or whether these were errors of practice. We offer them, however, as examples of child welfare errors implicated in a child tragedy that were ultimately made public.

References

Ægisdóttir, S., White, M.J., Spengler, P.M., Maugherman, A.S., Anderson, L.A., Cook, R.S., Nichols, C.N., Lampropoulos, G.K., Walker, B.S., Cohen, G. and Rush, J.D. (2006) 'The Meta-Analysis of Clinical Judgment Project: Fifty-Six Years of Accumulated Research on Clinical Versus Statistical Prediction', *The Counseling Psychologist*, 34(3): 341–82.

Arad-Davidzon, B. and Benbenishty, R. (2008) 'The Role of Workers' Attitudes and Parent and Child Wishes in Child Protection Workers' Assessments and Recommendation Regarding Removal and Reunification', *Children and Youth Services Review*, 30(1): 107–21.

Baird, C. and Wagner, D. (2000) 'The Relative Validity of Actuarial- and Consensus-Based Risk Assessment Systems', *Children and Youth Services Review*, 22(11/12): 839–71.

Bartelink, C., van Yperen, T.A. and ten Berge, I.J. (2015) 'Deciding on Child Maltreatment: A Literature Review on Methods that Improve Decision-Making', *Child Abuse & Neglect*, 49: 142–53.

Bartelink, C., van Yperen, T.A., ten Berge, I.J., de Kwaadsteniet, L. and Witteman, C.L.M. (2014) 'Agreement on Child Maltreatment Decisions: A Nonrandomized Study on the Effects of Structured Decision-Making', *Child & Youth Care Forum*, 43(5): 639–54.

Baumann, D.J., Law, J.R., Sheets, J., Reid, G. and Graham, J.C. (2005) 'Evaluating the Effectiveness of Actuarial Risk Assessment Models', *Children and Youth Services Review*, 27(5): 465–90.

Berrick, J.D. (2018) *The Impossible Imperative: Navigating the Competing Principles of Child Protection*, New York: Oxford University Press.

California Evidence-Based Clearinghouse for Child Welfare (2019) *Reducing Racial Disparity and Disproportionality in Child Welfare*. Available from: www.cebc4cw.org/topic/reducing-racial-disparity-and-disproportionality-in-child-welfare/.

City News Service (2018) 'Extensive DCFS Involvement and 12 Social Workers Didn't Save Lancaster Boy', *KEIB Radio*, 14 August. Available from: https://patriotla.iheart.com/content/2018-08-14-extensive-dcfs-involvement-and-12-social-workers-didnt-save-lancaster-boy/.

Clifford, S. and Silver-Greenberg, J. (2017) 'Foster Care as Punishment: The New Reality of "Jane Crow"', *The New York Times*, 21 July. Available from: www.nytimes.com/2017/07/21/nyregion/foster-care-nyc-jane-crow.html.

Cook, M. (2018) 'County Failed Repeatedly to Stop Sexual Abuse of Foster Children, Lawsuit Alleges', *San Diego Union Tribune*, 22 July. Available from: www.sandiegouniontribune.com/news/watchdog/sd-me-foster-care-20180722-story.html.

Crea, T.M. (2010) 'Balanced Decision Making in Child Welfare: Structured Processes Informed by Multiple Perspectives', *Administration in Social Work*, 34(2): 196–212.

Cuccaro-Alamin, S., Foust, R., Vaithianathan, R. and Putnam-Hornstein, E. (2017) 'Risk Assessment and Decision Making in Child Protective Services: Predictive Risk Modeling in Context', *Children and Youth Services Review*, 79: 291–8.

CWLA (Child Welfare League of America) (2001) *Cultural Competence Defined*, Child Welfare Information Gateway. Available from: www.childwelfare.gov/pubs/acloserlook/culturalcompetency/culturalcompetency2/.

D'Andrade, A., Austin, M.J. and Benton, A. (2008) 'Risk and Safety Assessment in Child Welfare: Instrument Comparisons', *Journal of Evidence-Based Social Work*, 5(1/2): 31–56.

De Jesús, A., Hogan, J., Martinez, R., Adams, J. and Hawkins Lacy, T. (2016) 'Putting Racism on the Table: The Implementation and Evaluation of a Novel Racial Equity and Cultural Competency Training/Consultation Model in New York City', *Journal of Ethnic & Cultural Diversity in Social Work*, 25(4): 300–19.

De Kwaadsteniet, L., Bartelink, C., Witteman, C., ten Berge, I. and van Yperen, T. (2013) 'Improved Decision Making About Suspected Child Maltreatment: Results of Structuring the Decision Process', *Children and Youth Services Review*, 35(2): 347–52.

DePanfilis, D. and Girvin, H. (2005) 'Investigating Child Maltreatment in Out-of-Home Care: Barriers to Effective Decision-Making', *Children and Youth Services Review*, 27(4): 353–74.

Douglas, E.M. and Cunningham, J.M. (2008) 'Recommendations from Child Fatality Review Teams: Results from a US Nationwide Exploratory Study Concerning Maltreatment Fatalities and Social Service Delivery' *Child Abuse Review*, 17(5): 331–51.

Douglas, E.M. and McCarthy, S. (2011) 'Child Fatality Review Teams: A Content Analysis of Social Policy', *Child Welfare*, 90(3): 91–110.

Drake, B., Jolley, J., Lanier, P., Fluke, J. Barth, R.P. and Jonson-Reid, M. (2011) 'Racial Bias in Child Protection? A Comparison of Competing Explanations Using National Data', *Pediatrics*, 127(3): 471–8.

Drake, B., Lee, S.M. and Jonson-Reid, M. (2009) 'Race and Child Maltreatment Reporting: Are Blacks Overrepresented?' *Children and Youth Services Review*, 31(3): 309–16.

Durfee, M. and Tilton-Durfee, D. (1995) 'Multi-agency Child Death Review Teams: Experience in the United States', *Child Abuse Review*, 4(5): 377–81.

Eubanks, V. (2018) 'A Child Abuse Prediction Model Fails Poor Families', *Wired*, 15 January. Available from: www.wired.com/story/excerpt-from-automating-inequality/.

Gainsborough, J. (2010) *Scandalous Politics: Child Welfare Policy in the States*, Washington, DC: Georgetown University Press.

Gelles, R. (2017) *Out of Harm's Way: Creating and Effective Child Welfare System*, New York: Oxford University Press.

Gilbert, N., Parton, N. and Skivenes, M. (eds) (2011) *Child Protection Systems: International Trends and Orientations*, New York: Oxford University Press.

Gillingham, P. (2011) 'Decision-Making Tools and the Development of Expertise in Child Protection Practitioners: Are We "Just Breeding Workers Who Are Good at Ticking Boxes"?', *Child & Family Social Work*, 16(4): 412–21.

Goddard, C.R., Saunders, B.J., Stanley, J.R. and Tucci, J. (1999) 'Structured Risk Assessment Procedures: Instruments of Abuse?' *Child Abuse Review*, 8(4): 251–63.

Guggenheim, M. (2005) *What's Wrong with Children's Rights?* Cambridge, MA: Harvard University Press.

Hacker, J. and Pierson, P. (2017) *American Amnesia: How the War on Government Led Us to Forget What Made America Prosper*, New York: Simon & Schuster.

Heimpel, D. (2018) 'Will L.A.'s Latest Child Death Drive Up Foster Care Numbers?', *Chronicle of Social Change*, 22 June. Available from: https://chronicleofsocialchange.org/analysis/will-l-s-latest-child-death-ignite-removal-machine/31410.

Hurley, D. (2018) 'Can an Algorithm Tell When Kids Are in Danger?', *The New York Times Magazine*, 2 January. Available from: www.nytimes.com/2018/01/02/magazine/can-an-algorithm-tell-when-kids-are-in-danger.html.

Janney, E. (2018) 'New Mother Reported to Child Protective Services over Bagel', *Towson Patch*, 8 August. Available from: https://patch.com/maryland/towson/new-mother-reported-child-protective-services-over-bagel.

Johnson, W.L. (2011) 'The Validity and Utility of the California Family Risk Assessment Under Practice Conditions in the Field: A Prospective Study', *Child Abuse & Neglect*, 35(1): 18–28.

Jonson-Reid, M., Drake, B. and Kohl, P.L. (2009) 'Is the Overrepresentation of the Poor in Child Welfare Caseloads Due to Bias or Need?', *Children and Youth Services Review*, 31(3): 422–7.

Keddell, E. (2015) 'The Ethics of Predictive Risk Modelling in the Aotearoa / New Zealand Child Welfare Context: Child Abuse Prevention or Neo-liberal Tool?', *Critical Social Policy*, 35(1): 69–88.

Kim, H. and Drake, B. (2018) 'Child Maltreatment Risk as a Function of Poverty and Race/Ethnicity in the USA', *International Journal of Epidemiology*, 47(3): 780–7.

Kim, H., Wildeman, C., Jonson-Reid, M. and Drake, B. (2017) 'Lifetime Prevalence of Investigating Child Maltreatment Among US Children', *American Journal of Public Health*, 107(2): 274–80.

Lawlor, J. (2018) 'Report Says DHHS Failures Preceded Abuse Deaths of 2 Girls, but Lack of Details Frustrates Lawmakers', *Portland Press Herald*, 24 May. Available from: www.pressherald.com/2018/05/24/state-failed-to-follow-procedures-and-share-information-in-deaths-of-two-girls/.

Los Angeles Daily News (2017) 'California Bets on Big Data to Predict Child Abuse', *Los Angeles Daily News*, 23 January, Available from: www.dailynews.com/2017/01/23/california-bets-on-big-data-to-predict-child-abuse/.

Magruder, J. and Shaw, T.V. (2008) 'Children Ever in Care: An Examination of Cumulative Disproportionality', *Child Welfare*, 87(2): 169–88.

Meyers, M.K., Gornick, J.C. and Peck, L.R. (2001) 'Packaging Support for Low-Income Families: Policy Variation Across the United States', *Journal of Policy Analysis and Management*, 20(3): 457–83.

Moran, G. (2018) 'Lawsuit Faults County for Placing Infant Who Later Died with "Overwhelmed" Foster Parents', *San Diego Union Tribune*, 28 June. Available from: www.sandiegouniontribune.com/news/public-safety/sd-me-foster-death-20180628-story.html.

Munro, E. (1999) 'Common Errors of Reasoning in Child Protection Work', *Child Abuse & Neglect*, 23(8): 745–58.

Palusci, V.J., Yager, S. and Covington, T.M. (2010) 'Effects of a Citizens Review Panel in Preventing Child Maltreatment Fatalities', *Child Abuse & Neglect*, 34(5): 324–31.

Putnam-Hornstein, E., Needell, B., King, B. and Johnson-Motoyama, M. (2013) 'Racial and Ethnic Disparities: A Population-Based Examination of Risk Factors for Involvement with Child Protective Services', *Child Abuse & Neglect*, 37(1): 33–46.

Reason, J. (1990) *Human Error*, New York: Cambridge University Press.

Roberts, D.E. (2008) 'The Racial Geography of Child Welfare: Toward a New Research Paradigm', *Child Welfare*, 87(2): 125–50.

SACHS (Southern Area Consortium of Human Services) (2012) *Review of Child Welfare Risk Assessments*. Available from: https://theacademy. sdsu.edu/wp-content/uploads/2015/02/SACHS_Risk_Assessment_ Report_and_Appendices_11_2012.pdf.

Therolf, G. (2017) 'Inside a Mom's Months-Long Fight to Get Back Her Children', *Los Angeles Times*, 16 February. Available from: www. latimes.com/local/la-me-dcfs-monique-baker-20170216-htmlstory. html.

US Census (2017) *Population Estimates*. Available from: https:// factfinder.census.gov/faces/tableservices/jsf/pages/productview. xhtml?src=bkmk.

US DHHS (US Department of Health and Human Services) (2018) *Child Maltreatment 2016*, Washington, DC: Administration for Children and Families, Administration on Children, Youth, and Families, Children's Bureau. Available from: www.acf.hhs.gov/cb/ resource/child-maltreatment-2016.

Vaithianathan, R., Maloney, T., Putnam-Hornstein, E. and Jiang, N. (2013) 'Children in the Public Benefit System at Risk of Maltreatment: Identification via Predictive Modeling', *American Journal of Preventive Medicine*, 45(3): 354–9.

WFLA Staff (2018) 'Child Welfare Officials Previously Investigated Tampa Mom Accused of Drowning Girl in River', *WFLA News*, 3 August. Available from: www.wfla.com/news/local-news/cps-previously-investigated-tampa-mom-accused-of-drowning-girl-in-river/1344979229.

Wildeman, C. and Emanuel, N. (2014) 'Cumulative Risks of Foster Care Placement by Age 18 for U.S. Children, 2000–2011', *PLOS ONE*, 9(3): e92785.

Winton, R. (2018) 'Jurors Blame L.A. Social Workers for Repeated Sexual Abuse of El Monte Girl and Award Her $45 Million', *Los Angeles Times*, 26 July. Available from: www.latimes.com/local/ lanow/la-me-child-abuse-lawsuit-dcfs-20180726-story.html.

14

Dealing with errors and mistakes in child protection: similarities and differences among countries

Kay Biesel, Judith Masson, Nigel Parton and Tarja Pösö

Our book so far has shown when and how errors and mistakes arise as a relevant topic in welfare states with different child protection orientations in Europe (England, Finland, France, Germany, Ireland, Italy, the Netherlands, Norway, Sweden and Switzerland) and the United States. In this concluding chapter, we draw together what are seen as errors and mistakes in these countries. We explore what events have triggered discourses on errors and mistakes in the countries and what actions, reactions and non-actions are taken, to avoid and learn from them. We show the similarities and differences in dealing with errors and mistakes across the countries. Based on this, we point out the six key responses to errors and mistakes we have identified through analysing the country-specific chapters; and the views on errors and mistakes, strategies and consequences associated with them. We also discuss how the different child protection orientations (child focus, family service and child protection) are related to the actions, reactions and non-actions associated with errors and mistakes in these countries. Finally, we examine the questions that remain and suggest what future research is needed.

Landscape of errors and mistakes in the countries

In the conceptual chapter (Chapter 2), it is apparent that errors and mistakes in child protection cannot be defined in a universally agreed way. They can be specified as deviations from legal and/or professional standards/care/duties (errors) and as actions or inactions based on misbeliefs, misconceptions or misunderstandings (mistakes). They are usually attributed to practitioners, who are seen as responsible. However, practitioners are not solely responsible for the origin and avoidance of errors and mistakes as errors and mistakes are influenced by several factors, for example by the predominant orientation towards child welfare – child protection, family service or child-focus (Gilbert et al, 2011). Consequently, the responses to dealing with them in services and organisations differ. In all chapters, we find a variety of understandings of errors and mistakes. They are seen and described differently, including as errors of decision making (false positive, false negatives), errors of practice (errors of omission, errors of commission), child perspective errors, procedural errors, mistreatments, (system) failures, tragic events, legal violations, abusive practices in institutions, irregularities, deficiencies or dysfunctions, organisational errors and policy implementation errors. The country chapters demonstrate that the definitions of errors and mistakes as well as related policy and research vary between the countries. Some authors report that there are no specific approaches to errors and mistakes in their countries whereas others report very established discourses and practices. Nevertheless, all chapters recognise that errors and mistakes occur in child protection.

One prominent group of errors and mistakes (errors of decision making, errors of practice, child perspective errors, procedural errors, mistreatments) mentioned in the country chapters describe situations where practitioners diagnose child abuse or neglect wrongly or do not identify children at risk as such; when they make mistakes and fail to protect children against harm or to prevent their death; or when parents are wrongly suspected of abusing or neglecting their children and as a consequence, children are separated from their parents. These occur because practitioners do not talk – or are not able to talk – to children or parents in a way that enables them to find out what can be done to help, or because they choose the wrong treatments. They also happen when practitioners do not record their casework accurately and information is lost. Children face life-threatening risks due to the lack of adequate care and upbringing, and the mismatched responses of practitioners' actions to these risks indeed belong to the shared repertoire of errors and mistakes in child protection across the countries.

Another common group of errors and mistakes highlighted in the chapters describes abusive practices in care: situations where practitioners or other caregivers abuse or maltreat children in residential or foster care or other institutional settings. In particular, the investigations into historical abuse of children and young people in childcare institutions as well as educational and religious facilities have underlined serious problems in the quality of the care provided by child protection authorities in many countries. Today, these abuses could be avoided if structures were established in organisations to prevent such violations against the rights of children and to disclose them if they occur (for example by using audits, inspections and forms of supervision). Such errors can be classified as organisational errors.

Closely related to organisational errors, the chapters discuss policy implementation errors as well. These errors describe situations where policy makers are unable to ensure the correct implementation of legislation or programmes, sometimes approached as 'systematic' or 'systems' failures. These failures are mentioned to describe the inability of policy to improve the practice of child protection. In this regard, the chapter on France provides an important example of the challenges created by translating country- and language-specific issues into English. The French term *faute* (failure) has a moral and legal dimension that is automatically linked to the notion of 'guilt'. Therefore, the term 'dysfunctions' is preferred in that chapter in order to avoid these connotations of liability and blame and to emphasise the system element. However, most commonly the term 'failure' is used in the chapters to describe situations in which practitioners are 'named and blamed' in reaction of a serious or fatal cases.

A special category of errors and mistakes approached in the country chapters is legal or procedural errors by practitioners (failures to comply with legal requirements). While practitioners aim to help families to achieve safe environments and supportive parent–child relationships, they may make, unintentionally, errors or mistakes for which they can be held responsible under civil or criminal law. The question addressed in some chapters is when practitioners' decisions and actions can and should be seen as illegal. Although practitioners should always act in accordance with the law and find ways to protect children within the existing rules and standards, they sometimes do not follow existing legal and administrative rules or standards because these undermine the goal of providing protection. In this case, practitioners fail to follow laws perhaps expediently as not all rules or standards in child protection are helpful from the point of view of front-line practice. Some are bad and do not fit very well with professional tasks. That is why it is essential to find out the reasons practitioners are not able or willing to respect rules or standards when errors and mistakes occur. When studying errors and mistakes in child protection, it is thus important to acknowledge the competing principles that shape child protection (Berrick, 2018) and which practitioners need to resolve in their everyday practice. The competing principles may also problematise very strict definitions of errors and mistakes.

What we did not see much in the country chapters is discussion about practitioners who choose to withdraw from good professional standards, legislation and codes of ethics or those who want to abuse children. Such people must be prevented from working with children and those working in child protection should be sanctioned for their misconduct and prosecuted. This group of errors and mistakes did not attract much political or media attention until relatively recently.

The triggers and responses to errors and mistakes in child protection

In most (but not all) countries, serious or fatal cases and public inquiries into historic, institutional abuse triggered discussion about child protection and errors and mistakes therein. Based on the country chapters, the overview on the triggers for action and reaction in response to errors and mistakes could look as follows.

In England, a fundamental starting point for discussion about errors and mistakes was the fatal case of Maria Colwell, in 1973. The more recent scandal case, Baby P from 2007, continues to reverberate through the system. Since the mid-1990s, extrafamilial abuse in institutional settings and abusive and exploitative behaviour of a series of high-profile celebrities has made headlines in the media and influenced practice (see Chapter 3).

In Ireland, the child abuse inquiry known as the Kilkenny Incest Investigation, at the beginning of the 1990s, was an influential starting point in debates on errors and mistakes in child protection. The inquiry was one reaction to a case where a father sexually and physically abused his daughters over more than a decade even though they were known to the authorities. Another seminal year for dealing with errors and mistakes was 2009 where the Ryan and the Dublin reports were published and 'uncovered' historical abuse of children in institutions run for the state the Catholic Church (see Chapter 4).

In the Netherlands, in the early 2000s especially, the fatal case of 'Savanna' had a major impact ('Savannaeffect') because a practitioner from a child protection agency was prosecuted for manslaughter. In reaction to this case and other tragedies, various initiatives to improve practice and to avoid errors and mistakes were taken (see Chapter 5).

In Finland, a case about a five-year-old boy named Niko influenced discussions in the 1990s not on errors and mistakes but on deficiencies in interview techniques for investigating child sexual abuse. Niko was taken into care because his father was unjustly accused of sexually abusing him. In 2012, another scandal, the death of a young girl called Vilja Eerika, who died as a result of violence by her father and stepmother, triggered extensive media publicity, criminal investigations and further national and local case reviews and also several reform programmes in child welfare (see Chapter 6).

In Norway, child protection is now well known around the world because of a series of cases taken to the European Court of Human Rights. However, in contrast to the other countries, the system has not (yet) been driven by scandal cases according to the Norwegian chapter. Errors and mistakes are identified in the context of system audits and case reviews but, as yet, have not resulted in pressure to act (see Chapter 7).

In Sweden, the practice of child auctions in the past and the Swedish Inquiry on Child Abuse and Neglect in Institutions and Foster homes during the period of the 1920s until the 2000s were important triggers for discussion on mistreatment and irregularities in child protection. Serious or fatal cases also influenced the system of child protection, resulting in further laws to increase the regulation of child protection (see Chapter 8).

In Switzerland, the Flaach case, where a mother killed her two children during a Christmas vacation in 2014 because she was afraid of losing them to the care authority was a starting point for a media campaign against the existence and work of the Child and Adult Protection Authorities and for debates on deficiencies in Swiss child protection. Debates about abusive practices in the past, on farms and institutions, also triggered discussion about the necessity for reform (see Chapter 9).

In Germany, the Kevin case in 2006 was a turning point in dealing with errors and mistakes. Kevin, two years old and under the guardianship of the local child and youth welfare authority, was discovered dead in the refrigerator of his drug-addicted (caregiver) father. The case was a scandal because the local child and youth welfare department knew about Kevin and allowed the father to take care of him even though he was a drug abuser. The social recognition of victims of abusive practices in institutions in the past has also been influential (see Chapter 10).

In France, failures or dysfunctions in the 1990s and later were relevant for improving child protection, for example institutional abuse, interventions not respecting parents' rights, misuse of children's testimonies in cases of sexual abuse and so on. Also, a fatal case of a girl named Marina, in 2009 attracted public attention and influenced child protection practice (see Chapter 11).

In Italy, cases of institutional abuse and satanic rites pushed forward debates about the function of the child protection system, but not on errors and mistakes in an open way (see Chapter 12). There are many parallels between practices in Italy and the other countries but there is no open, national acknowledgement of errors and mistakes in child protection.

In the US, false positive errors and false negative errors (as variations of errors) of decision making and as errors of omission and of commission (as variations of errors of practice) in child protection are mainly in the public and media spotlight (see Chapter 13).

Indeed in many countries, the triggers for naming errors and mistakes include scandals related with the fate of individual children, known by their names. The underlying social mechanisms are, however, more complicated. Those errors and mistakes in child protection are products of acts and they are recognised and named as such by different types of social practices. In other words, they are constructed in actions and reactions. We have identified six key forms of action, reaction and non-action in the country chapters: (1) professionalisation, (2) regulation, (3) responsibilisation, (4) scandalisation, (5) rights and empowerment and (6) non-recognition or non-action.

Professionalisation as form of action is taken when there is trust that errors and mistakes can be handled by practitioners. Errors and mistakes are seen as results of poor working conditions and a lack of expertise, competence and multi-professional cooperation. They are viewed as learning opportunities. Errors and mistakes could be avoided if practitioners have good education, training and supervision as well as good working conditions. Professionalisation may also include new types of duties given to practitioners to keep up a good standard of professional practice (for example using mandatory reports of mistreatment, failures or shortcomings in practice). In addition to increasing expert knowledge, this response may include some forms of regulating the required expertise: practitioners are, for example, required to be registered or to have a licence to practise in child protection. Trust in practitioners and their expertise leads to them being given a wide area of discretion, which may be accompanied by limitation – or even lack – of control and transparency.

The aim of *regulation* (proceduralisation and standardisation) is to limit practitioners' discretion and ensure more transparency and consistency. Practitioners should be made more accountable for their activities and subject to more organisational and external control. In this response, practitioners are seen as the main error-causers if they do not pay enough attention to existing rules and standards. Therefore, regulation is used to set out what is allowed and what is forbidden for practitioners. Guidelines, decision-making protocols and handbooks with detailed instructions are trusted to guide practice. The consequence of this form of response is deprofessionalisation, an increasingly technical (and often conflicting) view on 'good practice'. Errors and mistakes are then seen as deviations from the standards and procedural guidelines but not so much from the point of view of service-users' needs and rights or general professional standards.

Typical for *responsibilisation* is that errors and mistakes are viewed as individual phenomena of practitioners and other people (such as the parents). They are seen as resulting from actions by individuals who are personally accountable for them. Reactions relating to errors and mistakes focus on prosecuting them as crimes and/or establishing civil liability, not improving the working or living conditions of those who are seen as accountable. The nature of this response is punitive and includes a lot of blame. The consequences of this form are stress and fear among practitioners as well as parents. As a result, child protection work becomes less attractive and shortages of skilled workers occur. Parents, fearing loss of their children, react more reluctantly and unwillingly to the efforts of child protection services to help them. Responsibilisation could influence children as service-users as well but this is not explored in any of the chapters of this book. Trust, essential for relations between practitioners, service-users and the whole child protection system, fades or even disappears.

A variant of the response of responsibilisation is *scandalisation*. Errors and mistakes are viewed as 'disasters' or 'catastrophes', which are to be reported by the often outraged media. Individuals must be publicly named and blamed to demonstrate their culpabilities. This response aims to make the problem of errors and mistakes in child protection public and generate (political) pressure to act. Activities that are often undertaken include the use of investigations or reviews of serious or fatal cases, inspections of services and case audits without reference to the particular nature of child welfare. These may result in recommendations for legal and social reforms as some scandals can be useful for political purposes. The negative consequences of scandalisation are more serious than those of responsibilisation. Practitioners working with children and families fear the risks of blame and scandals and thus respond with increased rates of referral, investigation and intervention (risk aversion), overloading systems. In addition, the population generally, and parents specifically, have negative attitudes towards practitioners, seeing them as interventionist and incompetent. This again makes it more and more impossible to recruit people who want to work in child protection.

In contrast to these forms of response, we identified one that is focused less on the performance of practitioners or strategies to control or support them in dealing with errors and mistakes. The *rights and empowerment* response aims at strengthening the status and power of service-users in child protection. Errors and mistakes are viewed as violations of the rights of service-users. Specifically, the discovery and problematisation of abusive practices in institutions can be perceived as triggers for this response. Service-user associations, groups of experts by experience and other campaigners make efforts to ensure that service-users' rights are acknowledged in every part of practice, that errors and mistakes do not go unreported and associated damage is financially (or otherwise) compensated. In doing so, they take care that complaints are handled by practitioners and that they result in improvements to child protection. Also, they push for new services like an ombudsman or care-leaver services. This response is supported by other rights-based approaches in child protection in which human rights, particularly children's rights under the UNCRC are at the centre of child protection. Associated with this is the reformulation of professional power and expertise. The challenge for this rights-based response is whose rights in the family are given the priority, such as how to balance the rights, interests and needs of mothers, fathers and children against each other if they conflict.

The response *non-recognition or non-reaction* is characterised by practice and policy in which errors and mistakes are not recognised or not seen as problems. They are denied if they are detected and not constructed as deviations from legal and/or professional standards that can trigger fatal outcomes. The understanding that errors and mistakes in child protection are not a cause for concern and a high level of negligence are symptomatic of this response. This response ignores the needs and rights of the vulnerable families and children who might be mistreated because of the nature of the problem or their minority background, for example. This form is quite close to structural abuse or violence. Accordingly, strategies aimed at avoiding or at least handling errors and mistakes are diffuse. Because of this, nothing will be done to interrupt poor practice and public power will continue to be misused in ways that cannot help to improve the services given to children and families in child protection.

In most countries included in this book, those forms of response that focus on regulating practitioners undertaking child protection and empowering service-users are common. Only in a few countries (for example Italy or Switzerland) are discourses on errors and mistakes not widespread and therefore emerging responses are still difficult to spot. In most countries, responses are overlapping. What we could not find are forms that only apply in a single country. Although the existing research published in international journals suggests that England is the country where cases become scandals and where practitioners endure inquiries and need to follow procedures strictly, similar responses are to be found in other countries as well. Elsewhere child protection cases are also made into scandals and new guidelines and assessment tools introduced. Also, some countries implement strategies aiming to professionalise child protection further through training and licensing of professionals or quality development and assurance measures. Table 14.1 summarises the main elements of these six responses. The strategies to handle errors and mistakes will be looked more closely in the next section.

Main strategies to handle errors and mistakes in child protection

Strategies to handle errors and mistakes in child protection vary across nations and across different forms of response as Table 14.1 highlights. Typical strategies include *law reform* and *legislative amendment* as well as the establishment of *mandatory reporting and whistle-blowing systems* that may help uncover mistreatment, irregularities, deficiencies or dysfunctions. Also, the promotion of *serious case reviews* or *investigation systems* plays a major role – often connected with the publication of reports and recommendations for improving practice in child protection. A special variant of these investigation systems is the work of *inspectorates* that have the task of evaluating the quality of services or agencies and reviewing serious or fatal cases. In addition, the establishment of *ombudman's offices* or *ombudsmen* and the *improvement of legal safety of service-users* and *the possibilities of their complaining or appealing against unfair treatment or legal violations in child practices* are further strategies. For historical reappraisals of abusive practices in residential care or foster homes, *public inquiries* are central. Often, they have resulted in official apologies, financial compensation and prevention initiatives.

Other strategies in dealing with errors and mistakes in child protection are *registration, authorisation* or *licensing models for practitioners*. The models aim to regulate practitioners' access to the field of child protection, to ensure employees have specific professional profiles, skills and competences and to require them to undertake further training. The idea behind these models is to avoid errors and mistakes by guaranteeing that only well-educated, trained and experienced people are active in child protection. Another strategy is to improve *training* for practitioners and to support them by helping them to reflect on their cases better and to learn from errors and mistakes (*supervision*).

Implementation of assessment tools, the improvement of case documentation and *the development of model programmes* are also strategies in use to avoid

Table 14.1: Key forms of response to errors and mistakes and their characteristics

Characteristics/ responses	Professional-isation	Regulation (procedual-isation and standardis-ation)	Responsibil-isation	Scandalisation	Rights and empowerment	Non-recognition or non-reaction
Nature	Educating	Controlling	Punishing	Blaming	Politicising	Neglecting
View on errors and mistakes	Lack of skills, lack of experience, lack of learning and understanding; poor working conditions	Lack of control; too much discretion; too little accountability; lack of information sharing and cooperation	Individual failure of practitioners first, and other people, second	Disasters; catastrophes; outrage	Violations against the rights of service-users; abusive practices (in institutions)	Denial; lack of recognition or non-reaction
Who is forming the view?	Professional bodies and individual practitioners	Government (local and national); courts	Politicians; practitioners; public; service-users	Media; service-users; politicians (sometimes)	Service-users; non-governmental organisations; campaigner-like service-user associations	'Everyone'
Implications	External and internal regulation; training	Work based on instructions, procedures, standards and manuals	Loss of licence to practise; prosecution; imprisonment; civil liability	Raises profile of issue; public awareness of problem; need to act; destruction of confidence in the system	Rights to individual rights; systems obligations to recognise those rights	No one; but discrimination of some individual groups

Table 14.1 Key forms of response to errors and mistakes and their characteristics (continued)

Characteristics/ responses	Professional-isation	Regulation (procedual-isation and standardis-ation)	Responsibil-isation	Scandalisation	Rights and empowerment	Non-recognition or non-reaction
Strategies	Licensing; registration; supervision; education; training for all relevant practitioners; new methods, assessment tools and services; whistle-blowing rights and duties; Multi-professional cooperation	Laws – regulations, guidelines, assessment tools, procedures; reviews and inspections; interagency cooperation; registers; monitoring	Prosecution; registration/ deregistration; blaming	Biased use of inquiries and case reviews; inspections; law reforms; protocols regulation	Complaints systems; Ombudsman; involving service-users in service design; care-leaver services; compensation schemes	Diffuse strategies – actions are not taken to errors and mistakes
Consequences	Increased space for professional discretion; lack of control and transparency	Deprofessionalisation; increasing number of competing regulations, guidelines, assessment tools and procedures; more technical errors and substantive mistakes	Stress and fear; child protection work less attractive; leaving the profession; staff shortages	Stress and fear; risk aversion – increase number of cases – heavier workloads; staff shortages; negative attitudes in population and in parents	Difficulty of balancing between mothers and fathers and children rights (complicates); reformulation of power for practitioners	Nothing happens to interrupt poor practices; misuse of public power

and handle errors and mistakes. Assessment tools aim to minimise mistakes in decision making. The optimisation of case documentation has the purpose of supporting comprehensive knowledge in all cases, particularly complex ones. Model programmes are aimed at providing better support for parents and children. Alternative strategies are also important, for example: *legislation, inspection, whistle-blowing, assessment tools (based on evidence)* and *non-governmental/service-user movements*. Little is known about the effectiveness of these strategies or how they help avoid errors and mistakes or encourage learning from them.

The identified strategies can be schematised as in Table 14.2.

Each strategy has its shortcomings. Nevertheless, it is ethically doubtful to ignore errors and mistakes and not to learn from them and avoid reoccurrence in the future. Similarly ethically doubtful is blaming practitioners for errors and mistakes without taking account of the context in which they practise. The most ethically beneficial responses to errors and mistakes seem to be those aimed at supporting practitioners with effective tools as well as rules and standards to avoid and learn from previous errors and mistakes, and at strengthening the position of service-users to improve practice. That is why a way should be found to balance and to integrate the responses of regulation, professionalisation, and rights and empowerment with each other. In our view, practitioners should be regulated as far as is compatible with their codes of ethics and professional conduct and they should be respected and supported in carrying out their work. Service-users should be supported to express what they appreciate as right and wrong or good and bad in child protection and what they think needs

Table 14.2: Strategies to avoid or handle errors and mistakes in child protection

Main strategies	Reactive implementation	Proactive implementation
External regulation of practice and practitioners	Serious case reviews, inspections, public inquiries and so on	Model programmes, practice guidelines, law reform, inspections
Internal regulation of practice and practitioners	Registration of practitioners, professional bodies, whistle-blowing, mandatory reporting of professional misconduct and so on	Supervision, training, organisational and professional reforms
Empowerment of service-users	Appeals, complaints, support for service-users' access to their rights, compensation for wrongdoings	Service-user movements, the inclusion of experts by experience in developing child protection and so on

improvement. They should be respected as partners in learning and change practices and no longer seen as pariahs of the child protection system (Tobis, 2013; Falch-Eriksen and Backe-Hansen, 2018). They should regularly be compensated (financially or otherwise) if they suffer damage due to errors and mistakes. However, the question must be answered how exactly this balance between external and internal strategies, regulation and professionalisation in particular, and service-users' rights and empowerment is possible in practice. Figure 14.1 demonstrates the interdependence of these strategies.

Obviously, child protection relies on well-educated, trained and experienced practitioners who accept that errors and mistakes can happen and are aware that they can fail. Practitioners working in child protection are social workers but there are also others (judges, doctors, psychologists and nurses, for example), as shown in the country chapters. The requirements of high professional and ethical standards are relevant to them all. The codes of ethics and professional conduct should not be broken by, or removed from the control of, the professions. They are essential to prevent professional misconduct and malpractice, but not sufficient on their own for avoiding errors and mistakes. Practitioners need autonomy and flexibility to help families and to protect children against abuse and maltreatment. They require well-functioning multi-professional cooperation, organisational support (training, supervision, realistic caseloads), and guidelines and tools that

Figure 14.1: Balancing regulation, professionalisation, and rights and empowerment

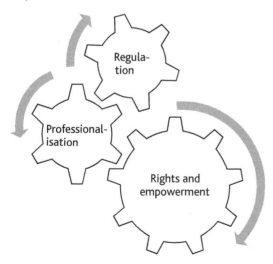

help them to avoid errors and mistakes and to learn from them. They are also reliant on informed service-users, adults and children alike, who know their rights and duties, work together with them on the basis of trusting relationships, and are not afraid to complain about errors and mistakes. Finally, they need a social and organisational environment where there is no shame in making unintentional errors and mistakes and therefore failing in child protection. Practitioners need to be respected in societies for their work and not seen as the primary source of errors. Furthermore, the media should not use serious or fatal cases for stoking system-wide scandals and for naming and blaming individual practitioners. When these new conditions prevail, errors and mistakes in child protection may no longer be drivers of fear and stress among practitioners and service-users.

Child protection orientations and dealing with errors and mistakes

How do the child protection, family services and child focus orientations (Gilbert et al, 2011) influence dealing with errors and mistakes? The attempt to identify a relationship between the forms of response to errors and mistakes and related strategies in each country, and their child protection orientations, is speculative. One should acknowledge, for example, that the knowledge on errors and mistakes in the countries presented in this book is based on contributions made by individual academics, written from their own perspective and disciplinary background. The chapters are well informed but may still lack some material that other writers might have included. Following from that, we have come to these conclusions:

- First, in those countries where child protection policy and practice are concentrated on families where risks of (re)abuse are immediate and high and the state functions as 'nightwatchman' to ensure a child's safety (child protection orientation), a great deal of the responses to errors and mistakes aim to regulate practitioners and to punish or create scandals in the event of serious wrongdoing (regulation, scandalisation and responsibilisation). Forms also focus more on parent's misbehaviour and maltreatment and aim to blame and punish them.
- Second, in countries where child protection policy and practice are more oriented towards supporting families and sustaining them to protect children (orientations towards family service), a great deal of the responses to errors and mistakes intends to educate

and train practitioners and to support them further by giving them practical guidelines, tools, and binding rules and standards (professionalisation). Forms also exist that are not directly linked to practitioners' errors and mistakes but aim to improve practice or to regulate activities of practitioners. There are also forms that turn serious mistakes into scandals (scandalisation) and ensure that practitioners will take responsibility for their wrongdoings (responsibilisation). In this orientation, it can also be that errors and mistakes of practitioners are not an issue (non-recognition or non-reaction).

- Third, in countries where child protection policy and practice are used to promote the well-being and development of children and strengthen their individual rights (child focus), the responses to errors and mistakes seek to empower parents and children and to give them the possibility of complaining and pushing forward new services (rights and empowerment). Responses that are associated with denouncing and blaming practitioners for their errors and mistakes are also widespread; this may be especially the case when a child dies or suffers severe harm (scandalisation and/or only responsibilisation).

These conclusions are summarised in Table 14.3.

As explained earlier, orientations in child protection have an influence on responses to errors and mistakes as they frame views on errors and mistakes and trigger strategies about how best to deal with them. Like the forms of response to errors and mistakes, the orientations in child protection in the countries treated in this book cannot be clearly distinguished from each other. There are main orientations but also orientations that are emerging and are in conflict with the existing ones. For example, there are countries where systems are both family oriented and child focused, or focused on the protection of children at

Table 14.3: Child protection orientations and forms of response to errors and mistakes

Orientation	Forms of response to errors and mistakes
Child protection	Towards regulation but also towards responsibilisation and categorising as scandals
Family services	Towards professionalisation but also towards non-recognition or non-reaction, responsibilisation and categorising as scandals
Child focus	Towards rights and empowerment but also towards categorising as scandals or only responsibilisation

risk and on the support of families. The orientations are in competition with each other in the countries, as are the responses to errors and mistakes. Sometimes these orientations complement each other well, at other times they are incompatible. From an analytical perspective, the combination of child-focused and family-service orientations seems problematic for dealing with error and mistakes. If both orientations apply in a country, errors and mistakes may be more common because practitioners may intervene either too early or too late where a child is abused, as they may be less willing to enforce child protection against the will of parents or children. An argument for this conclusion is that children in systems with these orientations are seen as *subjects with rights* or *objects of concern* (Butler-Sloss, 1988); in contrast, parents are viewed as *abusers* or *objects of support* and *partners in looking after the well-being of the child*. When orientations are in conflict, it is challenging for practitioners to do the right thing. On the one hand, practitioners have to introduce measures from the point of view of the child's best interest which might even imply separation of children from their parents and their assessment may conflict with the views of parents. On the other hand, they have to balance children's and parents' rights while at the same time promoting the well-being and development of children, protecting them from harm, supporting parents and strengthening families – and recognising parents' and children's rights to respect for private and family life. This challenging mission for practitioners provokes errors and mistakes, which is why level-headed responses to errors are wise without scandalising, responsibilising or (over)regulating.

These orientations towards child protection are constantly challenged by societal and global changes as described in the Introduction (Chapter 1). Those changes are likely to have their impact on errors and mistakes and the systems' strategies to handle them. When social inequalities increase, children and parents in vulnerable social conditions may experience growing social and economic insecurity in their own lives and have fewer and fewer opportunities to look after their rights as service-users. Social and economic insecurity will most likely influence the conditions for child protection practice: less time and fewer resources for practitioners and fewer services to help families and children. Decision-making processes will take place in haste due to the shortage of human resources. Trust in child protection practitioners and their expertise is contrasted by mistrust in expert knowledge in general, and relationship-based child protection will be more and more difficult to practise. Tendencies of this kind, evident in all chapters in this book to some extent, are self-evidently critical, even if not fatal, from the point of view of errors and mistakes.

Outlook

Even though we now know more about mistakes and errors in child protection, our book shows impressively what we do not know. As we have argued and seen in the chapters of the book, errors and mistakes are socially constructed in child protection. What is understood about them depends on the place and the time in which they are established and discussed. Exploring constructions and responses to errors and mistakes in a historical, cross-country perspective, taking into account the constantly changing family–state relations and child protection orientations would require further research. Indeed, we have seen in the chapters how important the history of child protection and society is to the present understanding of errors and mistakes. It would be helpful to explore further when, how and why abusive practices towards children's and parents' rights were socially recognised in different countries and when and why errors and mistakes as such were socially recognised and debated. Also, research is needed to better understand how it is possible to improve learning from these errors and mistakes and what we can learn from other fields such as healthcare and aviation, where the dealing with errors and mistakes has a longer history and is more advanced.

Many of the chapters acknowledge that scandals cause (non/re-) actions and sometimes reforms, and that the effects on practice are contingent. Exploring the conditions and factors influencing the effects of (non/re-)actions taken in order to respond to scandals could be a starting point for further cross-national research. In this context, research to examine the impact of reactive and proactive strategies to avoid errors and mistakes in child protection could be undertaken. The media also have a major impact on the constructions of errors and mistakes. Serious cases often lead to excessive media coverage of the deficiencies of child protection and the responsibilities of individual practitioners. In many countries, these tragic cases were turning points, which had a significant effect on child protection – even more so than the scandals of historic abuse in institutions or foster homes. The relationships between the media, service-users and strategies chosen to avoid and handle errors and mistakes in child protection and between governmental/managerial/organisational decisions and errors and mistakes of practitioners should be explored further. The growing use of different forms of social media may support the recognition of errors and mistakes but it may also increase blame and mistrust between families and child protection. Future research is needed to shed light on these relationships as well as on the role of open and public debate of errors and mistakes: how does it result in improving the quality of child protection?

Another area for insight from research is the position of children and parents from the minority groups – different in different countries – and children and parents with severe psychosocial problems. Such groups may be potential 'victims' of errors and mistakes in child protection as the weakest in society are highly vulnerable in this respect. In particular, children are not always seen as subjects with their own rights and meanings and therefore they have more limited opportunities to participate in decisions and actions than adults. People in vulnerable positions have limited options to defend themselves against errors and mistakes in child protection. Practitioners working for child protection share the ethical norms of equal human rights; yet, some service-users may experience erroneous and stigmatising child protection practices. Brave new research is needed to explore the mechanisms leading to the mismatch of service-users' rights and provision of services.

The outlook of research on errors and mistakes is overwhelmed by essential topics and standpoints to explore in the future. In addition to gaining a better knowledge base about the mechanisms of errors and mistakes and their relation to child protection orientations and social and economic changes, it is important to develop sustainable child protection practices and support people 'who are willing to take the moral risk' to work in child protection and to be wrong (Hollis and Howe, 1987: 132). Child protection is controversial and error-prone work. Practitioners must have courage to do their work knowing that their actions and decisions can have poor and unintended consequences for service-users as well as for themselves. If they fail to protect children from serious harm or death despite warning signals they are always morally responsible and will also lose their 'own innocence' (Hollis and Howe, 1987: 127). Sometimes they need 'moral luck' (Hollis and Howe, 1987: 123) as the consequences cannot be anticipated at the moment of making decisions. We hope that our book has succeeded in highlighting that the challenges of moral responsibility attached to child protection are widely acknowledged across these 11 countries. What is needed are systems, practices, research and policies that aim to share that moral responsibility and provide conditions to practise child protection in a fair and humane way towards children's and parents' rights.

References

Berrick, J.D. (2018) *The Impossible Imperative: Navigating the Competing Principles of Child Protection*, New York: Oxford University Press.

Butler-Sloss, E. (1988) *Report of the Inquiry into Child Abuse in Cleveland*, Cm 413, London: HMSO.

Falch-Eriksen, A. and Backe-Hansen, E. (eds) (2018) *Human Rights in Child Protection: Implications for Professional Practice and Policy*, London: Palgrave Macmillan.

Gilbert, N., Parton, N. and Skivenes, M. (2011) 'Changing Patterns of Response and Emerging Orientations', in N. Gilbert, N. Parton and M. Skivenes (eds) *Child Protection Systems: International Trends and Orientations*, New York: Oxford University Press, pp 243–57.

Hollis, M. and Howe, D. (1987) 'Moral Risks in Social Work', *Journal of Applied Philosophy*, 4(2): 123–33.

Tobis, D. (2013) *From Pariahs to Partners: How Parents and Their Allies Changed New York City's Child Welfare System*, New York: Oxford University Press.

Index

Note: Names of children are indexed as first name followed by a surname if available; e.g. Vilja Eerika rather than Eerika, Vilja.